KING GEORGE III
AND THE
POLITICIANS

KING GEORGE III
AND THE
POLITICIANS

THE FORD LECTURES
DELIVERED IN THE UNIVERSITY OF OXFORD
1951-2

BY

RICHARD PARES

OXFORD UNIVERSITY PRESS
LONDON OXFORD NEW YORK

Oxford University Press

OXFORD LONDON NEW YORK
GLASGOW TORONTO MELBOURNE WELLINGTON
CAPE TOWN IBADAN NAIROBI DAR ES SALAAM LUSAKA ADDIS ABABA
DELHI BOMBAY CALCUTTA MADRAS KARACHI LAHORE DACCA
KUALA LUMPUR SINGAPORE HONG KONG TOKYO

ISBN O 19 881130 6

First published by the Clarendon Press 1953
First issued as an Oxford University Press paperback 1967
Reprinted 1973

Printed in Great Britain
at the University Press, Oxford
by Vivian Ridler
Printer to the University

PREFACE

THESE lectures are published as they were uttered, with the addition of some detail which had to be omitted, especially from the fourth and fifth.

I wish to thank the University of Oxford for honouring me with the invitation to deliver the Ford Lectures—the highest honour, in my opinion, which an English historian can receive. I also take this opportunity of thanking the Wardens and Fellows, past and present, of All Souls College, for many years my home, whose library, traditions, and conversation formed my mind as an historian. But I owe most of all to my wife, whose lovingkindness has kept me alive to prepare this book. I dedicate it to her.

R. P.

I have taken the opportunity of a new impression to correct certain obvious mistakes of fact. For these corrections I am indebted to the reviewers, to Dr. Orlo C. Williams, and above all to Sir Lewis Namier. I wish to express my gratitude to them.

R. P.

October 1953

CONTENTS

I. AMATEURS AND PROFESSIONALS IN POLITICS   I

II. KING, LORDS, AND COMMONS   31

III. GEORGE III AND THE PARTIES   61

IV. THE APPOINTMENT AND DISMISSAL OF MINISTRIES   93

V. THE KING AND THE CABINET   143

VI. THE DECLINE OF PERSONAL MONARCHY   182

INDEX   209

I

AMATEURS AND PROFESSIONALS IN POLITICS

WHEN I accepted the invitation with which the University has been pleased to honour me, I resolved to offer, as the subject of my lectures, one which especially needs, at this time, a fresh general treatment, rather than another which I might have illustrated more profusely from my own researches into unpublished manuscripts. A circumstance which I cannot control has lately kept me from libraries and archive-rooms, and the only manuscripts I have been able to use, for this occasion, are those which I read before the war and for another purpose. Yet perhaps this undertaking is not so rash as it appears. Few things are more richly illuminated by printed documents than the politics of George III's reign: to take what is, admittedly, an extreme instance, the political activity of three generations of the house of Grenville is displayed in twenty-five published volumes, of which eighteen are devoted to the years between 1760 and 1812.[1] It is too early to say that, apart from the elucidation of special mysteries, such as the Fitzwilliam affair or Pitt's resignation in 1801, the marginal utility of unpublished material is beginning to diminish in this field; but at least, a new attempt at general discussion is needed much more urgently, and I hope I shall be able to show that such an attempt can be made with the help of documents which have been in print, some for ten years, others for anything up to a century. I believe that such a description is more likely to be superseded, soon or late, by a change in the outlook of historians than by the opening of new archives.[2] I am ready, as every historian must be, to take my chance of either; for the description is needed now.

[1] Not all of this material is edited well; some, such as Sir John Fortescue's edition of George III's correspondence, is edited very badly indeed. Yet an instructed reader with a little diligence should be able, at least, to correct and supply most of the defective datings and attributions, though he cannot hope to do so in the style of Sir Lewis Namier (L. B. Namier, *Additions and Corrections to Fortescue's Correspondence of George III*, i (Manchester, 1937)).

[2] Books like Sir Lewis Namier's great work on *The Structure of Politics at the Accession of George III* (London, 1930), which have transformed our attitude to eighteenth-

Let us begin by asking, what were politics about in the middle eighteenth century?—for here we have a question which has already been answered convincingly by a scholar of our own time. It has been the greatest of Sir Lewis Namier's achievements to exhibit the personal and local nature of political issues and political power at this time—to show how few members of parliament were, in the first instance, there for the purpose of taking a stand on political questions. They were there in their own right or for their own purposes, or as the relations or nominees of other people who held political power in their own right and for their own purposes. The political questions of the day were important to many of them—and to more and more of them as the reign went on; yet they did not, for the most part, enter parliament beforehand, nor did their electors send them there beforehand, in order to determine these questions.[1] This interpretation of British politics in terms of local or personal connexions and family prestige, first rendered popular by Sir Lewis Namier, has lately been confirmed by Professor Neale's discovery of very similar conditions in the reign of Elizabeth;[2] indeed, the same method can be applied to any society which is, in form or in substance, an oligarchy, as Dr. Scullard's and Professor Syme's researches into Roman politics have shown;[3] other historians have proved that a civil service can be permeated by the same influences as a senate or a parliament.[4]

As Sir Lewis Namier has pointed out,[5] these influences are likely to be strongest, when and where political interests, in the more usual sense of the term, are feeble and political questions unimportant. They may exist, as Mr. Walcott has shown,[6] even

century politics, have done so by virtue of a new outlook even more than by exploiting new manuscripts and exhibiting new detail.

[1] The idea of holding a general election on a given issue was practically unknown to the eighteenth century: the only occasions in George III's reign in which it could be said to have happened were 1784 and 1807.

[2] J. E. Neale, *The Elizabethan House of Commons* (London, 1949), especially chapters i, vii, and ix.

[3] H. H. Scullard, *Roman Politics, 220–150 B.C.* (Oxford, 1950); Ronald Syme, *The Roman Revolution* (Oxford, 1939).

[4] H. F. Schwarz (and John I. Coddington), *The Imperial Privy Council in the Seventeenth Century* (Cambridge, Mass., 1943).

[5] *Structure of Politics*, i. 21.

[6] Roger Walcott, Jr., 'British Party Politics (1688–1714)' in *Essays in Modern English History presented to Wilbur Cortez Abbott* (Harvard University Press, 1941), pp. 81–131.

when party differences mean something, but they are almost certain to prevail when party differences mean little or nothing. This accounts for their strength in Great Britain between 1714 and 1832. The dynasty had almost ceased to be an issue, though quarrels within the royal family (especially between the king and the heir apparent) had not. The ecclesiastical squabbles, which had distracted England in the reigns of the later Stuarts, had been laid to rest by a compromise: the tories were prevented from persecuting the Dissenters, but the whigs let them down by forbearing to press their claims to any more political power than could be exercised unofficially, almost furtively, in the constituencies. The distribution of political power between classes was hardly an issue in politics before 1815. There was social reform and economic development, and some of it was the subject of legislation; but most of this legislation was private, local, and facultative, setting up local agencies, such as turnpike, paving, enclosure, or improvement commissioners where such things appeared to be desired by the preponderant local interests.[1] These things only entered by accident into national politics; even legislation which was ostensibly national, imposing customs duties or regulating overseas trade, often had local implications and members of parliament handled it as agents of local interests.[2] Indeed, the House of Commons was in danger of becoming what Burke (who thought himself above this business but had to do it so long as he sat for Bristol), once called 'a confused and scuffling bustle of local agency';[3] though, unlike the contemporary Irish parliament, or the later Congress of the United States, it was saved from the worst kind of log-rolling by its own standing orders, which forbade a private member to propose the expenditure of public money.[4]

[1] One has only to look at the statute-book to see that bills of this sort accounted for most of the legislation in the middle of the century; and the *Journals* of the House of Commons show that these bills, and many, too, that were apparently national in scope, were treated as a matter for local representation, in that the members for the places or counties likely to be affected were regularly put on the committees which were to consider them.

[2] Bills on these subjects were particularly apt to contain, intentionally or unintentionally, provisions which raised issues between London and the outports; hence the frequent interventions of the M.P.s for Bristol in their passage. Mr. P. T. Underdown, of the University of Bristol, has given some illustrations in an excellent thesis on 'The Parliamentary History of Bristol, 1750–1790'.

[3] 'Speech at Bristol, previous to the election, 1780', in *Works* (1852 edn.), iii. 412.

[4] In Ireland the hereditary revenue was regularly raised without any reference to

Yet the age was not one of complete political torpor. There were, indeed, moments of boredom, especially in the calm which Henry Pelham so skilfully brought about in his later years, when Henry Fox could prophesy that 'A bird might build her nest in the Speaker's chair, or in his peruke. There won't be a debate that can disturb her',[1] and old Horace Walpole complained that 'the House of Commons is become a meer quarter sessions, where nothing is transacted but turnpikes and poor rates'.[2] But the political temperature was usually much higher than that, and there were political issues. They were necessarily and even rightly concerned with the composition and the behaviour of the executive.

The Government existed, in those days, not in order to legislate but in order to govern: to maintain order, to wage war and, above all, to conduct foreign affairs.[3] These things made up, in those times, nine tenths of government; and most of the controversies which divided politicians and parties concerned foreign affairs, or those questions about the distribution of the national effort in war-time, which were connected with foreign affairs.[4] The most prominent single issue was what one might call the 'German question'—that is to say, the expediency of opposing France in Germany, the choice of a German ally, the terms of the alliance, and, above all, the relation of British policy to the interests of the Elector of Hanover, who also happened to be king of Great Britain. Party politicians cannot easily take up attitudes beforehand to questions such as these, which arise unexpectedly in the course of executive government: it did

the demands upon it, and normally exceeded them. This left a surplus which the Irish politicians made every effort to disperse among public works, often of the most farcical kind, rather than leave anything for the king to spend. No doubt this was one thing which made the Irish House of Commons a scene of jobbery far worse than the British. Similar conditions in the United States gave rise to the so-called 'pork barrel' system in the later nineteenth century.

[1] Earl of Ilchester, *Henry Fox, First Lord Holland* (London, 1920), i. 179. Fox seems to have prophesied quite rightly, for Henry Pelham himself reported a little later to the Duke of Dorset that the session (1751–2) was the quietest for thirty years, 'no man unhappy but the Speaker, who finds some difficulty in procuring a decent attendance' (*Hist. MSS. Comm., Stopford-Sackville MSS.* i. 178).

[2] *Hist. MSS. Comm., Dropmore MSS.* i. 139.

[3] This can easily be seen from the most cursory analysis of the Newcastle Papers. Newcastle spent upon foreign politics scarcely, if at all, less energy than upon patronage and electioneering.

[4] See my article, 'American versus Continental Warfare', *English Historical Review*, li. 429–65.

not often happen, for example, that an Austrophile and a
Prussophile would refuse to sit in the same Cabinet.[1] For this
reason, though particular acts or negotiations were warmly
criticized, one cannot trace any consistent party attitude—not
even a whig and a tory attitude—to these issues.[2] Yet one can
trace a continual difference, not so much between parties as
between governments as such and oppositions as such, on this
question of isolation versus intervention: above all, though loyal
Protestants could not prudently express their dislike of the
dynasty, they could safely indulge it by denouncing any apparent
concession to the interests of Hanover. Since this was considered to be the great question of the age, the supposed apostasy
of the anti-Hanoverian Pitt surprised and shocked his contemporaries; it cost him much popularity and many political allies
—among them King George III, Bute, and George Grenville.
Only after George III's own isolationism, which he shared with
nearly all British statesmen after 1763, had robbed the anti-
Hanoverian agitation of its power to annoy the Government,[3]
could this great controversy be displaced from the centre of the
stage and room found for what we regard as the characteristic
issues of his reign.

When this controversy slept—as it often did—there was nothing to think about, in the middle eighteenth century, but the
control and composition of the executive government itself.
Indeed, when there is nothing to do but to govern, no other subject is worth thinking about. This consideration largely justifies
the attention given to what we should be inclined to dismiss as
questions of patronage, or of ins and outs.

It is easy for us to sneer at patronage; and we sneer in good
company. Even in the eighteenth century there were public

---

[1] This seems, however, to have happened in 1766: the Austrophile Egmont had,
no doubt, other reasons for refusing to serve under Chatham—for example, he disliked Chatham's domineering manners; but there was probably also a precise cause
of difference, viz. that he could not agree to a Prussian alliance, which was the
main plank in Chatham's platform (Lord George Sackville to General Irwin,
20 Aug. 1766, *Hist. MSS. Comm., Stopford-Sackville MSS.* i. 114; *The Duke of Newcastle's
Narrative of Changes in the Ministry*, ed. M. Bateson, pp. 15, 39).

[2] For instance, the whigs were expected to renew the war against France, or at
least to use their diplomatic strength against France, when they came to power in
1714; but, for good reasons, they did neither (Basil Williams, *Stanhope* (Oxford,
1932), pp. 157–68, 200, 229).

[3] George III thought and acted as a German prince very much more in the
1790's than in the 1760's.

men who valued their 'amateur status' absurdly high: Conway,
for example, believed that he could meet the criticism which the
Rockinghams directed against him for remaining in a Ministry
from which they were excluded, by refusing to take his salary,[1]
and Lord Grenville had some difficulty in persuading his
nephew that a man of rank and independent property could take
a salaried lordship of the Admiralty or Treasury without dis-
gracing himself.[2] Indeed, some went further, and acted on the
principle that the only money which it was a disgrace to take
was public money: thus Burke, who denounced every kind of
placeman, saw nothing odd in accepting £30,000 from Lord
Rockingham. Not everybody agreed with him: Dundas once
caused a scene in the House of Commons by asking 'if it was not
as honourable to be the King's pensioner as Lord Shelburne's',
which the savagely incorruptible Barré notoriously was.[3] But
the belief that disinterestedness, in the form of refusal to take
public money, qualifies a man for public respect and political
influence, has survived from that age to this.[4]

It was all very well for Rockingham and Shelburne, with their
enormous rent-rolls in England and Ireland[5] to vaunt their
disinterestedness. They could not expect even their own relations and dependants to emulate it.[6] They were not even disinterested themselves, where these dependants were concerned.
The heads of families (of whom more and more sat in the Lords)
did not expect to have to maintain their brothers, cousins, and
friends (of whom many sat in the Commons) out of their own

[1] Horace Walpole seems to have thought Conway thin-skinned, but encouraged
him in this proposal (*Memoirs of the Reign of King George III*, ed. Russell Barker
(London and New York, 1894), iii. 56).

[2] Grenville to Buckingham, 4 June 1800, printed by the Duke of Buckingham in
Courts and Cabinets of George III, iii. 75–78.

[3] Lord Fitzmaurice, *Life of William, Earl of Shelburne* (2nd edn., 1912), ii. 49.

[4] Sometimes it led to absurd and spectacular resignations, as when Leonard
Smelt, former sub-preceptor to the Prince of Wales, publicly renounced his pension
in a county meeting at York in order to have the pleasure of uttering some unpopular
royalist opinions (Rev. C. Wyvill, *Political Papers*, i. 15).

[5] Rockingham and Shelburne were reputed to be two of the richest absentee
proprietors of Irish soil (Arthur Young, *A Tour in Ireland*, ed. A. W. Hutton (1892),
ii. 115–16).

[6] Chesterfield had said of Rockingham's father in 1746, 'Though he has no place,
he recommends to about a hundred and fifty a year' (Chesterfield to Newcastle,
11 Jan. 1745/6, printed by Sir Richard Lodge in *Private Correspondence of Chesterfield and
Newcastle, 1744–6* (London, 1930), p. 103). The figure is an exaggeration, no doubt;
but there are letters from Lord Malton about patronage in the Newcastle papers.

pockets. The widespread descent of landed estates by primogeniture, even though mitigated, in favour of the younger children, by marriage settlements,[1] left many men of good family dependent upon some career. Here the head of the family might be able to help without consciously putting his hand in his own pocket. If he did not wish to spare from his building, his gambling, and his agricultural improvements any allowances over and above those which the settlements obliged him to pay, he might turn to account the political influence which happened to be annexed to his family and estate.[2] His own professional patronage would be limited in kind and degree: family livings might provide for brothers in holy orders,[3] and a great nobleman might control some military patronage in war-time if he happened to be Lord Lieutenant of a county or could obtain the privilege of raising a new regiment.[4] But this would not go very far. The bishoprics, the deaneries, the prebends, and the Crown livings were awarded by the Government; the higher posts in the regular army, the whole of the navy, the revenue offices, the colonial governorships, the political or civil services—in short, nearly everything that a gentleman could accept, had to be obtained from the Government.

[1] See Professor H. J. Habakkuk's article in *Transactions of the Royal Historical Society*, 4th series, xxxii. 15–30.

[2] Whether the political influence, which enabled him to command a share of the public patronage, did not cost him much more to keep up than the most generous allowances to his relations and dependants, was a question which he seldom had the common sense to consider. The Reverend John Brown described the matter well in the following words: 'We have seen that in a nation like ours, the great contention among those of quality and fortune will probably lie in the affair of *election interests*: that next to effeminate pleasure and gaming, this (for the same end as gaming) will of course be the capital pursuit: that this interest will naturally be regarded as a family-fund, for the provision of the younger branches, and that its force must arise from this principle, that in case the head of the family is not gratified in his lucrative demands, he and his dependents will raise a combustion in the state' (*An Estimate of the Manners and Principles of the Times* (1758), i. 127).

[3] Not all—perhaps not many—Church livings in private patronage were worthy of a well-born clergyman's acceptance until the century was well advanced: the Edmund Bertrams and Henry Tilneys were a less common phenomenon in the Church before the great rise of clerical incomes (see N. Sykes, *Church and State in the Eighteenth Century* (Cambridge, 1934), pp. 160, 417).

[4] George III's ceaseless struggles against 'raising regiments for rank' are exhibited in his *Correspondence* (edited by Sir John Fortescue, London, 1927–8, 6 vols., which I shall henceforward refer to without the editor's name), nos. 1702, 1773, 2096, 2130, 2146, 2157, 2164, &c.; see also *Private Correspondence of Lord Granville Leveson-Gower, 1781–1821*, ed. Countess Granville (London, 1916), i. 267, 270–2.

Not every landed proprietor in politics wished or needed to repay these favours by political support for the Ministry which bestowed them. We hear a very great deal, throughout the eighteenth century, about the 'independent country gentlemen' in the House of Commons, who were thought, or thought them-selves, the most upright and representative element in that assembly. In the first part of the century many of these men were Opposition tories: after 1763, many were Opposition whigs until the younger Pitt and the French Revolution rallied them to the cause of social order. Some of these men sat for the county seats; a fact which created the impression that there was something specially virtuous and important about the county constituencies,[1] and suggested to the early parliamen-tary reformers the idea of strengthening the forces making for virtue in the House by adding to the number of members for counties.

In reality the superior virtue of the counties was largely illu-sory. The study of any contested election, such as the great Oxfordshire election of 1754,[2] will dispel the belief that the forty-shilling freeholders were masters of their own votes, and the many elections uncontested because the big families would rather compromise than spend money, make it impossible to say whom or what these county members represented.[3] The real explanation of their so-called independence is a different one: the constitutional compromise of 1707, which allowed a member of the House of Commons to accept a place under the Crown but forced him to vacate his seat and stand for re-election, obliged a ministerial politician, who meant to climb the ladder of preferment, to choose a quiet, reliable, and inexpensive con-

[1] Sir Lewis Namier discusses some House of Commons divisions in which a pre-ponderance of county M.P.s voted against the Ministry or abstained (*Structure of Politics*, i. 183–91). See also Rev. C. Wyvill, op. cit. iii. 210, for a similar computa-tion of Sir George Savile's in 1780.

[2] R. J. Robson, *The Oxfordshire Election of 1754* (Oxford, 1949), pp. 44–51. According to Mr. E. G. Forrester (*Northamptonshire County Elections and Electioneering, 1695–1832* (Oxford, 1941), pp. 98–102) freeholders who were really dependent on their landlords used to compliment them with the disposal of one of their two votes, reserving the other for use according to their own judgement.

[3] The compromises were not always simple: sometimes two 'interests' would agree to divide the two county seats between them; at other times one interest would get both the county seats on condition of leaving a borough or boroughs within the county to the other. Mr. Forrester gives an instance of this, op. cit., p. 99.

stituency. There were many rungs in that ladder:[1] a beginner
or a junior minister must expect to go from a seat at the Admiralty or the Board of Trade to a seat at the Treasury, thence
to a minor 'Privy Councillor's office', such as the Treasurership
of the Chambers, before he could hope to reach the big posts,
such as the Secretaryship-at-War, the Presidency of the Board
of Trade, the Treasurership of the Navy, or the Paymaster-
Generalship, which were themselves graded according to seniority in their different lines.[2] At almost every move he must be
re-elected. Now a county constituency was not quiet, reliable, or
inexpensive: the pride of the local gentry made it bad tactics to
take their consent for granted, and even an uncontested election
cost hundreds of pounds, a contested one thousands.[3] A politician who sat for such a constituency must think twice before
he accepted even the highest and most tempting office: for
example, William Wyndham Grenville, most ambitious of men,
had to ask Pitt to postpone appointing him Secretary of State
because his re-election would hazard his brother's control over
the county of Buckingham which had cost him 'fifteen years'
slavery and £14,000'; and Lord Buckingham himself, though
he thought it had been worth it for the sake of his brother's
career, suggested that a county seat was such a nuisance to a
'political man' that it might be better to abandon it and buy
something cheaper in a borough.[4] This, I believe, was the real

[1] The importance of this systematic gradation of preferment is illustrated by the
fuss made in 1780 over Eden's request to be considered as having notionally 'passed
the Treasury Board' while serving in the Chief Secretaryship to the Lord Lieutenant
of Ireland, a post which was not exactly placed in the hierarchy (*Correspondence of
George III*, no. 3150); see also the letter of Lord Grenville to Lord Buckingham (*Courts
and Cabinets of George III*, iii. 75–78) answering the proposal that Lord Temple
should rise notionally in seniority while serving unpaid at the Committee of Council
on Trade.

[2] This explains why Henry Fox took it as a calculated insult when Pitt offered
him the Treasurership of the Navy in 1756: Fox knew quite well that he ranked
above George Grenville, whom Pitt proposed to promote to the Paymaster-General-
ship, a post of the same kind with higher prestige (Fox to Sackville, 4 Nov. 1756,
Hist. MSS. Comm., Stopford-Sackville MSS. i. 51; Fox to Bedford, 23 Nov. 1756,
Correspondence of John Russell, Duke of Bedford, ed. Lord John Russell, ii. 222).

[3] Philip Yorke's election for Cambridgeshire in 1747, which was virtually a walk-
over, cost £2,003, and was thought cheap at the price (P. C. Yorke, *Life of Lord
Chancellor Hardwicke* (Cambridge, 1913), ii. 161). In 1830 the Duke of Rutland said
that by great good management his brother had been elected for Leicestershire,
without a canvass, at a cost of less than £6,000 (*Correspondence of Charles Arbuthnot*,
ed. A. Aspinall (Camden Society, 1941), p. 130).

[4] See Buckingham's letter to Grenville, 30 Oct. 1786, *Hist. MSS. Comm., Dropmore*

reason why the county seats and those of Bristol, Westminster, and other popular constituencies were left to the unattached members—or would have been so, had not their very prestige made it worth while for the Ministry and the party leaders to contest them at vast expense, for the pleasure of claiming that their nominees represented the unbought suffrages of an independent electorate.[1]

However seated, there were members of parliament who could call themselves independent in the special sense that they did not demand favours from the Ministry, or else expected to receive them without seriously compromising their freedom of action in political questions. Systematic opposition probably meant going without, but those many others whose attitude was merely indeterminate might still expect a certain share of patronage. They could the more easily obtain it, because an independent member, when in doubt, and when present in the House at all (which was not always before Christmas and hardly ever after Easter),[2] would usually think it right to vote with his

MSS. i. 273, and their correspondence of 24 May–11 June 1788, ibid. i. 331–5. Other instances could be given: Welbore Ellis tried to avoid removing from the Secretaryship at War to the Joint-Paymastership (a removal which, in any case he considered unprofitable and undignified) by arguing that an unopposed election (for Aylesbury, never a very manageable constituency) cost him £1,200, a price too high to pay for an office worth £1,800 a year (*Correspondence of George III*, no. 128); George III himself, in 1780, used the argument for giving Lord Lewisham a double promotion, that 'Ld Lewisham stands for a county, his vacating frequently his seat is not therefore eligible' (ibid., no. 3155). Lord Stafford seems to have been discomposed because the king called up his eldest son to the House of Lords without his consent, thereby exposing him to the immense expense of getting a younger son elected for Staffordshire (*Private Correspondence of Lord Granville Leveson-Gower*, i. 240–3).

[1] Burke, Charles Fox, the younger Pitt, and Canning were all in possession of safe borough seats, or had every expectation of obtaining them when they chose to put themselves to the trouble of standing for Bristol, Westminster, Cambridge University, and Liverpool respectively, in order to claim that they represented some real public opinion. Lord North's election accounts for 1780–2 show clearly that a disproportionate amount of the ministerial election fund was spent in the open constituencies, including the counties (see his letters to George III, *Correspondence of George III*, nos. 3663, 3668; with which should be compared Robinson's statement of Apr. 1782, in *Parliamentary Papers of John Robinson*, ed. W. T. Laprade (Camden Society, 1922), pp. 57–59).

[2] The inability of the 'country gentlemen' to stay till the end of the session was so notorious that it was sometimes thought sharp practice to propose anything serious after the Easter recess: Rockingham, for example, used this argument in 1766 against asking parliament to vote allowances for George III's brothers (*Correspondence of George III*, no. 317; see also *Hist. MSS. Comm.*, *Stopford-Sackville MSS.* i. 123 and Bradshaw's argument in Grafton's *Autobiography*, ed. Sir W. R. Anson, p. 210).

Majesty's ministers. Even without this recommendation, a peer or a member of parliament, or any other person of good standing, might expect certain local favours, provided he was not known to be a systematic opponent of Government. Lord Gower's recommendation to the deanery or even the bishopric of Lichfield,[1] Lord Dudley's to a prebend of Worcester,[2] would be attended to almost as a matter of course, and Pitt promised, in the same spirit, to allow Lord Lowther to recommend the next Bishop of Carlisle.[3] Indeed, George III once laid it down, by way of a general maxim about Crown livings, that 'though Ld Archibald Hamilton had no promise of the living intended for Ld Hertford's son, yet that its being the Parish in which he lives unless he had [been] an avowed enemy to Government he had a better right to have his Recommendation attended to than any other person'[4]—a principle which Lord Chancellor Eldon repudiated on the ground that 'it is in fact making the Crown a mere trustee of its advowsons for every considerable family in the kingdom'.[5] Similar principles were often applied to lay patronage; the more so because no member of parliament, whatever his party, could hope to keep his constituents quiet unless he showed some power of obtaining personal or sectional favours for them. A Treasury which knew its business would try to reserve this great electoral asset for its own convinced supporters and, no doubt, it helped ministerial candidates to victory in all kinds of constituency.[6] But it was an open question whether unreliable or even hostile members of parliament could not claim the same rights.[7]

[1] *Correspondence of George III*, no. 1830; see also the somewhat puzzling letter of Pitt to Lord Gower (now Lord Stafford) in *Private Correspondence of Lord Granville Leveson-Gower*, i. 17, from which it appears that Pitt did not expect to control the next vacancy at Lichfield, but supposed that Lord Stafford could; and a letter from Granville Leveson-Gower to his father on p. 169.

[2] *Correspondence of George III*, no. 1976.

[3] *Hist. MSS. Comm., Lonsdale MSS.*, p. 154; but see Sykes, op. cit., p. 404.

[4] *Correspondence of George III*, no. 3352.

[5] H. Twiss, *Life of Lord Chancellor Eldon* (London, 1844), i. 390.

[6] Burke complained that 'almost all small services to individuals, and even to corporations, depend so much on the pleasure of the crown, that the members are as it were driven headlong into dependence' (Burke to Champion, 26 June 1777, *Works* (1852 edn.), i. 341).

[7] Sir William Meredith claimed in 1764 that the members of parliament for the port towns had an absolute right to nominate to certain offices in the ports; his claim was not allowed, and perhaps he did not expect that it would be, but only wanted an excuse for going into opposition (*Jenkinson Papers, 1760–1766*, ed. N.

Thus there were in the House of Commons some independent members of the governing class, who might, according to circumstances, sacrifice much or little for their independence; and these sat beside other members of the same class, who could only be regarded as professional politicians, in that they depended, more or less, on making a career in office. The exact difference between these two parts of the class is not easily stated. Naturally, in that age, the amateurs liked to think that the professionals were of inferior family. No doubt that was true sometimes: the 'men of business' Robinson, Whately, Dyson, Rose, and Huskisson were of mediocre parentage, and some of them lacked the advantage of university education. But the accusation was made far more often than it was justified. It is hard, for example, to see why Charles Jenkinson, first Earl of Liverpool, should have been universally regarded as a 'player' among 'gentlemen', for—as he was once driven to point out in the House of Commons[1]—he came from an old Oxfordshire family which sported a baronetcy, and he had been educated at University College, Oxford, even if his French accent remained odd to the end of his days. The careerists Gilbert Elliot and William Eden likewise came of excellent stock. It was mere social prejudice to insist on remembering that Canning's mother was an actress and to call Peel 'the spinning-Jenny', for both of them were indistinguishable, in education and attainments, from any other member of the governing class. But that was an age of social prejudice, even—indeed especially—among apostles of reform and progress—for it was Lord Grey, the great parliamentary

Jucker (London, 1948), p. 215). Dundas encountered and rejected a similar claim in 1791 (Holden Furber, *Henry Dundas, First Viscount Melville* (London, 1931), p. 240). In 1806 Lord Fitzwilliam denied, but Lord Grenville asserted, the principle that the sitting members had a right to custom-house patronage within their constituency; but as these sitting members were, on the whole, friends of Government, the incident does not prove the point conclusively (*Hist. MSS. Comm., Dropmore MSS.* viii. 286, 289). Wellington complained in 1829 that 'Certain members claim a right to dispose of every office that falls vacant within the town or county which they represent, and this is so much a matter of right that they now claim the patronage whether they support upon every occasion, or now and then, or when not required; or entirely oppose' (*Despatches, Correspondence, and Memoranda of Field Marshal Arthur, Duke of Wellington*, edited by his son, 1867–80, *Continuation* (hereafter cited as *Wellington, Despatches (Continuation)*, v. 407).

[1] Sir Henry Cavendish, *Parliamentary Debates*, ed. Wright, i. 448. Probably Jenkinson's failure to figure as a gentleman in politics may be attributed to a total lack of personal charm, which Mrs. Arbuthnot noticed also in his son.

reformer, who said of Canning 'The son of an actress is *de facto* disqualified from being Prime Minister of England', and Richmond, that earlier apostle of the same cause, who, when he wished to illustrate his party's weakness in men, said that if a Garter were to fall vacant, they should not know who to give it to.

The Opposition whigs, who transmitted to subsequent generations the legend of a contest between property and placemen, grossly over-simplified the picture by forgetting two things. In the first place, their own associates and 'men of business' were often inferior in social status to those of the Ministry: Creevey, the intimate of Sefton and Grey, was forever congratulating himself on his rise from a small house in Liverpool to toadyism in the mansions of the great, in the words 'Not bad for Old School Lane'; and, if we regard his social origins, we can only classify as an Irish adventurer the great Edmund Burke, the theorist and the high priest of snobbery, who had the grace to compare himself to a melon beside the ducal oaks, yet seems to have flattered himself, towards the end of his career, that such a melon might drop an acorn into the soil.[1] Moreover—and this is a much more important fact—the parentage of many placemen was not only respectable but illustrious. Even among the active politicians who worked their passage in the House of Commons, we find Lord George Sackville, son of the Duke of Dorset; George Grenville, brother of Lord Temple; Lord North, son of the Earl of Guilford; and, in a later generation, Lord Bathurst, the second Lord Camden, the Duke of Montrose, and so forth.[2] If we turn our eyes to the inactive placemen in the House who were not called upon to speak but only to vote,[3] or to those officeholders who, having obtained their posts for life by family influence in earlier dispensations, were free to vote against the Ministry, we see a more illustrious spectacle still.

[1] It is clear from Burke's retort to the Duke of Bedford's strictures upon his pension (*A Letter to a Noble Lord*) that he had more than half entertained, before his son's death, the hope that he might chance to found a political family, perhaps a peerage, as Bedford's ancestor had founded one 250 years earlier.

[2] Some of these names are given in Lord Grenville's expostulation to his brother, already quoted, p. 6, n. 2.

[3] There was a pretty distinct line between the 'efficient' places and the merely lucrative: Lord North, for example, said of two promotions in 1772, 'The Board of Trade brings a gentleman more into public business, but the Green Cloth is more profitable' (*Correspondence of George III*, no. 2014).

Burke himself, in a context which I shall have to discuss later, once boasted that: 'When we look over this exchequer list, we find it filled with the descendants of the Walpoles, of the Pelhams, of the Townshends; names to whom this country owes its liberties; and to whom his majesty owes his crown.'[1] A glance at such a publication as *The Extraordinary Black Book* confirms, for a somewhat later period, the impression that the holders of the most lucrative offices were, for the most part, not only of good families, but of the best.

Thus we cannot easily distinguish, in their origins and social status, the 'independent' members of the House of Commons from the placemen. At the most we can say that the 'independents' were more likely to be themselves heads of families (for the heads of many placemen's families were members of the House of Lords) and to sit in parliament by virtue of the property which they controlled rather than the property to which they were related.[2] The differences were largely accidental, and there were many exceptions on both sides: for a country gentleman like Dowdeswell or Gilbert Elliot might be tempted by ambition or circumstances into a career, or a placeman might have no dearer wish than to graduate into the ranks of country gentlemen, according to Hans Stanley's celebrated advice to careerists: 'Get into Parliament, make tiresome speeches; you will have great offers; do not accept them at first,—then do: then make great provision for yourself and family, and then call yourself an independent country gentleman.'[3] Such a placeman for life might behave like any other private gentleman with a secure income, as Horace Walpole devoted himself more and more to gossip and the collection of works of art, whereas contrariwise an 'independent' with strong political views, like Sir George Savile, might pursue his political duties so energetically

[1] This remark was made, rather surprisingly, in the *Speech on the Plan for Economical Reform*, 11 Feb. 1780 (*Works* (1852 edn.), iii. 386).

[2] The very fact that they sat in the House at all was often to be attributed to their property rather than to their personality. When Miss Crawford, in *Mansfield Park*, wishes to express her sense of the contrast between Mr. Rushworth's social opportunities and his personal insignificance, she can find no better words than 'A man might represent the county with such an estate' (*Mansfield Park*, vol. i, chapter xvii).

[3] Horace Walpole, *Memoirs of the Reign of King George III*, ed. Russell Barker, ii. 311. This was undoubtedly meant for George Grenville, who had attacked Stanley's appointment as ambassador at St. Petersburg.

that he only spent twenty-five or twenty-six days at home in the country in the course of a year. Yet, in spite of so many inter-changes and affinities, the placemen and the independents can be distinguished as classes, and their political behaviour often differed. It would hardly be too much to say that England had, at that time, not one political class but two—an active class within a passive one.[1]

If many gentlemen and noblemen looked to the public patronage as a proper means of providing for their relations and friends, the politicians of the middle and professional classes were even less likely to be independent of the executive power, though the reasons for their dependence might be somewhat different. The self-sufficient middle-class man was much rarer in the House of Commons than he became a hundred years later; for what could he live on? There were hardly any company directorships, and a partner in an industrial enterprise needed every penny and all the time he could get for his own business. A regular income from investments could, with very few exceptions, only be obtained from mortgages upon land or from the public funds; and these last seem to have served the politicians, down to 1800, rather for the casual profits of stock-jobbing than for the support of independent rentiers.[2] Almost

[1] This is only true of national, not of local politics, in which the independents must have been more active than the placemen, if only because they spent less time in the West End of London and in visiting each other's country-houses at opposite ends of England. Even a professional politician, if he happened to be in hopeless opposition, might fall back on the pleasures and responsibilities of local eminence. This helps to explain why Burke found it so hard to draw Rockingham and Richmond, who were uncrowned kings, respectively, of certain parts of Yorkshire and of West Sussex, from feasting with mayors, passing on political gossip at horse-races, and generally treating the maintenance of their local influence as an end in itself, to the parliamentary session which alone, in Burke's eyes, gave meaning to such activities. See, for example, Burke's letters to Rockingham, 5 and 20 Dec. 1774, 23 Aug. 1775; Rockingham to Burke, 6 Jan. 1777; Richmond's letters to Burke, 15 Nov. and 2 Dec. 1772; above all, Burke's heartfelt complaint to Charles Fox, 8 Oct. 1777 (*Works* (1852 edn.), i. 185, 198, 250–2, 257, 281–6, 324; v. 509–15).

[2] Politicians of all sorts seem to have gone in for stock-jobbing in the public funds, especially at the conjunctures of peace and war. Many ugly stories were told about the profits made by politicians and even office-holders out of the Peace of Paris and the Falkland Islands crisis. George III thought this a very disgraceful practice, and many of his Ministers took special precautions of secrecy to prevent it—often in vain (*Correspondence of George III*, nos. 3989, 4064; *Hist. MSS. Comm., Dropmore MSS.* i. 603–4, iii. 334; *Journal and Correspondence of William, Lord Auckland* (London,

the only rich business men with stable fortunes which would look after themselves were the absentee sugar-planters—a fact which goes some way to explain why a somewhat disproportionate number of them sat in the House.[1] To them were added a number of London merchants and financiers (mostly sitting for purchased seats in the southern counties).[2] Some of these merchants may have kept their politics and their business separate; but it would be far more natural, in an age when business activity was still relatively unspecialized and its financial side was receiving more and more emphasis, for them to aim at defending or increasing their fortunes by contact with politics. Of this sort were the business men who aimed at Government contracts, or the financiers who hoped for preferential treatment in the subscription to public loans before the younger Pitt virtually took such things out of politics; of this sort, too, were all those men connected with India or Indian trade, who wished to keep on the right side of a Government and a parliament which were beginning to intervene in Indian affairs.[3] It would be an anachronism if we were to expect to find many Gladstones and Chamberlains, keeping in the background a secure income from business or finance which could not—or at least need not—be increased by the touch of the executive power.

There were also some professional men in politics. Their situation too has changed in the last two centuries; but the changes have not all been in the same direction.

On the one hand, the enormous growth of the organized professions—perhaps the greatest change in the whole of modern

1861–2), i. 243, 279). Several celebrated hoaxes were perpetrated in order to affect the stock market: for instance, in 1787 there was a forged *Gazette Extraordinary*, reporting the march of a French army into the Low Countries (ibid. i. 430), and in 1801 the seal of the Secretary of State for Foreign Affairs was counterfeited for a similar purpose (*Private Correspondence of Lord Granville Leveson-Gower*, i. 148; the letter is misdated). In 1806 a British plenipotentiary, Lord Yarmouth, had to be recalled from Paris because he was credibly reported to have communicated his instructions to a French stock-jobbing partner, who instantly passed them on to Talleyrand (*Hist. MSS. Comm., Dropmore MSS.* viii. 272–8, 281).

[1] My researches in another field have convinced me that these incomes were very far from regular (*A West-India Fortune* (London, 1950), especially chapter vii). But the planters behaved as if they had been.

[2] Namier, *Structure of Politics*, i. 56–72.

[3] Ibid. i. 72; Cobbett, *Parliamentary History*, xxii. 1–47; see also the references given by Archibald S. Foord in his article on 'The Waning of the Influence of the Crown', *English Historical Review*, lxii, especially pp. 495–7.

history—explains, better than anything else, the difference between our attitude to patronage and that of the eighteenth century. We expect to provide for our children by educating them for professions, which can be entered without regard to official favour even when the state is the employer; in many of these professions, fixed pensions provide for old age and retirement, and in default, life insurance takes care of those contingencies and of the transmission of the family's status to the next generation in case of an accident to the bread-winner. It is easy for us, so circumstanced, to condemn the men of the eighteenth century, who provided for these things by cadging offices and pensions, for themselves or their children, from the holders of executive power. We do not need to do so; they did, for half the professions which secure our moral superiority did not then exist, or (like medicine and school-teaching) were regarded as scarcely fit for gentlemen; and life insurance itself was a new thing, at least not a widespread thing, in England.

Thus, on the one hand, those who were in search of a 'genteel' income were thrown into contact with the executive power far more often than we are, for want of purely professional opportunities; and, on the other hand, such professions as existed, were more intimately connected with politics than they are now. To put it concretely, certain professions which are not now compatible with a seat in the House of Commons, were so then —the army, the navy, and much of what we now call the civil services. In the law and the Church there has been less change, for the law has always been compatible with the House of Commons and the Church, in modern times, never has been. Yet the Church (including the universities) was then connected with politics as it is not now. These were the five great professions; and they were all, in different ways, affected by this connexion with politics.

Its effect upon the armed forces was bad, but not often powerful. The army (where professional skill does not seem to have been very necessary, and patronage might, therefore, reasonably have had free play) was saved from the worst intrusions of the politicians by the Hanoverian kings. George II was a soldier; George III was not, but he made the efficiency and contentment of the army, as an organized profession, his own concern—so much so, that his personal interferences, and resistances to interference, in military patronage were much more resolute than in civil.[1] Both these kings, moreover, handed over the army, towards the end of their reigns, to sons who were soldiers and administrators. This is not to say, however, that the army was altogether out of politics. Henry Fox, who managed the army under the Duke of Cumberland, seems to have considered it, as he considered everything else that he handled, in the light of a patronage machine, though the accusation, made by some contemporaries, of intending a 'military tyranny' was pure rant.[2] Moreover, there were ministers who could see no difference between dismissing soldiers and civilians for the enforcement of discipline in the House of Commons. Sir Robert Walpole—Henry Fox's first master—had acted on this principle, but the precedent was not a respectable one; and when George Grenville dismissed Conway from his regiment and his post in the Bedchamber, nobody flew to the rescue of the injured Conway more zealously than Sir Robert Walpole's son. The controversy was complicated by the question (which does not concern us here) whether Conway was dismissed for giving a single adverse vote on conscientious grounds or, as George Grenville said, for a systematic course of opposition; but many people agreed with Conway's brother, who distinguished between the Bedchamber and the regiment, adding that 'employments in the army have commonly been thought to be out of the reach of Ministerial influence; very few instances to the contrary have occurred in our time; and those have always been considered as violent and extraordinary'.[3] Nobody seems to have understood what was passing in George Grenville's mind, when he uttered the alarming words that 'the King cannot trust his army in the

[1] One could give a number of instances: perhaps it will suffice to mention George III's prolonged resistance to Lord Buckingham's various military jobs (*Courts and Cabinets of George III*, i. 403, ii. 134–45, 246–7); his veto, for which his ministers could only apologize, upon a scheme for raising volunteers in Staffordshire (*Private Correspondence of Lord Granville Leveson-Gower*, i. 270–2); and his extraordinary letter to Auckland, 29 Nov. 1799 (*Journal and Correspondence of Lord Auckland*, iv. 101–2).

[2] Such a charge could not have been believed, if the imagination of Englishmen had not been obsessed by a fear of the role of the army in civil affairs, which was partly justified by reminiscences of Cromwell and James II. Lord Waldegrave, like a sensible man, made light of it, but admitted that the distribution of military preferment added to Fox's strength, by furnishing the means of gratifying his dependents (James, second Earl Waldegrave, *Memoirs* (London, 1821), p. 21).

[3] Hertford to Grenville, 26 Apr. 1764, *Grenville Papers*, ed. W. J. Smith (London, 1852), ii. 308.

hands of those that are against his measures'. The day before he spoke them, the City mob had interfered with the solemn burning of No. 45 of the *North Briton*; and George Grenville (like the king himself) believed that riots, clandestinely encouraged by Opposition leaders for their own purposes, might offer a serious threat to social order and subordination.[1] In default of any other police, the king must have a trustworthy army to repress them. Horace Walpole and the other Opposition politicians, whose minds (as Dr. Johnson once said) were as narrow as the necks of vinegar cruets, had not the imagination to understand this, and interpreted Grenville's words in the context of parliamentary discipline. The outcry must have made an impression on the king, who himself declared in 1773 that he could never think it advisable to take away regiments. This, however, did not preclude him from disciplining officers in parliament for adverse votes; for in the army, as in many other branches of the public service, the 'plums' were not the regular regimental posts, but the accidental *douceurs*, such as governorships of forts, which were bestowed by favour—often by parliamentary favour. These, the king continued to think, were 'a very fair prey'.[2]

The opportunities for naval patronage were immense; the more so because the system for distributing prize money rendered certain stations, and certain kinds of ships, much more lucrative than others, and enhanced the advantages of an independent command.[3] A friend at the Admiralty could do much to help a captain push his fortune.[4] Yet the navy does not seem to have been more exposed to political interference than the army; perhaps less so.[5] On the one hand, the king had not quite the same personal concern in protecting its officers from political interference with their promotion, though he took an active interest

---

[1] The history of this affair can be followed in the *Grenville Papers*, ii. 296–351, *passim*, and in Horace Walpole's *Memoirs of the Reign of King George III*, ed. Russell Barker, i. 320–8, ii. 36, 47, 61.

[2] *Correspondence of George III*, nos. 1201, 2572.

[3] See my book, *Colonial Blockade and Neutral Rights, 1739–1763* (Oxford, 1938), pp. 33–42.

[4] George Grenville, as a Lord of the Admiralty in 1746–7, tried hard to obtain a lucrative cruise for his brother, and made an ugly scene when he did not get it (*Grenville Papers*, i. 53, 58–59). See also Rodney's letters on the unfair allocation of commands in 1757, ibid. i. 221.

[5] Perhaps for the obvious reason that a naval officer on a lucrative command could not, at the same time, be in the House of Commons to offend by his vote.

in some naval business, such as Captain Cook's explorations[1] and the coppering of ships, and administrators used sometimes to court his intervention when they wanted something important done in a hurry.[2] But perhaps his protection was less necessary because the politicians themselves may have felt that the interests of the navy, unlike those of the army, were a little too serious to be trifled with. The navy, unlike the army, was regularly represented in the Cabinet.[3] This might have exposed it to political jobbery, and, no doubt, sometimes did so.[4] But the First Lord was often a professional man, half outside the main stream of politics. It is doubtful, for example, if Hawke or Howe contributed much to Cabinet discussions on general questions.[5] Even when the First Lord was a politician, the Admiralty seems to have been a little kingdom of its own, administering its own patronage and only slightly concerned with House of Commons business.

Yet the armed forces could not escape from being dragged into politics in another way. The question of responsibility for failure in war is always likely to set ministers and serving officers by the ears—all the more so when the serving officers are members of parliament or of great political clans. Hence the scandalous interference of politics with the courts-martial of Matthews

[1] Various letters relating to Cook's expeditions were sent to George III and kept by him (*Correspondence*, nos. 1064–5, 1103), and he seems to have seen the 'Otaheita man' brought home by Furneaux in 1774 (ibid., no. 1490).

[2] Sir Charles Middleton to Spencer, 25 June 1795, in *Spencer Papers* (Navy Records Society), i. 45–46; *Barham Papers* (Navy Records Society), iii. 29.

[3] Some commanders-in-chief of the army were regular members of the Cabinet, especially in war-time; so was Granby as Master General of the Ordnance. The Secretary-at-War also attended on occasion. But the army was first represented permanently in the Cabinet when Windham became Secretary-at-War in 1794. The First Lord of the Admiralty, on the other hand, usually sat there, at any rate from Anson's time, if not from Sir Charles Wager's.

[4] Namier, *Structure of Politics*, i. 37–47.

[5] On such occasions the First Lord is often mentioned as absent, as Hawke was absent from the Cabinet which decided not to remove the tea tax (Grafton, *Autobiography*, ed. Anson, p. 230), or saying nothing, as Howe said nothing on the question whether to dissolve parliament, 25 Jan. 1784 (*Political Memoranda of Francis, Fifth Duke of Leeds*, ed. O. Browning (London, 1884), p. 95). When Howe retired in 1788, W. W. Grenville remarked that it would be a good thing to connect the Admiralty with the rest of the Administration, which Pitt had never yet succeeded in doing (*Courts and Cabinets of George III*, i. 385). Lord Barham seems to have gone to the Cabinet only when naval questions were to be discussed (*Barham Papers*, iii. 107–8, 118); this was suggested by the king (Stanhope, *Life of Pitt*, iv, Appendix, p. xxiii).

and Lestock—in which, incidentally, the members of the Administration were not all on the same side.[1] Hence the curious scenes in the houses of parliament, when members of Byng's court-martial (some of them M.P.s) were examined on a bill for dispensing them from their oath of secrecy, and one of them, knowing which side his bread was buttered, remarked, 'It will hurt my preferment to tell'.[2] In the War of the American Revolution both services became the sport of party politics. Generals returning home under a cloud or in dudgeon allowed or even encouraged the Opposition to use them against Lord George Germain. The fleet was torn in two by the quarrel between Palliser and Keppel. Keppel was already the naval mascot of the Rockingham whigs, and the First Lord of the Admiralty struggled most injudiciously to save Palliser, who was, indeed, one of his most capable advisers.[3] The entire Opposition repaired to Portsmouth in order to grace Keppel's court-martial, and Opposition admirals resorted to the meanest subterfuges to avoid taking command of squadrons, in order to force the Ministry to take Keppel back.[4] The command in the Channel had finally to be conferred on a series of neutral septuagenarians, whose greatest good fortune it was that they did not encounter the enemy. One of the first acts of the triumphant Rockingham ministry was to send out another of their party admirals to the West Indies to replace Germain's friend Rodney who, rather unluckily for them, had in the meantime won the greatest victory of the war.[5]

I do not say that none of this would have happened if serving officers had been excluded from parliament. It was part of the general disintegration and indiscipline of Lord North's era. But it might not have reached such proportions if the admirals and

[1] H. W. Richmond, *The Navy in the War of 1739–1748* (Cambridge, 1920), ii. 55–57, 268–71. Both Henry Fox and George Grenville spoke and voted against Henry Pelham on this issue (*Grenville Papers*, i. 36; Ilchester, op. cit. i. 113).

[2] Horace Walpole, *Memoirs of the Reign of George II* (1846 edn.), ii. 318–71.

[3] George III himself seems to have thought that Sandwich took Palliser's part imprudently and even unfairly (*Correspondence*, nos. 2540, 2547–51).

[4] See, for example, *Barrington Papers* (Navy Records Society), ii. 337–40, 349–52; *Sandwich Papers* (Navy Records Society), iii. 299–300. George III's efforts to find commanders for the Channel squadron can be seen in his *Correspondence*, nos. 2209 (misplaced by Fortescue; the date should clearly be 1779), 2584, 2585, 3125–6.

[5] Admiral Pigot, though a very good sort of man, was chiefly distinguished by the assiduity with which he played for heavy stakes at Charles Fox's Faro Bank (*Hist. MSS. Comm., Carlisle MSS.*, pp. 490, 497, 544).

generals—Burgoyne, Howe, and Keppel—had not had political associations and even seats in parliament.

The services and the politicians recovered some discipline and restraint in the even greater wars which followed. The gravity of the issues at stake had reunited most of the parties, and the commanders of forces, who were now fighting Frenchmen, not Americans, had no excuse for doubting the justice of the cause in which they were engaged. There were political campaigns against an unsuccessful general—especially when he happened to belong to the royal family—and acrimonious political disputes over naval administration, especially Lord St. Vincent's attempts at reform and his commissions of inquiry.[1] But these were disputes of politicians over naval questions, such as might occur today, not civil feuds within the fleet.

There is less to say about the law; for the modern conventions were already established, whereby the Law Offices and the chief seats on the Bench are conferred in return for services rendered, or to be rendered, in parliamentary debate, and the highest post of all, the Lord Chancellorship, is held during pleasure, the Chief Justiceships during good behaviour. Some of these parliamentary lawyers grudged the price of their preferment, tried to extort the maximum of promotion in exchange for the minimum of debating, and evidently looked upon their professional rivalries as the reality, their House of Commons careers as a disagreeable farce.[2] The Lord Chancellors did not

---

[1] St. Vincent had himself been one of the leaders of the Keppel faction in 1778; but I do not think there was any connexion between the two things.

[2] The professional rivalries of Charles Yorke and Pratt, of Wedderburn and Thurlow gave George III and his ministers plenty of trouble. Charles Yorke thought himself a better lawyer than Pratt (which he very likely was) and his main object was to catch up with Pratt, or even get ahead of him, in the race for high promotion. Since Pitt had insisted on putting Pratt over his head and keeping him there, Charles Yorke could not ally himself with Pitt, and did his best to prevent his friends from doing so. After 1763 this personal rivalry took a constitutional form, for Yorke differed from Pitt and Pratt on some (though not all) aspects of the General Warrants case. Charles Yorke's contortions and 'delicacies', in his efforts to even the score with Pratt without too obviously betraying his friends, put everybody to great inconvenience. Lord Chancellor Northington said: 'It makes one sick' (*Grenville Papers*, ii. 525–32; G. Harris, *Life of Lord Chancellor Hardwicke* (London, 1847), iii. 446–75 (especially 450, 457); P. C. Yorke, op. cit. iii. 472, 533–7; *Correspondence of George III*, nos. 106, 125, 126, 135). George III had scarcely less trouble with Wedderburn, who disliked Thurlow's promotion before him, and made himself disagreeable until North obtained for him a Chief Justiceship with a peerage (ibid., nos. 2372, 2635, 2637, 2648, 2818, 2834).

willingly retire at changes of Administration, but tried to get themselves carried over from one Cabinet to another. For this purpose they would dissociate themselves from their colleagues at moments of danger—it was a sure sign that the ship was likely to sink, when the Lord Chancellor began to create a scene about nothing[1]—though we should not believe all the stories we read about Lord Chancellors shamming sleep when awkward questions were discussed in Cabinet.[2] Their endeavours had a great measure of success, for many of them—notably Northington, Thurlow, and Eldon—survived several changes of Administration, including some quite violent ones.

Although churchmen, unlike lawyers, could not sit in the House of Commons, they were very much in politics: for one thing, their exclusion from the Commons was more than compensated by the seating of the bishops in the House of Lords, and by the great inequalities of their incomes, which made translation to a better diocese as strong a temptation as the original appointment to the bench.[3] Since the bishops of most sees appointed to their own prebends and some other livings, besides exercising, directly or indirectly, such discipline as then existed in the Church, to control the bishops was to influence the politics of a large part of the clergy. The bishops knew this quite well: Lord Hardwicke implored Archbishop Herring to come from York to Canterbury, in the name of his duty to the whig

---

[1] Northington showed peculiar dexterity at this in 1765 (*Grenville Papers*, iii. 136, 151; *Correspondence of George III*, no. 52). He did not contrive to retain the Great Seal at the next change; but having made sure beforehand that Pitt would recommend him for a pension as well as the Presidency of the Council, he refused to co-operate with the existing ministers, so giving George III an excuse for dismissing them and delivering the power into Pitt's hands (*Correspondence of George III*, nos. 303, 304, 342, 346, 347; Albemarle, *Memoirs of the Marquess of Rockingham and his Contemporaries* (London, 1852), i. 353–5). Thurlow was thought to be behaving in the same way in 1779 and again in 1781 (*Correspondence of George III*, nos. 2823–5, 2839, 3481), and looked like doing so again in the Oczakoff crisis of 1791 (*Political Memoranda of Francis, Fifth Duke of Leeds*, pp. 149, 159).

[2] Thurlow is described as shamming sleep at the Cabinet of 31 Mar. 1791 (ibid., p. 157) and Erskine at that of 9 Feb. 1807 on the Catholic question (Holland, *Memoirs of the Whig Party* (London, 1852), ii. 184. Sometimes one can sympathize with the reluctance of a Lord Chancellor to discuss a question quite unlike anything he was called upon to deal with in his profession—as when Thurlow complained that he, a lawyer, was called upon to decide whether Admiral Darby's fleet should sail (*Hist. MSS. Comm. Carlisle MSS.*, p. 520). The only Lord Chancellor in this period to show real insight into strategy was the great Lord Hardwicke.

[3] N. Sykes, op. cit., especially pp. 49–66.

party and the whig clergy,[1] and Archbishop Markham did not scruple to remind his clergy, in a visitatorial charge, that membership of associations for parliamentary reform was 'foreign to their clerical functions, and not the road to preferment'.[2] From this, as from all other attempts at political dragooning, the established clergy were partly saved by the great variety of private patronage in the Church, which sheltered hundreds of tory clergymen from whig bishops or, later, whig clergymen from tory bishops. But friends of the Government could be rewarded, even though enemies might not be punished.

Political interference with the Church and universities was seldom scandalous. Newcastle, who set up for an expert in bishops and regius Professors during more than twenty years, was pious beneath his worldliness, and would never have claimed that learning and sanctity were quite unnecessary: it was reserved for Charles Fox (who, after all, was not a Christian)[3] to say openly that he thought classical scholarship more important in an Irish bishop than residence in the diocese.[4] But the learning and sanctity of Newcastle's candidates were usually taken for granted: they certainly are not insisted upon in his correspondence.[5]

The political managers valued the control of Church patronage, not so much for the sake of controlling the electorate through the clergy (though the clergy had widespread influence, and bishops could sometimes procure the return of a reliable

[1] P. C. Yorke, op. cit. ii. 82.

[2] There was a hullabaloo about this in the committee meeting of the Yorkshire Association, 17 Oct. 1781; and no wonder, for many clergymen were enrolled in the associations: nine members out of thirty-two committee men in Yorkshire, Dec. 1779, and fourteen out of seventy in Sussex, Apr. 1780 (Wyvill, op. cit. i. 50, 183-4).

[3] In spite of Sidmouth's pathetic attempts to convince himself that Fox made a good end (G. Pellew, *Life and Correspondence of Viscount Sidmouth* (London, 1847), ii. 434).

[4] *Memorials and Correspondence of Charles James Fox*, ed. Lord John Russell (London, 1853), iv. 143-4. The episcopal church in Ireland seems to have had too many clergymen of this sort already: see Shelburne's bitter remarks (in Fitzmaurice, *Life of William, Earl of Shelburne* (2nd edn., 1912), ii. 362), they 'content themselves with delivering or preaching now and then some cold essay, or with publishing once in their lives some literary book, and God knows how rarely they do so much, which has as little to do with the real duty of a parochial clergyman . . . as so much Mathematics or Natural Philosophy'.

[5] Sykes, op. cit., pp. 277-82, 437-9; see also his article on 'The Duke of Newcastle as Ecclesiastical Minister', *English Historical Review*, lvii. 59-84.

member or two for their cathedral towns), but because it was a way of rewarding powerful lay politicians. Every great man had a relation, or a chaplain, or an old schoolfellow, or a former tutor or bear-leader on the grand tour, whom he wanted to reward, preferably at the public expense, by promotion in the Church.[1] Perhaps not many noblemen were so single-minded as the Marquess of Carmarthen, who, when asked what post he desired under a new administration, demanded nothing for himself, but a prebend of Westminster for a friend.[2] But many men in public life were ready to take some clerical preferment for a friend or relative in part payment for their own services. So long as this was so, the exclusion of the lower clergy from parliamentary life could not isolate the Church from politics. (Exactly the same thing, incidentally, could be said of the various civil posts whose holders were debarred from parliament by Place Acts: so long as members of parliament could obtain them for others, it mattered comparatively little that they could not themselves hold them.)

This consideration probably explains the steady intrusion of the politicians and their influence into the professions. It would be rash to suppose that any profession had ever been quite free from politics; and it is an open question, at any time, what professions ought to be free from politics: for example, at the very end of the nineteenth century Lord Salisbury still thought it

---

[1] See the magniloquent remarks of Burke, who believed that Church and State both gained by this practice, in *Reflections on the French Revolution* (*Works* (1852 edn.), iv. 232). As an example of Danegeld paid, at the Church's expense, to a politician who had threatened to turn nasty, see North's letter of 19 Sept. 1775 on the expediency of giving the deanery of Rochester to Thurlow's brother (*Correspondence of George III*, no. 1715). Thurlow himself, as Lord Chancellor, once asked to see the Secretary of the Treasury's parliamentary list, as it would help him to award Crown livings (*Hist. MSS. Comm., Abergavenny MSS.*, p. 34) Questions of ecclesiastical preferment often aroused violent feelings among politicians. Grafton, who had very lately accepted from Shelburne assurances of the purity of his political principles, decided that they were 'rendered of little effect' when he heard that the Opposition Bishop Hinchcliffe (for the late Opposition had their mascots among bishops as well as admirals) was not to be translated to Salisbury because the king had promised it to Bishop Barrington, who, to make matters worse, had spoken for the American War. Soon afterwards he learnt from another source that the late Lord Rockingham 'had declared . . . that he would sooner have seen the conclusion of his Administration, than that he could consent to have it disgraced, through such an injustice done to the worthy bishop' (Grafton, op. cit., pp. 325–6). I have little doubt that Rockingham would have done this.

[2] *Political Memoranda of Francis, Duke of Leeds*, p. 65.

right for a Conservative Government to make Conservative judges, though he did not think the same rule applied to bishops or civil servants.[1] There is no doubt that political interference increased after 1714, especially where other influences diminished. In the Church, for example, recommendations to preferment had been made in earlier generations by commissions, sometimes of bishops and laymen, at other times of churchmen alone:[2] but for over twenty years in the middle of the century, they were virtually controlled by a single layman who had no qualification for it but that of being the greatest political boss of his time. It was generally agreed that the efficiency of the revenue services had been likewise debauched by political nominations, though it might be harder to fix the responsibility upon any one man.[3] When the East India Company acquired vast revenue and administrative powers in Bengal, the politicians, as a class, instantly—within a decade—prepared to move forward into this new field of imperial patronage. They could not easily effect this through the resistant medium of the East India Company, with its own feuds and its unmanageable political structure; but their incursion resulted in a weird dance of East India factions and parliamentary factions joining and parting hands in ephemeral partnerships of dazzling intricacy. The implications of this contact for British politics were thought so ominous that a halt was called and, for the first time, in the 1780's, an attempt was made to take out of politics something that had got into it.

So far, I have dealt with the influence of politics upon the professions, and have said nothing about political patronage properly speaking—the award of incomes, with or without duties, in the service of the Crown or its agencies. Everybody knew that it was increasing, and many people ascribed it to its true causes: wars, which required more ships and regiments to fight them, more taxes (which somebody had to collect) to pay for them, and—since they were mostly successful wars—brought more colonies to govern. This was enough, without any extension of the scope of governmental activity, to account for great in-

---

[1] Lady Gwendolen Cecil, *Life of Robert, Marquis of Salisbury*, iii. 193.
[2] Sykes, op. cit., p. 25.
[3] Edward Hughes, *Studies in Administration and Finance, 1558–1825* (Manchester, 1934), chapter vii.

creases in the public services. Besides this, there were the debris of the medieval services, many of them now divorced from any intelligible duties and others easily performed by an underpaid deputy; and the quiet backwaters of the law-courts, not so obviously related to politics (for the judges sold some of the offices, esteeming this as a regular and respectable part of their income) but furnishing the wherewithal to support an active politician like the young Charles Abbot. The tendency to increase was accentuated by the practice of breaking down great offices into what one may call small change—the substitution, for example, of five lords of the Treasury and five lords of the Admiralty for a single overmighty Lord Treasurer and Lord High Admiral. Even so, there were those who complained that there was still not small change enough.[1]

Much of this patronage was irrational or at least unnecessary; but some of it was not quite as bad as it looked. For one thing, electioneering was expensive, and a member of parliament might well wish to recover his costs of production—though this argument might be, and often was, inverted by claiming that those costs would have been much smaller if they could not have been recovered in this way. Many of the active posts were insufficiently paid and brought their holders into debt: thus North owed £18,000 in 1777 after years of office, and the younger Pitt's debts were much greater.[2] The Lord Lieutenant of Ireland, so Lord Temple said in 1783, must spend £15,000 of his own money every year.[3] There were no regular pensions

[1] Lord Buckingham, Lord Lieutenant of Ireland in 1789, spoke of two great posts as 'too large to be marketable', and wished to put them into commission (*Hist. MSS. Comm., Dropmore MSS.* i. 445–6). In the same spirit Lord North, to whom George III had offered a Tellership of the Exchequer for one of his younger sons, declined it because he did not wish to have one of them so very well provided for while the others had nothing at all (*Correspondence of George III*, no. 2351).

[2] *Correspondence of George III*, no. 2060; Earl Stanhope, op. cit. iii. 341. See also Professor Aspinall's valuable note on Canning's finances, on p. lv of the Introduction to *The Formation of Canning's Ministry* (London, 1937): he shows that Canning had spent, during his political career, £67,500 out of his wife's fortune; a circumstance which justified her request for a pension after his death.

[3] *Hist. MSS. Comm., Rutland MSS.* iii. 73. It is hard to believe that he was right: he had only been in Dublin a few months in his first term of office, and the first year was generally the most expensive, because of the outfit. Other Viceroys, such as the Duke of Richmond, were said to have lived within their income or even saved money (*Hist. MSS. Comm., Bathurst MSS.*, p. 183); but perhaps a comparison with Viceroys after 1801 is misleading, since there was then no Irish parliament to seduce with good dinners.

schemes in the public service, and the king could not, in any case, have spared enough money from the Civil List to pension all public servants. It was therefore established—at least, it was very strongly claimed—that a minister or an under-secretary had some right to a 'permanency', in the form of a sinecure office, for himself or his children, against the time when he left office. Thus the Prime Minister usually received the Lord Wardenship of the Cinque Ports if it happened to fall vacant in his time.[1] Tellerships and Auditorships of the Exchequer, Clerkships of the Pells, and so forth were the normal patrimony of Prime Ministers' sons—Sir Robert Walpole, George Grenville, and Sidmouth provided for theirs in this way. Under-secretaries could not pretend to anything so grand; but we find them similarly claiming a right to a 'permanency', and arguing 'All my colleagues have a certainty already apart from the emoluments of office', in order to obtain the post of German Translator, Gazette Writer, or Master of the Revels in Ireland.[2]

It was not a good system of family endowment. Some of the posts claimed ought not to have been treated as sinecures.[3] Families were endowed partially and uncertainly, for sons might die before their fathers, and the prosperity of one child did not necessarily ensure that of the family as a whole.[4] Even as a system of pensions for retirement it was rather haphazard. But it served some useful purpose by enabling the leading men to recover for their children some of the money they had spent on the pleasures and responsibilities of political life; a consideration all the more important for those who followed the almost uni-

[1] North, the younger Pitt, and Hawkesbury (as 'Prime Minister for a day') all received this reward. North struggled hard to have it granted for life, but George III (not that he foresaw North's behaviour in 1783) would only grant it during pleasure, which North took as an unmerited insult. In 1782, however, George III converted the grant during pleasure into a grant for life; he must have regretted it next year (*Correspondence of George III*, nos. 2346, 2347, 2358, 2370).

[2] *Correspondence of George III*, no. 1307.

[3] For example, the German Translatorship (*Correspondence of George III*, no. 1345).

[4] Sidmouth's and Auckland's sons both died before them. Auckland's case was very hard, for the virtuous youth had regarded his income as an endowment for his hordes of younger brothers and sisters. His father hoped, not without reason, that as the office had been a reward for his own services, it might be transferred to another son; but in vain. Spencer Perceval had other uses for it: though he showed remarkable restraint by declining to confer it upon his own son (for he was no less philoprogenitive than Auckland) he gave it to a fellow politician in order to facilitate a political arrangement (*Hist. MSS. Comm., Dropmore MSS.* viii. 330; *Journal and Correspondence of Lord Auckland*, iv. 347).

versal fashion of perpetuating their political eminence by a peerage.

It would be wrong to infer from this description that politics was an utterly sordid affair. That it was not, even for the careerists. They could not afford to throw away thousands on politics, like Lord Rockingham. They wished, as very few of us do not, to leave the world richer than they had entered it. But above all, the characteristic of the careerist, the so-called 'man of business', was what his name implied. George Grenville and his son William, Charles Jenkinson and his son Robert, Lord Auckland, Speaker Abbot—whatever their station in life, were all 'men of business' fascinated by the details of policy and administration; especially by those most businesslike kinds of business—trade, revenue, and the reform of administrative machinery. No doubt the desire to do something useful and the desire to get on in the world were unconsciously mixed in much of this reforming activity, and jointly account, for example, for the young Charles Abbot's zeal on such unpromising subjects as the census, the public records, and the publication of Acts of Parliament. Only once, in the younger Pitt, were these tastes and this temperament united with supreme political talent; perhaps that is one reason why conscious amateurs like Rockingham and Charles Fox looked down upon the 'man of business' as something dusty, even a little shady. But amateurs themselves liked business, and pursued it without hope of reward: what else, for example, could have induced people like Lord Falmouth and Lord Berkeley of Stratton to spend their days so assiduously in attendance upon the committee of Council for hearing appeals in prize causes?[1] Finally, let us look at that veteran careerist Lord Auckland in 1806. Office made little difference to his income, for his pension was correspondingly diminished. But he took on the Presidency of the Board of Trade, as well as the trusteeship of the Hunterian Museum and the special commission for the Westminster improvements, and wrote with glee to the Prime Minister about all their affairs, besides attending the impeachment of Lord Melville pretty regularly in the House of Lords.[2]

---

[1] See the table in my book, *Colonial Blockade and Neutral Rights* (Oxford, 1938), p. 104.

[2] See his letters to Lord Grenville in volume viii of the *Dropmore Papers*, especially pp. 142–3.

In short, we see him (as somebody said of Gladstone) 'splashing about like a baby in its bath'. It is a pity that historians should so seldom have recognized the fact that men were in politics not only for party and for profit, but most of all for the due exercise of the talents God gave them, and for fun.[1]

[1] In 1761 Shelburne said (I dare say, with truth): 'The only pleasure I propose by the employment is not the profit, but to act a part suitable to my rank and capacity such as it is' (Fitzmaurice, op. cit. i. 88).

II

KING, LORDS, AND COMMONS

ALTHOUGH the politicians of the eighteenth century did not go into politics with the original purpose of dealing with any particular political issues, yet political issues inevitably arose, and were settled in accordance with certain political and constitutional understandings. These understandings saved politics from degenerating into mere administration or mere faction. Nobody could follow the discussion of political questions in parliament without becoming aware that Great Britain was, in some manner or other, a constitutional state.

It was a commonplace of the time that the elements were mixed, or balanced, within this constitution. This mixture was believed to have been brought about by extraordinary skill or luck: George III once called the British constitution 'the most beautiful combination that ever was framed'.[1] Probably neither George III himself nor many of his subjects could have explained very convincingly the advantages of mixed over simple constitutions: it was foreigners, such as Montesquieu, who could see and express most clearly the truth that the dispersion of political power between independent sovereignties or agencies, by neutralizing the strength and efficiency of government as a whole, enlarged the scope of civil liberties. Burke came near to saying this, towards the end of his life;[2] but more often, when he harped upon the theme of 'a combination of opposing forces', describing it as 'a work of labour long and endless praise,'[3] he seemed to hold that its beauty consisted in the inherent magnificence of subtlety and complication.[4] For Burke, however, as

---

[1] *Correspondence of George III*, no. 2991. George III spoke of himself as trying to preserve this beautiful combination unspoiled by the assaults of the Opposition: one of the assaults which he had in mind was Dunning's famous resolution, 'That the influence of the Crown has increased, is increasing, and ought to be diminished', which the House of Commons had passed less than a week earlier.

[2] *An Appeal from the New Whigs to the Old*, in *Works* (1852 edn.), iv. 486; *Second Letter on a Regicide Peace* (ibid. v. 339).

[3] *A Letter to a Member of the National Assembly* (ibid. iv. 389).

[4] See, for example, the passage in *An Appeal from the New Whigs to the Old* (ibid. iv. 486–7). Burke had, at least once in his career, denied by implication the opinion that the constitutional powers of the branches of the legislature were evenly

for his contemporaries, the contrast between the liberties enjoy-
able under a mixed and a simple constitution was immensely
heightened after 1789, when the muddled and compunctious
absolutism of the Bourbons, who had allowed their power to be
frittered away among corporations and vested interests, was
replaced by the dreadful single-minded energy of the Jacobins.

There could be no guarantee that this mixture or balance
would amount to very much in practice—that the internal con-
tradictions of the balanced powers would act forever as a protection of private liberties. Blackstone could see that King,
Lords, and Commons, when united, made up an omnicompetent
parliament. Denials of this omnicompetence, such as Burke's,[1]
were beginning to have a medieval look; and in the most celebrated trial of strength on this subject—the controversy over
parliament's legal right to tax colonists—Chatham's attempt
to limit omnicompetence by an exception was made to look
rather silly by the antiquarians and the theorists.[2] It was still,
however, the fashion to preserve and insist upon the balance as
a thing of some practical importance. The most dangerous
charge that could be made against George III was that of
upsetting or falsifying it, and he, in his turn, was able to rally
a powerful public opinion to his side, in 1784 and 1807, by
claiming that the dominant parliamentary gangs were the
aggressors against this balanced constitution, himself its up-
holder.

But what were the elements so mingled or balanced? The

balanced: in moving a *Representation to His Majesty* in the House of Commons,
14 June 1784, he had criticized phrases in the King's Speech about the need 'to
support, in their just balance, the rights and privileges of every branch of the legislature'. He had suggested that it was not 'safe to admit anything concerning the
existence of a balance' and the remonstrance had gone on to imply that the constitution was, at least, in this sense unbalanced, that the king must, in the last resort,
do what parliament wanted (ibid. iii. 522). But he wrote this under the influence of
passion, and I do not feel sure that it represents his true opinion.

[1] For example, in *Reflections on the French Revolution* (*Works* (1852 edn.), iv. 276),
'We entertain a high opinion of the legislative authority; but we have never dreamt
that parliaments had any right whatsoever to violate property, to overrule prescription, or to force a currency of their own fiction in place of that which is real, and
recognized by the law of nations.'

[2] I am aware that this is still an open question, and was debated, not very long
ago, between Professor C. H. McIlwain (*The American Revolution* (London and New
York, 1923) and Professor R. L. Schuyler (*Parliament and the British Empire* (London
and New York, 1929)). I can only say that, in my opinion, Professor Schuyler had
the better of the argument.

idea of a trinity was popular, but its terms were not always the same. Locke had spoken of executive, legislative, and federative powers as separate; Montesquieu of legislative, executive, and judiciary. Locke's terminology was soon forgotten. Montesquieu's had better luck, for he not only flattered the English, but pointed to an institution which had a real though, perhaps, subordinate importance in politics—the virtual independence of the higher judiciary.[1] But the preoccupations of Montesquieu, an antiquarian *Parlement* lawyer and a political pluralist, were not those of most Englishmen. They thought more about the old English trinity of King, Lords, and Commons. This might or might not be identical with the trinity of monarchy, aristocracy, and democracy; and that might or might not be identical with the trinity of executive power, landed property, and money. Yet other trinities might be conceived, such as that of king, property, and administrative talent.

It is best to begin with the most concrete of these trinities— that of King, Lords, and Commons. At least we know the meaning of the terms.

The distribution of power between the king and the two houses of parliament was commonly believed to have been fixed by the so-called 'Revolution Settlement'. Taking the term in the broad sense, by including in it not only the Declaration of Rights and the Act of Settlement but also the constitutional innovations and encroachments of William III's reign, this was partly true. Absolute monarchy was expressly excluded, by proscribing the use of certain prerogatives without which it could not live. The king could not rule without parliament, for both money and military discipline depended upon laws passed annually.[2] But this was all negative: it was clear enough what the king could not do—much less clear, what he could. The authors of the 'Revolution Settlement' probably did not mean, and certainly did not say, that the king was to be a figurehead.

[1] F. T. H. Fletcher, *Montesquieu and English Politics* (London, 1939), *passim*.

[2] Supplies were never actually refused, nor was the Mutiny Act openly rejected, even in the crisis of 1784. But the Opposition toyed with the idea of postponing both, in order to intimidate (Gilbert Elliot to Harris, 26 Feb. 1784, in *Diaries and Correspondence of James Harris, First Earl of Malmesbury* (London, 1844), ii. 61). The reality of the financial sanction is proved by the number of occasions when the Ministry calculated how long they could postpone the meeting of parliament without running into money difficulties. Twice—in 1784 and 1807—the time-table of a general election was affected by this consideration.

William III was not a figurehead; he was, to a very remarkable degree, the leader of the country. He was, therefore, an example of what a British king could do within the limits laid down in 1689; and George III, who likewise aspired to leadership, may have had him in mind.[1] But William III had got into many difficulties, and sometimes had to acknowledge defeat. Later generations of parliamentary politicians remembered those defeats. Lord North, who certainly had not passed as an opponent of royal power, reminded George III in 1782 that his predecessors had sometimes sacrificed 'their private wishes, and even their opinions' (note the *crescendo*, for it does George III no more than justice)

to the preservation of public order, and the prevention of those terrible mischiefs, which are the natural consequences of the clashing of two branches of the sovereign power in the State . . . Your Majesty [North continued] has graciously and steadily supported the servants you approve, as long as they could be supported: Your Majesty has firmly and resolutely maintained what appeared to you essential to the welfare and dignity of this country, as long as this country itself thought proper to maintain it. The Parliament have altered their sentiments, and as their sentiments whether just or erroneous, must ultimately prevail, Your Majesty having persevered, as long as possible, in what you thought right, can lose no honour if you yield at length, as some of the most renowned and most glorious of your predecessors have done, to the opinion and wishes of the House of Commons.[2]

Many people of that age would have considered this to be the pure milk of the Revolution gospel; they would only have been surprised at finding it in the mouth of Lord North.[3] But it had never been expressed in any document of constitutional validity, therefore it had no clear authority. Moreover, it was one-sided: it assumed that there was nothing which the king could not, in the last resort, be called upon to give up at the wish of the parliament; no real balance of powers between executive and legislature; and (as North himself was to show by his conduct within a year) no holds barred in the game of getting up an

---

[1] See his letter to Pitt, 21 Feb. 1784, published by J. Holland Rose in *Pitt and Napoleon* (London, 1912), p. 205.

[2] *Correspondence of George III*, no. 3566.

[3] It was not really surprising at all: Lord North was, above all, a House of Commons man. See p. 48, n. 1.

overwhelming parliamentary combination with which to force
the hand of the king. George III held that there were some
prerogatives—and very important ones—which even parliament could not take from him; that there was a balance, which
it was his duty to preserve even against parliament; and that
there were some limits, in morals if not in law, to the validity of
parliamentary manœuvres. These opinions were then just as
constitutional as that expressed by Lord North; indeed, they
had this much more prescription on their side, that the prerogatives in question had undoubtedly been annexed to the monarchy in the past.

This conflict was the main constitutional theme of George III's
reign; and it is the main theme of these lectures. I do not wish
to develop it further at this stage—only to point out that in the
distribution of power between the king and the parliament there
was a question which—although some politicians might think it
had all been settled long ago[1]—had not yet been resolved by any
enactment, or open admission, or irreversible course of precedents.

The relations between the other two members of the trinity—
Lords and Commons—exhibited some paradoxes. On the one
hand, the age was justly regarded as an aristocratic age; and,
in particular, the possessors of electoral influence were extremely
well represented in the House of Lords. In Robinson's list of
borough patrons, drawn up at the end of 1783, out of 11 men
who influenced or controlled more than 3 seats, only 4 were commoners; and 2 of these 4 were soon afterwards ennobled, so that
in the list published by the 'Friends of the People' in 1793, only
2 commoners were credited with influence over more than
3 seats—the rest were lords.[2] These men were not borough
patrons because they were lords: indeed, it was deemed strictly
unconstitutional for a peer of parliament to meddle with elections to the Commons, and interested parties sometimes raised
an outcry against these noble wire-pullers. On the contrary,
they were lords because they were borough patrons. For instance,
of the two commoners in Robinson's list who were ennobled

---

[1] Charles Fox asked in the House of Commons 'Had not a majority of the House
of Commons, almost from time immemorial, governed this country?' (*Parl. Hist.*
xxiv. 597.)

[2] *The Parliamentary Papers of John Robinson*, ed. W. T. Laprade, pp. 105–9;
Wyvill, op. cit. iii. Supplement, pp. 238–46.

between 1783 and 1793, neither had acted a part on the public
stage which wholly justified the honour; but Lowther controlled
nine seats in Robinson's list, including that for which the Prime
Minister himself sat, and Eliot seven: that was enough.[1] This
motive for ennoblement was even commoner in Ireland than in
England: finally the suppression of a number of Irish borough
seats at the Union was compensated by the biggest wholesale
promotion ever made in the peerage. Nor was the practice quite
extinct in England itself: as late as 1857 Lord Palmerston thought
it relevant to mention the electoral influence of a candidate
whom he recommended to Queen Victoria for a step in the
peerage.[2]

Thus the heads of many families sat in the Lords, their younger
brothers and dependants in the Commons. The elder Pitt once
described the House of Commons as 'a parcel of younger
brothers'.[3] One might naturally expect that when the elder
brother exercised the rights of a borough patron, as well as the
prestige and, perhaps, the financial control which went with the
headship of the family, he would determine the conduct of the
family as a whole, and the younger branches in the House of
Commons could only follow. For the rights of a borough patron,
especially in those close constituencies where his influence was
incontestable, were usually regarded as absolute. There might
be half-hearted patrons like the Duke of Leeds, who felt com-
punction about coercing his nominee Charles Abbot; but even
the Duke of Leeds was provoked to ask what was the use of
electoral influence if your M.P.s never did what you wanted,
and Abbot finally chose, or was forced, in 1802, to change constituencies by changing dukes.[4] Other patrons had less scruple:
as late as 1827, W. H. Fremantle had to apply for the Chiltern
Hundreds because he would not follow his patron, the Duke of
Buckingham, into opposition against Canning.[5] Even a young
man of obvious distinction like the younger Pitt was regarded
as being, in a manner, his patron's property: Lowther was

---

[1] According to the report of the committee of the Society of the Friends of the
People, 1793, nine persons, controlling twenty-four seats, had been elevated to the
peerage in the last nine years (ibid. iii. Supplement, 236).

[2] H. C. F. Bell, *Lord Palmerston* (London, 1931), ii. 158.

[3] P. C. Yorke, op. cit. ii. 238.

[4] *Diaries and Correspondence of Lord Colchester* (London, 1861), i. 13, 17, 124–31.

[5] *The Formation of Canning's Ministry*, ed. A. Aspinall, p. 83.

congratulated on Pitt's maiden speech and received the earliest information about Pitt's intention to take office; it was understood between them that if ever their lines of conduct should become opposite, Pitt would 'give him an opportunity of choosing another person'.[1]

Many borough patrons exercised this power over their own relations, already indebted to them for help and favours of other kinds. There were some families whose heads used these means of control to the full. Charles Townshend, for example, although a somewhat more important politician than his elder brother, usually insisted on consulting him before accepting a new office; and when Rockingham tried to negotiate with Charles without first observing this formality, Lord Townshend was exceedingly displeased.[2] The Yorkes were kept together as a clan for two generations after the great Lord Chancellor's death; so strong was the family feeling that Charles Yorke died of his brother's reproaches for his acceptance of the Great Seal, and the third Lord Hardwicke seems to have decided, more than once, whether his somewhat better-known brother should accept office or go into opposition.[3] But the best instance of family solidarity, and the power of the head of the family, is that of the Grenvilles. Perhaps this family was unusual in certain respects. For three generations the eldest son was a proud, passionate man who claimed the right to manipulate the careers of better-known

[1] *Hist. MSS. Comm.*, *Lonsdale MSS.*, p. 140; Stanhope, op. cit. i. 47.

[2] Charles Townshend was reported, in 1764, to have said that he would 'receive no proposals, but through his brother, and those must be in writing' (Lord George Sackville to General Irwin, 25 Nov. 1764, *Hist. MSS. Comm.*, *Stopford-Sackville MSS.* i. 98). According to the Duke of Newcastle, Charles Townshend refused to come into the Rockingham Ministry, 'declaring his own inclination to accept, but that his brother, my Lord Townshend, would not permit him to do it' (*The Duke of Newcastle's Narrative of Changes in the Ministry, 1765-7*, ed. Mary Bateson (London, 1898), p. 25). A few days later Lord Townshend was alleged to have refused a Secretaryship of State on his brother's behalf, and 'alleged the injury he felt as having been done to him in attempts having been made to seduce his brother from him, by negotiating with him at least ten days before he himself had received any message' (George Grenville's diary in *Grenville Papers*, iii. 211).

[3] See Basil Williams, 'The Eclipse of the Yorkes' in *Transactions of the Royal Historical Society*, 3rd series, ii. 129-50, especially pp. 148-9; also an unpublished thesis by Mr. J. T. Park, of the University of Manchester, on Charles Yorke. The third Lord Hardwicke, who had announced his family's adhesion to Lord Grenville's cause in 1807 (Grenville to Auckland, 19 Mar. 1807, *Journal and Correspondence of Lord Auckland*, iv. 299), is said to have refused to let his half-brother Charles take office in Perceval's Ministry, 1809 (Spencer Walpole, *Life of Spencer Perceval* (London, 1874), ii. 11).

younger branches for the purpose of obtaining a step in the
peerage for himself; in addition, the first Lord Temple seems to
have had most of the family property (his brother George
thought, too much), and, being childless, was not tied up by
marriage settlements, so that he could use a great income to
reward brothers (or brothers-in-law) who agreed with him and
punish those who differed from him. His nephew, the first Marquis of Buckingham, though not childless, seems to have had
money to spare for similar purposes; and, though there was
more real generosity and less calculation in the offers which he
repeatedly made to his brothers, their freedom of political action
must have been all the more effectually impaired.[1] This financial

[1] The first Lord Temple offered Pitt £1,000 a year as a compensation for the
office from which he had been dismissed in 1755 (*Grenville Papers*, i. 149–52). In
1761 he rewarded his brother James, who resigned with him and Pitt, by a post-obit
bond for £5,000, which obviously must be paid out of the estate to be inherited by
the sons of his brother George, who had not resigned (ibid. i. 408). When George
became a Secretary of State next year, and had to stand for re-election at Buckingham, Lord Temple 'left him at liberty to offer his service at Buckingham, but did
not intend to recommend any person upon this vacancy'. George put a good face
on this, but it must have indicated displeasure (ibid. i. 453). Only after the brothers
were reconciled did Temple send George Grenville £1,000 for answering the 'vile
misrepresentations' of his brother-in-law Pitt, who was now the enemy (ibid. iii.
227). In the negotiations over the formation of Pitt's Ministry in 1766, Temple, as
the head of the family, played the cards of George Grenville, the former Prime
Minister, as well as his own, and saw fit to exhibit the family's dignity and moderation, by asking nothing for his brother, a great deal for himself (ibid. iii. 267–8,
275). No wonder that George Grenville once criticized his mother for having
sacrificed the younger branches of her family too much, in the settlement of the
Stowe and Wotton estates, to make her eldest son a great man (ibid. i. 428). No
wonder also that Shelburne said of Temple, in the remarkable character which he
drew of him, that, 'From his dependants and the other branches of his family, he
expected a degree of deference to his opinions and inclinations, which was not consistent with their interest or dignity' (Fitzmaurice, op. cit. ii. 26).

The second Earl Temple, and first Marquis of Buckingham, seems to have used
his power peevishly rather than ruthlessly. He was very much cut up when his
brother Tom threw up his mission in France as a political gesture in support of
Charles Fox (July 1782); and indeed, he might well be annoyed, since, for all Tom
Grenville knew, Temple himself was about to become Fox's successor. Yet, though
he wrote with resentment that Tom had sacrificed for his political friends 'that
political and intimate connexion, which nature had pointed out', he does not
appear to have cut off Tom's income (*Courts and Cabinets of George III*, i. 272). But
he exploited the loyalty of his much more distinguished brother William: he
accepted his offer to resign the Speakership for his sake (*Hist. MSS. Comm., Dropmore MSS.* i. 444, 447) and came near, more than once, to breaking off all relations
with him when his own unreasonable pride was offended by the rejection of a job
or the readmission to favour of anybody whom he had ever discountenanced as
Lord Lieutenant of Ireland (ibid. ii. 647–50, 655–6). On the other hand, when Lord
Grenville offered to resign in December 1793, because Pitt could not do one of Lord

control did not prevent George Grenville from becoming Prime Minister against Lord Temple's will, or Tom Grenville from following Charles Fox for a dozen years while the Marquis of Buckingham supported Pitt. But Lord Grenville, even after he became a Secretary of State and the second man in the Ministry, was forever being torn between his family allegiance to his brother and his political allegiance to Pitt: more than once he seems to have been on the point of sacrificing the latter to the former for wholly insufficient causes. Finally, the first Duke of Buckingham believed that upon a junction of his forces with those of Lord Liverpool's Ministry in 1821, he had been invited to designate his own representative in the Cabinet; he wrote the Duke of Wellington letters, in 1827, which could only mean that, having withdrawn his confidence from his cousin Charles Wynn, the President of the Board of Control, he had a right, if not to demand the expulsion of Wynn from the Cabinet, at least to appoint another representative or to claim some equivalent compensation, namely the Governor-Generalship of India, for himself.[1]

Yet these examples of the *patria potestas* in politics would give a wholly misleading impression of the relation between the two Houses as institutions. The House of Lords, as a body, was very much the weaker of the two. Its debates were sometimes more brilliant than those of the Commons—for example, in the later years of Sir Robert Walpole—and ministers were very far from

Buckingham's military jobs and Lord Grenville had unwittingly been made to tell his brother a lie about it, Lord Buckingham had the grace to say he did not expect him to do so (ibid. ii. 482–6). Lord Buckingham felt hurt because his brother did not give him advance news of the Duke of Leeds's resignation from the Cabinet (ibid. ii. 56) and, perhaps most unreasonable of all, expected his brother to consult him before putting anybody (other than the holders of efficient offices) into his Cabinet (ibid. vii. 342).

[1] *The Formation of Canning's Ministry*, ed. Aspinall, pp. 45–46, 50–51; *Journal of Mrs. Arbuthnot*, ed. Bamford and the Duke of Wellington (London, 1950), i. 434; see also *Wellington, Despatches (Continuation)*, iii. 589. There is no evidence in his son's *Memoirs of the Court of George IV* to show that Liverpool interpreted the invitation to Wynn in the same sense, though it was clearly meant to earn Buckingham's support (see Liverpool's letter to the king, 7 Oct. 1822, in Yonge's *Life and Administration of Lord Liverpool* (London, 1868), iii. 204–5). I have already referred to the duke's arbitrary action in forcing W. H. Fremantle to vacate the Buckingham seat because they no longer agreed in politics (p. 36, n. 5). They seem, however, to have made it up soon afterwards, and the duke promised support to Canning's successor Goderich (Duke of Buckingham, *Memoirs of the Court of George IV* (London, 1859), ii. 347–52).

thinking an adverse vote in the Lords of no account: Grafton, for instance, was desperately anxious about the narrowness of his majorities there in the summer of 1767,[1] and the rejection of a Government bill, procured in the Lords by somewhat questionable means in 1783, was deemed to give George III enough excuse for dismissing the Coalition Ministry.[2] Yet the House of Lords was not usually considered to have the same weight as the House of Commons; still less could it stand up to the king or impose its will upon him as the House of Commons was believed, at least by some people, to have the right of doing.[3]

Indeed, most people considered the House of Lords as an occasionally useful longstop, which could be perfectly relied upon to reject any measure which the Ministry could not, or durst not, resist in the Commons. This was particularly true of bills or motions which the members of the House of Commons were obliged to patronize because the electorate and the public, generally, were known to favour them. George III, for example, advised North in 1772 not to force his supporters in the House of Commons to vote against the Dissenters' Relief Bill, if it would expose them to losing their seats at the next election; North should content himself with opposing it in person, and if he should be beaten, 'the House of Lords will prevent any evil'. North's lieutenants in the Commons advised him not even to vote against the bill himself, and all said that this was the kind of bill that should be thrown out by the Lords, not the Commons.[4] It was obvious enough that the Lords would reject this bill, for nearly all the twenty-six bishops would vote against it

[1] Grafton to Chatham, 27 May 1767, in *Correspondence of William Pitt, Earl of Chatham*, ed. Pringle and Taylor (London, 1838–40), iii. 255. The king seems to have been less worried (see his letter of 30 May, ibid., pp. 260–1), but he had not, like Grafton, to face the music. Perhaps Grafton, too, would have minded less had he sat elsewhere, e.g. in the House of Commons.

[2] See Temple's memo. 1 Dec. 1783 in *Courts and Cabinets of George III*, i. 288; the king clearly tried to bring the House of Lords into play against the Commons in Feb. 1784 (D. G. Barnes, *George III and William Pitt* (Stanford U.P. 1939), p. 82). Not until 1836 did a Ministry declare that it should not regard an adverse vote in the Lords as a reason for resigning office. (See also Melbourne's letter of 22 Mar. 1839 to Queen Victoria, in *Letters of Queen Victoria*, 1st series (London, 1907), i. 188–9).

[3] This was clearly understood by Burke, the partisan of aristocracy (*Observations on the Conduct of the Minority*, in *Works* (1852 edn.), v. 126–7).

[4] *Correspondence of George III*, nos. 1048, 1049. The king did not see why the leader of the House should not court defeat for a good cause; the parliamentarians could see more clearly that his prestige would suffer by *any* defeat.

without any prompting. But the king was just as ready to rely upon the House of Lords to throw out the Contractors' Bill, a measure without any ecclesiastical reference;[1] and, in general, most people would have agreed with Lord Stormont in describing the House of Lords as the place 'where the great support of Government should naturally lie'.[2]

The reasons for this subserviency of the Lords to the executive were often discussed. The Ministry controlled the election of most of the sixteen Scottish peers. Most of the episcopal bench, even if not appointed by the present Ministry, hoped that the present Ministry would translate them. Some of the British lay peers had been created by the present Ministry, or at least the present king. Still more of them hoped that the present Ministry or the present king would give them a further step in the peerage. Some members of the upper House, as of the lower, were placemen and, in particular, lords of the Bedchamber, a post which brought them into fairly close personal contact with the Crown. Party leaders often gibed at this phalanx, especially the Scots peers, the Bedchamber and, above all, the bishops. These, for example, were held responsible for the defeat of Fox's India Bill in 1783.[3] The bishops were almost a laughing-stock for their subservience. They could not even stay away without exciting comment: when only seven of the twenty-six appeared in parliament during the ticklish Regency crisis of 1788, Lord Bulkeley remarked that it was 'a proof that crows soon smell powder', and Lord Auckland pointedly called the Prime Minister's attention to a conspicuous absence of bishops in 1807.[4] This outcry against

---

[1] Ibid., no. 2536. (It was not necessary on this occasion, for the House of Commons itself rejected the bill.)

[2] Ibid., no. 3131. The Irish House of Lords was likewise useful as a longstop. Before the Renunciation Act of 1782 it was not the only one, for both British and Irish Privy Councils could put a spoke in the wheels of legislation; but when they lost this power, the House of Lords became more important in this respect, as the Government immediately recognized (Sydney to Rutland, 28 Apr. 1784, *Hist. MSS. Comm., Rutland MSS.* iii. 91).

[3] Fox, in *Parl. Hist.* xxiv. 210–11; Fitzpatrick to Ossory, 15 Dec. 1783, in *Memorials and Correspondence of Charles James Fox*, ii. 220. Lord Loughborough hoped that the bench would stand firm against royal influence (*Journal and Correspondence of Lord Auckland*, i. 67), but he was mistaken: even the Archbishop of Canterbury, Eden's brother-in-law, voted against the bill.

[4] *Courts and Cabinets of George III*, ii. 14; *Hist. MSS. Comm., Dropmore MSS.* viii. 148. George IV, in 1827, gave Canning a written authority to ensure that the bishops behaved properly in the House of Lords (*Formation of Canning's Ministry*, ed. Aspinall, p. 236).

the bishops was, perhaps, exaggerated. Professor Sykes has shown, for example, that Newcastle's joke about the bishops forgetting their maker was not wholly justified, since nearly half of his nominees stuck to him for some years after he lost power; and if he could not persuade them to enter systematically into opposition, their refusal can hardly be blamed.[1] Indeed, the resistance of the House of Lords as a whole to popular legislation can be misinterpreted. There were, no doubt, occasions when the ministers tipped the wink to the Archbishop or to other supporters in the upper House about legislation which they did not wish to oppose in the Commons: but more often they had only to rely on the peers' spontaneous dislike of all change, which indeed often showed itself in the rejection of measures which the majority, at least, of the ministers would have favoured: thus the younger Pitt was seriously nettled by the resistance which the peers (abetted by his own Lord Chancellor) put up to the smallest interference with the slave trade, and it was not until the Prime Minister was himself in the Lords that this resistance was overcome.[2]

An institution which normally submitted to so much executive influence, and only resisted when it was even more conservative than the executive itself, was not likely to overbear the House of Commons, whose goodwill the executive had to

[1] Sykes, op. cit., pp. 51–54. I only know of one occasion when a prospective bishop was asked his political intentions before he was appointed: this was in 1827, when Canning, hard pressed in the House of Lords, asked Dean Percy (whose relations had just voted against the Ministry's Corn Bill) what his politics would be. According to Canning, the dean did not resent the inquiry (*Correspondence of George IV*, ed. Aspinall, no. 1359). I do not reckon George IV's inquiries about Dr. Copleston's attitude to the Catholic question (ibid., nos. 1420, 1426) as a strictly political interference.

[2] Pitt was ready to bring on a dispute between the two Houses, and even to break up his Cabinet, if the House of Lords rejected Dolben's bill (*Hist. MSS. Comm., Dropmore MSS.* i. 342). This proved unnecessary. See also *George Canning and his Friends*, ed. Joceline Bagot (London, 1909), i. 149–51, for evidences of Canning's indignation, which he believed Pitt and Grenville to share, against the constant sniping of Government supporters in the Lords against bills for regulating the slave trade. Grenville has not been given enough credit for the abolition of the slave trade. Fox and Grey, in the Commons, had done no more than Pitt had done before: they had not introduced the bill as a Government measure, but only as one favoured by members of the Government (see Howick's declaration in Cobbett's *Parl. Debates*, ix. 279). Grenville would have compromised if necessary in order to get something through the House of Lords (see his letter to Sidmouth, *Hist. MSS. Comm., Dropmore MSS.* viii. 168–70), but he finally got the measure entire through the Lords—a remarkable achievement, in view of the Lords' record of obstruction.

cultivate. The primacy of the House of Commons in politics—its ultimate superiority not only over the Crown, but also over the House of Lords—was beginning to be generally assumed, in one way or another.

This primacy of the House of Commons is better explained by its historical role than by any direct appeal to the representative principle; for that principle was by no means generally accepted at the time and, in any case, the House of Commons was obviously not representative as we should use the word: both in theory and in fact many people looked upon the House as 'a second rate aristocracy'.[1] The theories of virtual representation were invoked in order to explain how a House of Commons which only represented opinions and interests in a most haphazard fashion was nevertheless entitled to prestige and preponderance. Burke admitted that virtual representation—the undefined community of interests and sympathy in feelings and desires—must have a substratum in actual representation;[2] but only a substratum—and he reduced the role of the people in politics to that of uttering cries of distress, whose interpretation and remedy was a matter for a sanhedrin of skilled legislators, collected with more regard to variety of experience than to the proportion of the interests represented.[3] So little was the principle of actual representation valued that the early parliamentary reformers themselves ignored or even denied it. All the emphasis, at first, was on making the House of Commons more virtuous, or more independent of the Crown, or more economical; only gradually did the inequalities of representation come to appear as the chief part of the grievance.[4] Thus it would not

---

[1] Flood's phrase, in his speech of 4 Mar. 1790: 'The House of Commons is a second rate aristocracy instead of a popular representation' (Wyvill, op. cit. ii. 554).

[2] *A Letter to Sir Hercules Langrishe, Bart.* (1792), in *Works* (1852 edn.), iv. 540.

[3] See, for instance, his remarks at the end of the *Speech on the Plan for Economical Reform* (ibid. iii. 401).

[4] The change can be traced in the proposals. Pitt's scheme of 1783 provided for 100 additional members for counties; this shows that the emphasis, in his mind, was still on strengthening that part of the House which had the reputation of virtue and independence (*v. supra*, pp. 8–9). In 1785 he proposed 72 additional members for counties and 36 for big towns; but the process of enfranchisement was to depend on the voluntary and, presumably, gradual extinction of rotten boroughs, and all the 72 county seats were to be allocated before the big towns got anything. In 1793 his former supporter Wyvill proposed to reverse this priority, in favour of 'those great unrepresented towns and districts of the metropolis, whose total

be exactly true to say that the House of Commons founded its claim to supremacy upon the representative principle. It founded that claim rather on its historical function as a check on the Crown.[1] Probably the two things were mingled in most people's minds. But, whatever the justification, this claim to supremacy was made and passionately supported: the exaltation of the House of Commons as a body came to be thought the essential principle of the constitution.

This exaltation took many forms. Firstly in the formation of Ministries, the claims of the House of Commons were set against those of the House of Lords, especially during the long period of wrangles and manœuvres which followed the death of Henry Pelham. For a whole generation before that date (with the exception of two years in which Pelham shared the power with Carteret) the chief minister, so far as there was one, had apparently sat in the House of Commons.[2] In 1754, when George II reverted to the older practice of taking his chief minister from the House of Lords, the pride of the House of Commons was affronted. Moreover, as experience was to show, it was becoming very difficult to manage the Commons by remote control: the members of parliament who received, or were ready to receive, favours from the Government, needed some leader to discipline them and negotiate with them, or the Ministry would soon cease to get value for money.[3] There must, therefore, be an accredited leader of the House; but if he was kept in the dark as to patronage or policy, if he was treated as a mere mouthpiece without any voice in the policy he expounded, his leadership

privation of the fundamental right of representation must be considered as the most oppressive grievance' (Wyvill, op. cit. ii. 388, 391, 599–602). It is an open question, how Wyvill's own development in the direction of the representative principle may best be explained: possibly he had to play it down at first, in the hope of getting the support of the Rockingham whigs, whom he distrusted but wished to use; also his dislike of aristocracy seems to have been increased by the coalition of 1784, which he treated as a mere manœuvre of aristocratic gangs. Whatever the cause, he began by laying stress on the *freedom* of parliament and ended by laying it on the *representative* principle.

[1] 'What, Sir, is the purpose of Parliament, but a balance against the power of the Crown?' (Thomas Pitt, in the House of Commons, 7 May 1782, in Wyvill, op. cit. i. 460).

[2] I say 'apparently', because the exact distribution of power between Henry Pelham and his elder brother the Duke of Newcastle is obscure (*v. infra*, pp. 176–7).

[3] As Murray told Newcastle, 'It is necessary where different colours may fly by surprize, that there should be a standard which may be followed by the eye' (Ilchester, op. cit. i. 217).

would be neither wholehearted nor efficient, and the House, as a body, would soon come to resent its relegation to the status of an 'appendage', or 'a parcel of younger brothers'.[1]

The Duke of Newcastle seems to have been genuinely blind to the importance of these feelings, or over-confident of his ability to manage the House by the distribution of loaves and fishes from the background. But those ambitious rivals in the Commons, Henry Fox and William Pitt, did not intend to acquiesce in such a slight to the House. Fox seems to have aimed at becoming chief minister himself, a position for which he was wholly unfitted because he had no interest whatever in questions of policy. Pitt knew he could not aim so high, for the king disliked him and he had not, like Fox, a supporter within the royal family; but his parliamentary *esprit de corps* was far more genuine than that of Fox, who seems to have secretly considered the House as an ill-conditioned talking-shop which distracted time from the business of administration.[2] Though they agreed in nothing else, and regarded their rivalry with each other as the burning question in politics, Pitt and Fox combined to make Newcastle's attempt at remote control impossible. Fox refused office at first because Newcastle would not tell him what he did with the Secret Service money;[3] Pitt demanded an office of advice as well as execution, and refused to talk, like a lawyer, from a brief.[4] Both insisted on entry to the Cabinet and free access to the king's closet, independent of the permission of any senior colleague. Newcastle only gave way to these demands

[1] The phrases are the elder Pitt's. Fox demanded 'some such mark only of your Majesty's favour, as may enable me to speak like one perfectly informed, and honoured with your Majesty's confidence in regard to the matters I may be speaking of' (*Chatham Correspondence*, i. 129).

[2] See his letter to Bedford, 4 Nov. 1756: 'Richelieu, were he alive, could not guide the councils of a nation if (which would be my case) he could not from November to April have above two hours in four-and-twenty to think of anything but the House of Commons' (*Bedford Correspondence*, ii. 210; see also Fox's and his nephew Digby's letters, in Ilchester, op. cit. ii. 10). Pitt, on the other hand, was a real House of Commons man; he may have been sincere when he told Newcastle that he would have served under another House of Commons politician such as Fox or even Murray, but implied that he could not bear to have a mere diplomat like Sir Thomas Robinson put over him (*Chatham Correspondence*, i. 100).

[3] As Sir Lewis Namier has pointed out (*Structure of Politics*, i. 213–90) the Secret Service money was not very important in politics; but the objection is characteristic of Fox: believing, as he did, that corruption was three-quarters of political influence, he would not take service with Newcastle unless he could share in its direction.

[4] P. C. Yorke, op. cit. ii. 238.

inch by inch: at first he admitted that 'he did not intend Mr. Fox should have any power whatever out of his own office', and asked 'Who desires Mr. Fox should be answerable for anybody but himself in the H. of Commons?' Then he tried to fob him off by promising that he should be 'constantly and early informed of all advices that may come from abroad, and all other matters that may in any way relate to the business of the House of Commons', but limited this concession by the reservation that 'it was not His Majesty's intention to confer any power or confidence independent of such Ministers as His Majesty should think fit to entrust with the conduct of his affairs', which amounted to saying that the leader of the House was to be a mere mouthpiece. Finally, when Fox, Pitt, and Legge had defeated all these attempts at limitation by the curious expedient of opposing his measures from the Treasury Bench, Newcastle had to make his bargain with one of them. Even then he was not safe, for Fox, whom he had chosen as the least exacting in questions of policy and not, after all, likely to rival him in the affections of the king, proved to be without the courage to face the terrific House of Commons storm which the misfortunes of war and Pitt's demagogy were likely to conjure up. Not until Pitt himself had come to terms with Newcastle, was the problem of keeping the House of Commons quiet under the king's ministers settled for the time being.

The claims of the Commons, however, had a permanent or, at least, a recurrent influence upon the balance of power within the Ministry. These claims were exploited by George Grenville, a commoner surrounded in the Cabinet by lords. Even before he became Prime Minister, Grenville jealously asserted his rights, as leader of the House of Commons, against both Newcastle and Bute. The fall of Newcastle in 1762 was caused, in part, by the refusal of the leader of the House to demand from it the money which the First Lord of the Treasury believed to be necessary;[1] and Grenville attributed his own degradation from the leadership a few months later to 'the opinion I had

---

[1] *Grenville Papers*, i. 440; see also George III's letter in *Letters from George III to Lord Bute, 1756–1766*, ed. Romney Sedgwick (London, 1939), p. 100; Newcastle to Barrington, 8 Apr. 1762, British Museum Additional MSS. 32926, f. 440; to Hardwicke, 10, 17, and 30 Apr., vol. 32937, ff. 13, 183, 450; Mansfield to Newcastle, 3 May, vol. 32938, f. 28; Newcastle to Rockingham, 4 May, f. 50; to Devonshire, 5 and 7 May, ff. 67, 105.

declared some time ago of the difficulties to carry on the business of the House of Commons without being authorized to talk to the members of that House upon their several claims and pretensions, and having them communicated through me to Lord Bute and the King which was a circumstance that Lord Bute could not consent to'.[1] When he became Prime Minister, his noble colleagues seem to have agreed that he alone should have the disposing of offices to members of the House of Commons, and only disputed his claim to have the whole patronage.[2] He was succeeded by three Prime Ministers in the Lords, and they experienced some of the Duke of Newcastle's old difficulties in managing the Commons from a distance. One of these was the great Earl of Chatham who, as William Pitt, had so mercilessly pressed the claims of the House of Commons and its leader against Newcastle. He was now resisted, one might say defied, by his own House of Commons ministers: by disregarding their advice he lost the support of the Rockingham party, and they turned so insubordinate that he had to use a completely unofficial mouthpiece, his friend Beckford, in the House of Commons for his opinions upon the East India question.[3] Even before he retired from the scene, the House and the Treasury Bench were quite out of hand, and a psychologist might suggest that the consciousness that he could not cope with them was one of the things that turned his gout to madness.

The problem of managing the House of Commons was not dealt with satisfactorily until the promotion of North, a House of Commons man. Whether, and in what sense, North was a Prime Minister, is a matter to be discussed later: but at least it can be said that if the real Prime Minister was elsewhere—namely, on the throne—North was an ideal leader of the House, for,

---

[1] *Grenville Papers*, i. 483. It is interesting that Grenville should have thought this important, but in fact his degradation was probably to be accounted for by something else, namely Bute's distrust of his loyalty in defence of the terms of peace (see my book, *War and Trade in the West Indies* (Oxford, 1936), pp. 604–8).

[2] *Grenville Papers*, ii. 207, 211–12, 221. Grenville himself seems to have confused the two things, for he told Sandwich 'that in the situation he stands in the House of Commons, he must be known to have the patronage, or the whole must break'.

[3] Horace Walpole, *Memoirs of the Reign of King George III* (1894 edn.), ii. 267–92 (Walpole is a good authority here, because much of his information came from Conway, one of the House of Commons ministers concerned); Grafton, op. cit., pp. 103–28; *Chatham Correspondence*, iii. 176, 188, 199, 201, 218; *Hist. MSS. Comm., Stopford-Sackville MSS.* i. 119.

though he always took the House, its claims and opinions, seriously, he did not try to use it for the purpose of claiming for himself, against his superiors, the last word on policy or patronage.[1] Perhaps the necessity of a trustworthy House of Commons minister was best illustrated in the crisis of 1783, when most of the talent of the House was arrayed against the king, and happened to command a majority of the votes. Any number of Ministries were sketched on paper; but none of them had the slightest chance of life without a commanding figure in the House of Commons, who durst put himself at the king's service and would consent to do so on tolerable terms. George III hunted all over the place for such a person—'Mr. Thomas Pitt or Mr. Thomas Anybody'. William Pitt alone could fill the bill; and this was why he was able to make terms which the king cannot altogether have liked.[2]

Thus the necessity of conciliating the goodwill of the House of Commons repeatedly strengthened the ministers who belonged to it, against their noble colleagues in the Cabinet. This was one way of exalting the House of Commons as an institution.

Many people, as I have said, regarded the exaltation of the House of Commons as the main achievement of the 1688 Revolution. But this exaltation, like the Revolution itself, could be understood in more ways than one.

It could be treated simply as a legal fact, without any political implications of a democratic or even popular kind, just as the Revolution itself could be treated as a unique historical event, defensive in character, which had brought about a state of affairs definable only in terms of itself. As Burke pointed out early in his career, 'To be a Whig on the business of an hundred years ago, is very consistent with every advantage of present

---

[1] North looked upon himself as a House of Commons man, and once spoke as if his political advancement had been due to his eminence in that House. (See his speech of 7 May 1783, *Parl. Hist.* xxiii. 852.) This was only partly true: North had been a very useful speaker in the House, but his career had been that of a 'man of business', not that of a party leader—he brought with him no party of his own when he became First Lord of the Treasury, though he took a large one away with him when he left office. He never really cared for anything except the House of Commons: he took reverses there much more seriously than the king (*Correspondence of George III*, nos. 1405, 1406, 2179, 2182, 2292, 2295, 2322, 2535, 2536, 3568), and his Secretary of the Treasury had once to implore him not to take to heart a defeat in a division over university almanacs (*Hist. MSS. Comm., Abergavenny MSS.* p. 25).

[2] For these terms, *v. infra*, p. 130.

servility'—and, he might have added, of political conservatism:[1] a curious remark, for Burke himself later became the best possible instance of 'a Whig on the business of an hundred years ago', when he appealed from the New Whigs to the Old, and represented the 1688 Revolution as an event from which no general consequences—least of all, democratic consequences—could be drawn.

Other members of the House of Commons could not understand any but a purely legal interpretation of their privileges, or see any sense in the proposition that those privileges ought to be used for the enlargement of popular influence. This was the significance of the Wilkes episodes, which showed up, as by a flash of lightning, the hidden differences between the whigs upon the business of a hundred years ago and the whigs upon the business of today: for the House was suspected, first of limiting its own privileges in order to assist in the punishment of one whose real offence was that of setting up for a tribune of the people; and, later, of refusing to allow the electorate to elect him. The majority in the House of Commons which favoured these undemocratic proceedings was probably, for the most part, sincere. If the persecutions of Wilkes had only had the support of those who perverted judgement in order to gratify the personal vengeance of the king, they would never have been carried into effect.[2] They had also the consent—sometimes the enthusiastic consent—of the legally minded, the conservative, and the unimaginative, such as Mr. de Grey who exclaimed in the House that: 'Such is the levelling principle that has gone forth, that the people imagine they themselves should be judges over us'; or that feeble purist Conway, who warned the Opposition not to set up the liberty of the people against the liberty of parliament;

---

[1] *Thoughts on the Cause of the Present Discontents* (*Works* (1852 edn.), iii. 115–16).

[2] This is not to deny that George III strained his influence to the full in order to get Wilkes suppressed: according to George Grenville, he treated it as a personal matter in 1763, and was hot for dismissing Conway from the Bedchamber for his vote (*Grenville Papers*, ii. 162, 223). He proposed Wilkes's expulsion from the House to North in 1768, and described the question next year as 'a measure whereon my Crown almost depends'. Conway's brother, a courtier who knew his business, found it necessary to apologize for Conway's lukewarmness in this business even in a private meeting, and the king collected lists of those whose vote was unsatisfactory, with a view to intimidating them by rudeness in the Drawing-room (*Correspondence of George III*, nos. 613, 690–3, 703; the last of these documents may possibly refer to a division on another subject).

or George Onslow, son of the great Speaker, who claimed
that the rejection of Wilkes was pure whiggism, that the House
of Commons was contending, not with the people of England
but with a few individuals of the county of Middlesex, and that
any opposition to the privileges of the House, even in such a
cause as this, would necessarily increase the power of the Crown
and the House of Lords.[1] The question of American taxation
divided the politicians in a similar way: for there were many
who thought all general principles of 'no taxation without representation' beside the point, and could only see what they supposed to be the historical and legal fact that the British parliament exercised the right of binding the colonists, as it had
bound the people of the county palatine of Chester, in all cases
whatsoever.[2] George III, who had far less initial responsibility
for the American troubles than for the Wilkes affair, could say
in all good faith that in attempting to restore control over the
colonies, he was 'fighting the battle of the legislature'.[3]

The partisans of this sovereign body were very jealous of any
pressure from the general public, even from constituents. The
right of constituents to instruct their members of parliament on
political affairs was an open question. Some constituencies with
well-defined interests in trade habitually sent such instructions
on proposals which might affect them, even when such proposals
took the form of bills of general interest. Bristol, for example,
must have instructed its members dozens of times—a fact which
adds topicality to Burke's famous harangue on this subject.[4] At
certain times in the past, especially about 1740, waves of instruction had flowed to Westminster upon the political questions of
the day. There was another wave from 1768 to 1770. But the
practice was a controversial one: the right to instruct was both

[1] Sir Henry Cavendish, *Debates*, i. 230, 352, 367.
[2] The Yorkes are a good instance of this kind of legal conservatism: probably
their opinions had almost as much influence as those of the king in obliging the
first Rockingham Ministry to pass the Declaratory Act along with the repeal of the
Stamp Act. (Albemarle, op. cit. i. 284; see also Mr. J. T. Park's unpublished thesis
quoted above.) Charles Yorke was also against allowing Wilkes to plead his parliamentary privilege against a charge of seditious libel—either because he had un-
guardedly committed himself on the subject, or because his enemy Pratt held the
contrary opinion, or because he really believed that the privilege did not extend so
far in law.
[3] *Correspondence of George III*, no. 1709.
[4] See Mr. P. T. Underdown's unpublished thesis, quoted above.

attacked and defended, for example, in the House of Commons debate of 1 March 1769 on the civil list, and echoes of the controversy came from the shores of Jamaica, where the vestry of St. Ann's parish thought fit to pass a resolution affirming the right.[1]

The right to petition parliament was limited, in the interest of public order, by the Act of 1664 against tumultuous petitioning. The attempt to narrow this limitation still further, in the case of the Kentish Petition, might be held to have been discredited; and it was generally agreed that a meeting held, conformably to this Act, in order to petition parliament for the redress of grievances, was the one clearly unexceptionable form of public political assembly.[2] Even so, there were people who did not feel quite happy unless the meeting was called by the high sheriff of the county, which would presumably give it some of the status of a meeting of the historic county court, now decayed.[3] There was also, perhaps, a lingering feeling that there

[1] Sir Henry Cavendish, *Debates*, i. 280, 288; St. Ann's Parish, Jamaica, Vestry Minutes, 1767–91, p. 31. Even the politicians of the Opposition who claimed the lead in a popular cause, disliked the idea that they acted under any impulsion from their constituents: for example, the members for the city of York, replying on 26 Aug. 1769 to an address of thanks, went out of their way to say: 'We feel ourselves extremely happy that in the free exercise of our own judgements, we have acted in a manner agreeable to your sentiments' (Wyvill, op. cit., vol. i, p. xv). Burke, introducing his Bill for Economical Reform in 1780, said that he had not followed the sense of the people, but 'met it on the way'. One of the most remarkable instances of obedience to instructions was that of Alderman Sawbridge, member for the city of London, who announced in the House that although he had voted twice for Fox's East India Bill, he should now vote against it in committee because his constituents had instructed him to do so; but he should use no arguments against the bill as his constituents had not furnished him with any (*Parl. Hist.* xxiv. 55).

[2] Wyvill, op. cit. ii. 287–303 (see, especially, the remarks of Lord Fauconberg). The rarity of public meetings for political purposes helps to explain the importance of race-meetings, which served as a means of retailing political gossip and discussing political plans. There is a good instance of this in Burke's letters: he was expecting Lord Temple to put up his nephew for Buckinghamshire in the general election of 1774, and could not make out why he had not done so at the Aylesbury races; a few days later the mystery was cleared up—Lord Temple did announce the candidature at the Newport Pagnell races, in his own corner of the county (Burke to Rockingham, 16 and 25 Sept. 1774, in *Works* (1852 edn.), i. 235, 238). In 1812 Lady Downshire was said to have commenced an extensive canvass in County Down at 'a ball under cover of a christening'.

[3] For example, the signatories to the advertisement in the *York Courant*, 14 Dec. 1779, calling a meeting to consider a petition for parliamentary reform, state that the death of the High Sheriff made it impracticable to obtain a county meeting called in the usual mode (Wyvill, op. cit. i. 1). They would, however, have called

were some things for which it might be unconstitutional for any-body to petition—among them, the dissolution of parliament itself. It is clear that in the debate of 17 February 1769 North was inclined at first to think that a petition to the king for this purpose would be a breach of parliamentary privilege, and only recollected himself a little later.[1]

If the zealots of the House of Commons felt so much doubt about the rights of the constituents and of the general petition-ing public, they looked still more jealously on any unofficial political organization which could claim to represent that public. Aware, perhaps, that the electoral system by which they were returned was haphazard to the point of fantasy, they were afraid of any association, still more any delegate confer-ence of associations, which might claim, in virtue of a more rational system of representation or a more widespread con-stituency, to be an anti-parliament. This objection was often made to the county associations for parliamentary reform, which sprang up in 1780; and not only by conservatives who wished to obstruct by a technicality, but also by many parlia-mentary reformers themselves, who were haunted by the idea that pressure ought only to be put upon parliament by an *ad hoc* meeting for presenting a petition, such a meeting being, in a sense, an appendage of parliament itself.[2] The leaders of the parliamentary reform movement might point to the respectable precedents of the association to preserve the life of King William III and the association which the Archbishop of York had promoted in 1745 for the purpose of resisting the Pretender; a far more sinister precedent, or rather parallel, was in most people's minds in 1780—the Protestant Association of Lord

the meeting themselves, even if the High Sheriff, when asked, had refused (ibid. iii. 108–14; see also Sir William Anderson's letter to Wyvill, 30 Nov. 1779, ibid. iii. 118, and the discussion at the York county meeting, 17 Dec. 1783, ibid. ii. 287–303).

[1] Sir H. Cavendish, *Debates*, i. 229, 234.

[2] For denunciations of associations by adversaries of parliamentary reform, see, for example, Rigby's speech in the House of Commons (Wyvill, op. cit. i. 478) and the resolution of the Corporation of Leicester (ibid. ii. 108). See also Dunning's letter to Wyvill, 13 June 1781 (ibid. i. 351). For the misgivings of reformers, see the speeches of Coke, Mann, and Rolle in the House of Commons (*Parl. Hist.* xxii. 96, 144, 157) and Lord Fauconberg's remarks in the York county meeting (Wyvill, op. cit. ii. 293). Fauconberg was a real reformer; indeed, the whole movement in Yorkshire may have arisen out of private meetings held by him (ibid. iii. 120): but in 1783 he was particularly annoyed by the Association's apparent attempt to influence a by-election pending in the county (ibid. ii. 277, 300).

George Gordon.[1] Still more did the parliamentary politicians fear a central committee or delegate conference of associations, sitting in London, and, as Burke later said, 'nosing parliament in the very seat of its authority'.[2] It was thought the more ominous because Wyvill, for his own reasons, had tried to exclude all members of parliament from its meetings.[3] Did not this look like an anti-parliament? The word 'anti-parliament', indeed, was actually used, not wholly in jest;[4] and the idea continued to haunt the minds of politicians for many years—so long, indeed, as the imperfections in the electoral system might plausibly entitle an unofficial convention to claim that it was the most faithful extant image of the Commons of England.[5] The

---

[1] Wyvill, op. cit. i. 151–2, 258.

[2] *A Letter to a Noble Lord*, in *Works* (1852 edn.), v. 220. This whole passage of reminiscence grossly exaggerates the danger: there is no evidence that George III or Lord North was much alarmed by the conference, though they both disapproved of it and of the associations which gave rise to it.

[3] It can hardly have crossed Wyvill's mind that his conference could usurp the place of King, Lords, and Commons; he wanted the parliamentary politicians excluded because he meant to use them, not to be used by them, and rightly suspected them of trying to get his wind to fill their party sails (see his letter to Lord Mahon, 28 Feb. 1780, in *Political Papers*, iii. 180; and H. Butterfield, *George III, Lord North and the People* (London, 1949), pp. 220–8, 269–83).

[4] Savile to Wyvill, 21 Jan. 1780, in Wyvill, op. cit. iii. 204.

[5] Good examples of this obsession are King William IV's desire for the dissolution of the Political Unions, and the uneasiness which was caused by the Chartist Convention of 1839. The fear of associations and conventions was still more acute, and much better justified, in another context. In America and Ireland the established representative institutions of the country were so obviously controlled or frustrated by the British Government that nationalism could only take extra-official forms. These could not be recognized in England. The House of Commons would not receive a petition from the Stamp Act Congress in Jan. 1766, because that congress had no official status. The petitions of the first Continental Congress were treated in the same way. In Ireland there was a whole series of unofficial bodies which existed to organize the political life of the country and put pressure on parliament. In 1783–4 there was tension in Dublin between the Irish parliament and the convention called by the Volunteers to consider parliamentary reform; when Flood went down from the convention to the House of Commons to propose in the latter a bill approved by the former, he gave the Lord Lieutenant and the enemies of reform an excellent excuse for refusing to pass it under duress, and the president of the convention had some difficulty in restraining it from violent resolutions against parliament (R. B. McDowell, *Irish Public Opinion, 1750–1800* (London, 1944), pp. 97–103; *Hist. MSS. Comm., Charlemont MSS.* i. 123–33; *Memorials and Correspondence of Charles James Fox*, ii. 185). Further, and more deliberate, attempts were made at assembling anti-parliaments next year (McDowell, op. cit., pp. 107–10). In the next generation the proceedings of the Catholic Association gave scandal to British politicians, and destroyed what hope there may have been of an agreed compromise on Catholic Emancipation.

worst of these morbid fears was never justified: no such usurpation was ever attempted. But the associations of 1780 were, in a
different way, a portent, for they introduced a new and indispensable adjunct to our political life—the voluntary association
for promoting political objects by means of public pressure
upon parliament.

The conservative whigs, who exalted the status of the House
of Commons without any real regard for its representativeness
or its popularity, were, perhaps, mistaking the letter of the constitution for its spirit. But they were not the only kind of whigs;
perhaps not the best kind. The popular significance of the House
of Commons was not forgotten by politicians like the elder Pitt,
lawyers like Pratt, and writers like Thomas Hollis and Richard
Price. These last regarded the commemoration of the 1688
Revolution, not merely as an excuse for a good dinner followed
by comfortable reflection upon the blessings of life, but as an
incentive and indeed a justification for a democratic movement
in the present day.[1] Pitt's ideas were, perhaps, not so definite;
indeed, they were prejudices rather than ideas. Patriotism and
demagogy were curiously jumbled in his mind, and one could
never tell which would be uppermost.[2] He was a House of
Commons man—none better—when the prestige of the House
had to be upheld against a clique in the Lords; but he never
thought of the House of Commons as the be-all and the end-all
of the constitution, and he would readily appeal from it in all
directions. Sometimes he appealed to some wider constituency,
which his friends called the people, or public opinion, but his
enemies called the City mob.[3] At other times he appealed to

[1] For Thomas Hollis, who distributed copies of Locke's and Sidney's writings in
the belief that they would stimulate some kind of democratic action, see F. Black-
burne, *Memoirs of Thomas Hollis* (London, 1782) and an article by Caroline Robbins
in *William and Mary Quarterly*, 3rd series, vii. 406–53. It was Price's anniversary
sermon 'On the Love of our Country' that started the celebrated controversy over
the meaning of the 1688 revolution and its relation to the modern democratic movement.

[2] See the amusing story (in Ilchester, op. cit. i. 121–2) about the occasion on
which he allowed his prejudice against Hanover to run away with him and abused
the Londoners, whose support he usually courted, as 'shopkeepers' because they
did not share it. In the same vein, he denounced the City's resistance to press-
warrants, in his speech on the Falkland Islands crisis, although he had very lately
been backing the City for all he was worth against the Government (*Chatham
Correspondence*, iv. 11 note).

[3] The difficulty of knowing exactly what was Chatham's public, and how much

some popular maxim of the constitution, or some natural right which even parliament itself could not infringe: he was one of the last politicians to tell the House that there were some things which even parliament had no legal right to do. Some of these guarantees of freedom were enforceable in the law courts; perhaps this is why he made such a fetish of Charles Pratt, Lord Camden. Pratt would hardly have been called an erudite lawyer, but that did not matter to Pitt, who openly preferred bad lawyers to good.[1] Pratt was a popular lawyer, and justified Pitt's patronage by giving some celebrated decisions, by which popular causes were favoured and popular liberties enlarged.

The elder Pitt was, in some respects, more like a politician of the seventeenth century than of the eighteenth;[2] and when he used the word 'whig'—which he very often did after 1762—he gave it a different sense from that which it bore among the noblemen and lawyers who took their whiggism so much for granted that they had almost forgotten what it meant. He seems to have been responsible—even earlier than Burke—for the vogue of calling a bad whig a tory—which is the more curious,

its influence weighed, sometimes puzzled his fellow politicians, for they did not know how far they could safely disregard him. In 1755-7 it was stronger than they reckoned, for all the calculations of Newcastle and Fox, grounded on their knowledge of the two Houses of Parliament, were set at naught by the popular outcry and the 'rain of gold boxes'. If George II really said to Pitt, 'Sir, you have taught me to look for the sense of my subjects in another place than in the House of Commons', he was speaking no more than the truth. In 1761, on the other hand, Pitt's public was less formidable than it was expected to be: some people expected his resignation to be followed by an outcry like that of 1757, but nothing more happened than a few minor demonstrations in the City.

[1] He had a long feud with Mansfield and, to a less degree, with Hardwicke—the latter he called 'a slow man whom the law had made,' the former 'a man of fine parts whom the law had unmade, both equally unfit to govern' (G. F. S. Elliot, *The Border Elliots and the Family of Minto* (Edinburgh, 1897), p. 368). The disagreement with Hardwicke was aggravated by disputes with his son, Charles Yorke, about Wilkes's privilege (P. C. Yorke, op. cit. iii. 463-5, 501). The feud with Mansfield (who had once been Pitt's rival in the House of Commons) seems to have started because Mansfield denied that a judge must, in all cases, grant a writ of Habeas Corpus when applied for; but it was maintained because Mansfield denied to juries in libel cases the right of determining the question of law as well as that of fact. Pitt's hatred may have overreached itself, for in 1771 he would not support the Rockingham section of the Opposition in a bill which should enact that Mansfield's doctrine should be reversed for the future, insisting on one which should declare that it always had been wrong (*Chatham Correspondence*, iv. 99-112).

[2] Perhaps he might rather be called a medieval politician, in that he was not satisfied with enacting that what he thought right should be the law of the land, but insisted on declaring that it was the law of the land already.

because he had himself had the support of most of the tory M.P.s during the Seven Years War. His somewhat heated imagination began to perceive new issues which prolonged or renewed the relevance of whiggism; and he was disappointed, though not wholly surprised, to find that not all the great whig families and luminaries would follow him in these new crusades.[1] One personal grievance crowded upon another in his mind; and he hardly knew whether he most disliked Newcastle, who had long retarded his rise to power and had defended him too feebly against Bute, or Bute himself, the king's 'favourite', or Bedford, the maker, in his opinion, of a shameful peace. But there were moments when he would have taken some of them, at least, under the whig banner, provided it were understood that he himself bore the banner, and that it should be dipped once more in the brighter and more popular colours which had faded since 1688. The lucky hour was missed: Pitt lost the opportunity to return to power as leader of a united whig party, largely because his whiggism was so ostentatiously pure as to require the proscription of many politicians whom the king felt himself bound to protect.[2] Pitt then drew apart once more from the great families, because they would not wholeheartedly accept the cause of Wilkes and all that it implied.[3] When next he approached power it was not as Pitt the whig champion but as Chatham the enemy of all party. In the last of his metamorphoses he reappeared once more on the extreme left as Chatham

[1] Pitt told Thomas Walpole on 13 Nov. 1762 that the old distinction of whigs and tories was reviving (P. C. Yorke, op. cit. iii. 431; see also iii. 506). Note the early date, before the Wilkes cases had begun to impinge upon politics; Pitt can only have been thinking, at this stage, of Bute's 'transcendency of power' as the great offence against whig principles. In Aug. 1763 he told the king that Grenville's Ministry 'was not founded on true revolution principles; that it was a tory administration' (*Grenville Papers*, ii. 199). By that time he may have begun to think of the cause of Wilkes (whose character, incidentally, he disliked and despised) as true whiggism.

[2] In August 1763 (ibid.; also P. C. Yorke, op. cit. iii. 469, 523). See the happy little notes of the whig dukes when they thought Pitt was leading them back into the promised land (*Chatham Correspondence*, ii. 237–41).

[3] Above all, Pratt. Pitt, who attached enormous importance to the outward symbols of his opinions and wishes, demanded that Newcastle and his party should bow down to his fetish Pratt. This was awkward for them, as they felt some obligation to their own fetish, Pratt's enemy Charles Yorke (*v. supra*, p. 22, note 2). It really looks as though this battle of the lawyers, with all that it symbolized, had a great deal to do with the failure of Pitt and the Newcastle whigs to agree in 1763–4 (P. C. Yorke, op. cit. iii. 472–3, 504, 506, 516–23, 535, 547, 552, 554–5).

the tribune of the people, chiding the 'gentle warblers of the grove' and urging them into an agitation more popular, more nearly democratic, than anything they had known.

The whig nobles—Newcastle, Devonshire, Rockingham— and their followers, were not all inert: they were not altogether 'whigs upon the business of a century ago'. But if they defended and cultivated whiggism as a living tradition, it was not a popular tradition like that of Pitt. It was, strictly speaking, anti-monarchical; and if the question of the rights of the monarchy had not been reopened after 1760, this kind of whiggism would, in all probability, never have burst into flame again.

We should be putting the matter in too simple terms if we were to speak of an antagonism between monarchy and aristo-cracy. No king was ever less fond of plebeian society than George III.[1] He liked to be surrounded by lords at court: he even thought it right that one of them should be 'plagued into his service', and once, when reserving a court post for another lord, he expostulated thus: 'Ld. North cannot seriously think that a private gentleman like Mr. Penton is to stand in the way of the eldest son of an earl, undoubtedly if that idea holds good it is diametrically opposite to what I have known all my life.'[2] He was accused of diluting the peerage and, indeed, did dilute it; but not willingly, still less of malice prepense.[3] He took it as a matter of course, just as the Duke of Newcastle had done, that the Crown ought to assist a nobleman in financial difficulties. Although Burke suspected him of trying to use the moneyed men in politics against the aristocracy and gentry, there is not the

---

[1] Burke's accusations—or rather, insinuations—on this subject were ridiculous. In his *Speech on the Plan for Economical Reform, 11 Feb. 1780* (*Works* (1852 edn.), iii. 388) he explained why he did not abolish more offices at court by saying that kings are naturally fond of low company, and hate rather than love their nobility; they ought therefore to be surrounded by noblemen, even against their will. See also his remarks about the King of France, in *Thoughts on French Affairs* (1791) printed in *Works* (1852 edn.), iv. 581.

[2] *Correspondence of George III*, nos. 1756, 3155.

[3] 'I desire I may hear no more of Irish marquises, I feel for the English earls and do not choose to disgust them' (ibid., no. 1837). He seems to have thought that only a peer of a very old creation should be raised a step in the peerage (*Letters from George III to Lord Bute, 1756–1766*, ed. Sedgwick, p. 231). Even to a privy councillor-ship he applied the principle that 'the husbanding honours is the only means of keeping up their value' (*Correspondence of George III*, no. 2031). He was particularly reluctant to ennoble judges (ibid., no. 2299). See also *Memoirs and Correspondence of Viscount Castlereagh*, ed. Londonderry, iii. 320–2, 333–4.

slightest evidence of this: on the contrary, when he communicated to Lord North his intention of suddenly dissolving parliament in 1774, he said: 'I trust it will fill the House with more
gentlemen of landed property as the nabobs, planters, and other
volunteers are not ready for the battle.'[1] Those were exactly
Rockingham's sentiments.

Nor were the noblemen, as a class, hostile to monarchy or to
the king, though the difference between his and their tastes and,
sometimes, moral standards made it difficult for some of them
to regard the court as the head of society, as they did in the
reign of his son.[2] Many of the most assiduous 'King's Friends'
were noblemen—for example, Barrington and Hillsborough—
and many others must have thought it right to support the king's
Government as such. Yet it is not wholly wrong to speak of an
aristocratic opposition to the king, or at least of an aristocratic
inclination to belittle his power. Much was heard of the 'great
Revolution families'—of whom some of the proudest, as Sir
Lewis Namier has pointed out, were in fact descended from
Charles II's bastards. These families—above all, perhaps, the
Cavendishes—could not forget that their ancestors had, as it
were, conferred the crown upon the king's ancestors, and they
did not mean to let him forget it either, for they alluded to it in
season and out of season.[3] They looked upon themselves as his

---

[1] *Correspondence of George III*, no. 1501.

[2] His mother is said to have encouraged him to confine himself to the society of
his brother Edward, because young people of quality were so vicious that none of
them were fit to keep company with him (*Diary of George Bubb Dodington*, ed. H. P.
Wyndham (London, 1784), p. 172). The resulting difference of tastes may have
been increased by the privacy of his family life, especially after the purchase of
Buckingham Palace. There seems to have been some contrast in this respect
between George III and his predecessors: Horace Walpole, who often talked nonsense but seldom without something at the back of his mind, dilates on the 'privacy
and lifeless solitude' of the king's life, and refers to the queen several times as
being in a 'prison' (*Memoirs of the Reign of George III*, ed. Russell Barker, i. 125,
iii. 159). The privacy must, however, have been only partial, if we may believe
Fanny Burney, who describes the way her father tried to cadge a court job by con-
triving to meet the royal family on the Terrace at Windsor after church on Sunday
(*Diary*, ed. Barrett (1893 edn.), ii. 57–58).

[3] Lord John Cavendish, for example, managed to drag this into a speech at
York about the Middlesex Election: he spoke of 'opening the eyes of their sovereign
to his real friends, who had at the hazard of their lives and fortunes supported his
Crown in former days of danger' (Wyvill, op. cit., vol. i, p. xxxiii). Burke, in his
speech on economical reform, Feb. 1780, seemed to imply that the services of these
families were rightly rewarded by the lucrative offices conferred upon them (*Works*,
(1852 edn.), iii. 385).

creators rather than his creation: one would almost say they had forgotten that the dukedom of Devonshire itself had been established, less than a century earlier, by the merely human agency of a king.[1] 'No wise king of Great Britain', as Burke once said, 'would think it for his credit to let it go abroad that he considered himself, or was considered by others, as personally at variance with a Lord Rockingham, a Duke of Richmond, a Duke of Portland, an Earl of D——, the families of the Cavendishes, with a Savile, a Dowdeswell, &c.'[2]

This feeling of self-subsistence and self-sufficiency did not depend wholly on birth; indeed, birth alone did not qualify those who were without some other recommendation of connexion, utility, celebrity, or amusement which brought them into the social and political swim,[3] whereas possession of those recommendations without birth was often enough. It was not so much a class as a clique which claimed the monopoly of political responsibility—a very broad clique which could embrace almost any man whose celebrity or usefulness to the right people could not be overlooked, for neither the aristocracy nor the peerage itself was rigidly fixed. This clique identified itself with a political party: consisting, as it originally did, of those members of the whig party who had come to terms with the Duke of Newcastle or revolved around his orbit, it appropriated the title of 'whig' as exclusively and pertinaciously as Chatham, and with more permanent success. Though it opened its doors to such talent as might be necessary, it was an aristocratic clique: nobody without a profound respect for birth could have

---

[1] Burke himself was capable of remembering that these great families had had a beginning, and an unpleasant one; but one might almost say that it took the Duke of Bedford's insolence to himself to put him in mind of it (*A Letter to a Noble Lord*, in *Works* (1852 edn.), v. 231–40).

[2] Burke to Bishop Markham, ? 1771, *Works* (1852 edn.), i. 147. George III, on one occasion (June 1765), saw fit to appeal to this feeling of caste: when he wanted Rockingham's friends to rescue him from Grenville, he said he did not think they would 'approve of seeing the Crown dictated to by low men' (*Correspondence of George III*, no. 88).

[3] For instance, Devonshire, when complaining that the king ought not to have made Bute his chief minister because he was not one of those 'that the nation have a good opinion of', did not deny that Bute had the recommendation of birth (Ilchester, op. cit. ii. 203). When Lord Fitzwilliam wished to sneer at the young William Pitt he alluded, among other things, to 'his predilection for court, and seclusion from those social circles where his equals in rank and fortune and years commonly resorted' (*Parl. Hist.* xxiv. 499).

thought Portland or Rockingham fit for the Treasury and the leadership of a party,[1] or Grafton and Richmond for the Secretaryships of State which they held at so early an age. The theory of this clique became, in the writings of Burke, an aristocratic theory.[2] Its parliamentary existence depended to a great degree (though not exclusively) on the private electoral patronage which the aristocracy happened to possess, and the hospitality in London which the great houses best afforded. In these senses I think it not unfair to say that the most permanent opposition to George III was an aristocratic opposition: it did not arise in the House of Lords, nor was it ever patronized by the whole body of the nobility, but it was led by nobles conscious of their claims, and inspired by an aristocratic sentiment.

[1] There was, as I hope to show, something more to be said for Rockingham: he had, at least, this qualification for leadership of a party, that he devoted his life (when he happened to be in London) to leading it.

[2] Many exquisite passages substantiate this view, such as the letter of 17 Nov. 1772, to Richmond, in which he compares himself to a melon, Richmond and Rockingham to great oaks, and says of the Claudii and Valerii of Rome 'that the balance of that famous constitution was kept up for some ages, by the personal characters, dispositions, and traditionary politics of certain families, as much as by anything in the laws and orders of the state' (*Works* (1852 edn.), i. 190) and the passage in the *Appeal from the New to the Old Whigs*, in which he discusses the true natural aristocracy (ibid. iv. 465–6). It comes out in his discussions of religious toleration in Ireland, for he objects to the domination of Catholics by Protestants precisely because this constitutes a *plebeian* oligarchy, and the Protestant cobbler's triumph over the Catholic peer whose footman's shoes he mends is reprehended as an inversion of the natural order of things in which the Catholic, as a peer, would have been recognized as superior to the Protestant, as a cobbler (*Speech at Bristol, previous to the Election* (1780), ibid. iii. 440; *A Letter to Sir Hercules Langrishe*, ibid. iv. 514). It comes out also in his discussion of the French Revolution, as in *Heads for Consideration on the Present State of Affairs* (1792; ibid. v. 8) and in *Remarks on the Policy of the Allies* (ibid. v. 25, 33–34) where he blames the Allies for crusading on behalf of the King of France rather than the exiled princes and nobles and 'the intermediate orders of the state, by which the monarchy was upheld'. In *A Letter to a Noble Lord* (ibid. v. 229) Burke truly claims that the Duke of Bedford might have given him some credit for having 'supported with very great zeal, and I am told with some degree of success, those opinions, or if his grace likes another expression better, those old prejudices, which buoy up the ponderous mass of his nobility, wealth and titles'.

III

GEORGE III AND THE PARTIES

I<small>N</small> a mixed constitution, where the bounds of the respective powers are not precisely and effectively fixed, their actual relations at any time will be determined by the accident of personalities and the advantage which the need of surmounting emergencies, or the prestige of emergencies already surmounted, may give to one institution or to another. The mixture is never quite 'as before'. That is a commonplace; and it can be no surprise to discover that the British constitution did not work in the reign of George III exactly as it had done in that of George II. Indeed, it was no surprise to contemporaries. They may have awaited the change with hope or fear, but they assumed that it would be a change: as Henry Fox observed, 'I was at Court this day, & pleas'd to see it by many examples prov'd, how rightly I had ever call'd a new reign a new world, of which we could know nothing before hand.'[1]

Fox was thinking of men rather than measures. So, perhaps, was George III, for his policy, so far as he had one in 1760, was made up almost entirely of vindictive personal grudges against everything and everybody who had been connected with his despised grandfather. But he designed a change of system too, in that he meant to do his duty better than George II had done it; and in this sense it is fair to say that the new reign differed intentionally from the old, that the drift of the constitution in a certain direction was now deliberately arrested with a sharp jerk.

In later years, when George III's attempts to regain and exercise the leadership of his country had begun to provoke opposition, his adversaries used to speak of George II, 'the late good old king', with some misplaced affection. There is no great reason to think that George II willingly or deliberately accepted any constitutional limitations which his grandson tried to flout. George II knew that there were some things he could not do: that there was a thing called the constitution; and he claimed to

---

[1] Fox's 'Memoir', printed by Lady Ilchester and Lord Stavordale in *Life and Letters of Lady Sarah Lennox* (London, 1902), i. 37.

have observed it, though he was nettled by Newcastle's tendentious appeals to it.[1] But he did not like it; and whatever he may have meant by saying, 'They must not expect to find me a Stuart', it does not appear at all likely, from the context, that he was declaring his preference for constitutional monarchy. He spoke of the 'damned House of Commons' without admiration; and he thought himself the sovereign of a very extraordinary people, which passed nearly a hundred laws every session for the sole purpose of breaking them, and allowed politicians to occupy Secretaryships of State without having even read Wicquefort, let alone made any serious study of foreign affairs.[2] In many of these respects he differed little from his grandson, however much they might dislike each other.[3] If we are only to regard principles and preferences, there certainly is not much difference between the two kings. Yet contemporaries perceived a difference, and rightly: they were right in contrasting 'the quiet court' of the first two Hanoverians, 'whose only object was to get through', with the more active royalty of George III.[4]

The difference was not one of principle, but of personality. George II might stamp his foot, might turn his back on people he disliked, might call people 'puppy', and use fine words about 'striking a great stroke' or 'seeing who is king of this country'; but very little came of it. His rudeness, deliberate or not,[5] was enough to make people feel uncomfortable, but it was the rudeness of a weak-minded man who takes it out of servants to whom he has had to yield.[6] If they did not much mind taking no for an

[1] P. C. Yorke, op. cit. i. 370; *v. infra*, pp. 95–96.

[2] Horace Walpole, *Memoirs of the Reign of George II* (1846 edn.), ii. 267; Waldegrave, *Memoirs*, p. 132.

[3] For example, George III might have spoken the same words that George II used in his conversation with Waldegrave, just quoted.

[4] Shelburne's opinion (Fitzmaurice, op. cit. i. 39). Shelburne exaggerated, however, when he described the first two Hanoverian kings as telling the people, 'We are your slaves and blackamoors' (ibid. i. 17).

[5] It is hard to be sure whether George II's rudeness to politicians was calculated, but I have the impression that it was spontaneous, and therefore not really formidable. The rudeness of George III, on certain occasions, was quite deliberate and was meant to affect conduct (see his *Correspondence*, nos. 703, 1036).

[6] P. C. Yorke, op. cit. i. 357, ii. 97, 401. There are numerous references to George II's weakness and rudeness in *Private Correspondence of Chesterfield and Newcastle, 1744–6*, ed. Sir R. Lodge (London, 1930). Newcastle describes 'the greatest dissatisfaction showed at the very measures that are awkwardly yielded to', and prophesies that a piece of business on which Chesterfield insists will not be refused

answer, he sometimes got his way; indeed, he was an excellent Jorkins, and his personal dislikes may really have obstructed the promotion of those whom his ministers did not very much want to promote. (The best example is the elder Pitt, who fell behind Fox in the race for nearly two years, because nobody thought it worth while to force him on the king.) But when they really wanted to get their way, they got it, or took shame to themselves if they did not: as his daughter-in-law said, when they tried to put her off,

if they talked of the King, she was out of patience; it was as if they should tell her, that her little Harry below would not do what was proper for him; that just so, the King would sputter and make a bustle, but when they told him that it must be done from the necessity of his service, he must do it, as little Harry must when she came down.[1]

It was weakness, and weakness alone, that prevented this active and businesslike king from exercising the influence which the constitution would have allowed him, outside the departments, such as the army and the Bedchamber, which the politicians did not mind leaving to him. Had his strong-minded wife lived, the royal power might have been exerted more effectively; and perhaps (though they did not formulate the thought) the politicians feared the Duke of Cumberland because they guessed that he alone, of the royal family, had the will to govern, in person or through his father.[2] If Sir Robert Walpole could have lasted for ever, perhaps he too would have protected the king's weakness, at a price. But without his queen or Walpole near him, George II did not know how to deal with the politicians. He suffered public defeat, three times, in his attempts to use the most important of the surviving royal prerogatives, that of choosing his own ministers,[3] and the leadership which he should

but 'disagreeably done'; George II threatens to be rude to Pitt if he is forced to make him Secretary-at-War (pp. 40, 64, 108).

[1] Dodington, *Diary*, pp. 205, 212–13.

[2] They talked of 'military tyranny' but, though British politicians had a morbid fear of the army as a political force, it may have been the duke's strength of character that impressed them (see p. 18, note 2). Fox, in 1765, commenting on the degeneration of the Duke of Cumberland, said 'The having any fears, any diffidence of the power of the Crown, when there was spirit to exert it. These traits have none of them the least resemblance of the Duke of Cumberland I knew' (Ilchester, op. cit. ii. 297).

[3] The ministerial arrangements of 1744 and 1757 were made by the politicians without respecting the king's wishes except on comparatively unimportant points;

have exercised passed to the Pelham family, indeed to the political class as a whole. The royal family did not even keep itself in the limelight by furnishing an heir apparent who could be looked up to as the active king of the next generation; for Frederick, Prince of Wales, was one of the most futile leaders of opposition that ever existed, and for nearly a decade after his death the heir was an unpromising youth who kept himself, or was kept, in the background. George III grew up to deal with a generation of politicians who, having had the run of the place for twenty years, had almost ceased to take account of anybody's opinions but their own, and had accustomed themselves to think not of the court but of the two houses of parliament, or London and country-house society, as the theatre of action and reputation, the real centre of political power.[1]

George III was not, at first sight, very well equipped for dealing with this class. He was a virtuous but not a brilliant youth; and the virtue was almost as great a handicap as the lack of brilliance, for it was both unfashionable and uncharitable. He had been brought up too carefully, and segregated from the gilded youth which might have corrupted him.[2] His censorious chastity and sobriety—or, as Junius called it, his 'unforgiving piety'—which many of his principal subjects did not care to imitate, affected his behaviour towards them too much and too publicly. He would have liked to reform their morals as well as their constitutional practices.[3] He would have liked to surround himself only with ministers who were known to lead regular lives: he did not want, for example, to send Weymouth or Sandwich to Ireland as Lord Lieutenant, and he welcomed the evangelical Dartmouth to his Cabinet with unusual warmth just as he welcomed a countess of 'unfashionable propriety' to a court office about the queen.[4] But this effort to insist on private

and his attempt to reverse the arrangement of 1744 was frustrated, in a humiliating manner, by the collective resignation of Feb. 1746 (*v. infra*, pp. 95–96).

[1] Burke's use of the term 'faction' is an interesting example of this: he spoke of the politics of the Court as 'factious', contrasting them with the operations in the real political arena, the House of Commons. George III must have considered this a total inversion of the word's true meaning.

[2] Dodington, *Diary*, pp. 172, 255, 258–9.

[3] *Letters from George III to Lord Bute, 1756–1766*, ed. Sedgwick, pp. 166–7.

[4] *Correspondence of George III*, nos. 139 (p. 165), 577, 674; *Grenville Papers*, ii. 514. The Lord Lieutenant of Ireland was the king's personal representative; this was a special reason for refusing to fill the post with a *roué*.

virtue as a qualification for office was bound to fail laughably, and Junius did not miss the opportunity of pointing out the incongruity of Grafton's appearance as first minister of a court 'in which prayers are morality and kneeling is religion.'[1] George III had to limit himself to more practicable endeavours: in 1780 he still thanked heaven his morals and course of life had but little resembled 'those too prevalent in the present age', and therefore he was scrupulous about the character of his eldest son's attendants, 'though in other cases I never wish to be informed, unless of those great enormities that must make every man of principle shun the company of those persons.'[2] His private virtues, which were known and never denied, probably help to account for his great popularity with the middle class in the second half of his reign; but they were not a bond of union between him and fashionable whigs such as Charles Fox, whose early career in London society offered such a violent contrast to his own.

If George III's private morals were respectable from first to last, in some other respects he was not so promising. He seems to have been backward, shy, rather lazy (especially at his books), conscious of his mission but almost hysterically diffident of his power to fulfil it. No trace here of the dogged energy, the self-confidence, or even the incessant loquacity of his later years. Indeed, the youth revealed by Mr. Sedgwick's edition of his letters to Bute is so unlike the George III of the 1770's that I am tempted to describe his mature character as an artefact, deliberately created by a sense of duty in order to meet the needs of a constitutional monarchy.[3] Perhaps his madness can best be explained as the breakdown of a too costly struggle to maintain this artificial character—the reserve and equanimity imposed upon a hot temper and anxious nerves, to say nothing of his resolute fidelity to a hideous queen, and a regimen of violent exercise and exaggerated abstinence designed to counteract strong passions and a tendency to fat.

[1] Junius to the Duke of Grafton, 8 July 1769. There was a great deal of church-going at court: the equerries used to complain to Fanny Burney of the horrors of morning prayers in winter-time at Windsor. As it happens, Grafton ended his life as a pious Unitarian.

[2] *Correspondence of George III*, no. 3201.

[3] Junius, whose claim to understand George III's personal character is not without foundation, was alluding to this when he said: 'Nature intended him only for a good-humoured fool. A systematical education, with long practice, has made him a consummate hypocrite.'

The rather lazy boy who had to make good resolutions to keep up his reading developed into one of the most energetic, though not the most discerning, highbrows of his day. George III is generally assumed to have been a Philistine because he once said to Fanny Burney: 'Was there ever such stuff as great part of Shakespeare? Only one must not say so! But what think you? What? Is there not sad stuff? What? What?'[1] This stricture on the author of *Titus Andronicus* and *Love's Labour's Lost* appears to me both just and prudent, and many of his other conversations with Miss Burney show, at least, that he had read widely. His remarks on Voltaire and Rousseau are not worth much; but how many of his ministers could have distinguished them at all? How many of their wives read the *Paston Letters* or the *Sorrows of Werther*, or kept a servant to go round the bookstalls for bargains? How many of George III's Prime Ministers would have run up a bill for astronomical instruments, copied out the manuscripts of astronomers in their own hand, and manifested genuine eagerness to see a new comet through a new telescope? No doubt much of this intellectual activity was mere curiosity, for George III was forever asking questions about things which did not concern him.[2] But one must respect the curiosity which was directed to the foundation of the Windsor collection, the patronage of Herschel and the furtherance of Captain Cook's voyages.

His will developed even more remarkably than the range of his interests. If he had not, as a young man, deeply distrusted his own capacity for decision, he would not have misplaced his confidence so wholeheartedly in the inept Lord Bute, as a shield between himself and the difficulties of life.[3] Only as he learnt to do without Bute did he begin to grow up; and even after that, if he could have found in Cumberland or Chatham an older man to

---

[1] *Diary and Letters of Madame D'Arblay*, ed. Barrett (1893 edn.), ii. 47.

[2] See the strange letter of Lord Hertford (*Correspondence of George III*, no. 3241) satisfying the king's curiosity about an odd-looking woman he must have seen on his way to or from the play; also Sir William Young's letter of 16 May 1788, describing the king's minute inquiries about Lord Buckingham's domestic arrangements. Young says, 'He was, as usual, much more particular in his inquiries about *persons* than about *business*' (*Courts and Cabinets of George III*, i. 387). Possibly this habit of asking questions, as well as his ejaculations of 'What? What?' and 'Hey? Hey?' were the tricks of a nervous man, who disliked awkward silences, for preventing the conversation from flagging, a thing it is apt to do when the interlocutor of royalty does not know whether he is expected to reply.

[3] *Letters from George III to Lord Bute, 1756–1766*, pp. 4, 20, 21.

whom he could have looked up for guidance, he would probably have been glad to accept it. But they all failed him. Bute ran away from the battle, Cumberland died, Chatham went mad—which was perhaps only another manner of running away. George III soon changed when, surrounded by the irresolute and the incompetent, he had to take matters into his own hands: he developed a self-assurance which may, perhaps, betray some traces of nervousness by its uncompromising rigidity, but also derives from a religious man's consciousness of fulfilling his task as he understands it.

His maxims, in mid-career, were those of a conscientious bull in a china shop. 'I know I am doing my duty and therefore can never wish to retract.' 'Men of less principle and honesty than I pretend to may look on public measures and opinions as a game, I always act from conviction.' 'I will rather risk my Crown than do what I think personally disgraceful, and whilst I have no wish but for the good and prosperity of my country, it is impossible that the nation shall not stand by me; if they will not, they shall have another King.' 'It has ever been a certain position with me that firmness is the characteristick of an Englishman', and so forth. In the summer of 1779, when he thought he had rallied North and his colleagues who had nearly run away, he said, 'I begin to see that I shall soon have enfused some of that spirit which I thank Heaven ever attends me when under difficulties', and went on to express his trust in the Almighty and in the uprightness of his own intentions.[1]

His idea of firmness was extremely simple: flat refusal to make any political concessions to anybody. Even the sanction which he occasionally gave to tactical retreats in the House of Commons usually took the form of making light of a defeat after it had happened.[2] He was particularly concerned to resist any threat to established institutions, enforcement of law, or the general principle of 'subordination';[3] and this, no doubt, was one of his reasons for hating Wilkes, though he may have had

---

[1] *Correspondence of George III*, nos. 1683, 2221, 2230, 2451, 2678.

[2] Not quite always: he was more willing than North to throw Palliser to the wolves, but North was, at this period, an absolute zero, for he could not take any decision at all (*Correspondence of George III*, nos. 2540, 2542, 2547–9, 2551).

[3] Very few of his subjects (Dr. Johnson was an exception) could see at the beginning of his reign that there was any problem about preserving 'subordination'.

private grudges as well.[1] The only great concession he ever made concerned the Stamp Act: he had not much liked the Act originally, but he would rather have modified it than repealed it altogether,[2] and he never ceased to repent it, for he believed that it had awakened an insatiable appetite for concessions.[3] To yield nothing to dependencies became a general maxim with him,[4] and thus, though George Grenville and Charles Townshend were responsible for the taxes which caused the original trouble, it was George III's rigidity which prolonged the war for years after it had lost its original popularity and prospect of success. Historians have blamed his obstinacy and applauded the ready acquiescence of the Rockinghams in defeat; but surely one could hardly expect the king to preside with equanimity over the dissolution of the British Empire?—and that, as he not unreasonably supposed, was the issue before him.[5] After Yorktown, he was coerced but never convinced; he felt that his parliament and his people had disgraced themselves and him, and here, for a time, his obstinacy lost all dignity.[6] Even now he tried, with a little help from Shelburne, to preserve some sort of political connexion with America, praying Heaven 'to guide me so to act that posterity may not lay the downfall of this once respectable empire at my door'.[7] When all was over, and the separation complete, George III was, for many years, an isolationist in foreign affairs, holding that, having lost the only war worth fighting, we could have no inducement to fight another.[8] In the struggle with revolutionary France, he showed his unimaginative rigidity once more: he would never see any advant-

---

[1] No doubt George III, who had sworn revenge upon anybody who insulted his mother (*Letters from George III to Lord Bute*, p. 3), was incensed by Wilkes's probably unjustified references to Isabella and Mortimer.

[2] *Correspondence of George III*, nos. 242, 247–8; *The Duke of Newcastle's Narrative*, ed. Bateson, pp. 51–52.

[3] *Hist. MSS. Comm., Various Collections*, vi. 260; *Sandwich Papers* (Navy Records Society), iii. 25.

[4] *Correspondence of George III*, nos. 2254, 2449.

[5] Ibid., nos. 2451, 2649. In Mar. 1780 he 'could never suppose this country so far lost to all ideas of self-importance' as to acknowledge the independence of America; if it did so, we should fall 'into a very low class among the European states' (ibid., no. 2963). 'The giving up the game would be total ruin, a small state may certainly subsist but a great mouldering one cannot get into an inferior situation but must be anihilated' (ibid., no. 3155; see also nos. 3357, 3439, 3501).

[6] Ibid., nos. 3962, 4004, 4414, 4422, 4441, 4470.   [7] Ibid., no. 3923.

[8] Stanhope, op. cit., vol. i, Appendix, p. xix; D. G. Barnes, op. cit., p. 185.

age in entering into a negotiation with the enemy for the sake of putting him in the wrong or satisfying our own pacifists, and thus was nearly always on the side of the unbending Grenville against the opportunist Pitt.[1] In the last great controversy of his reign, over Catholic Emancipation, his obstinacy, reinforced by genuine religious and constitutional scruples, became madness; indeed, he knew this himself, and when he refused to discuss the question, or demanded pledges against its future discussion, he was probably concerned as much for the protection of his own sanity as for the defeat of the measure before him.[2]

George III was, in many ways, the spiritual ancestor of Colonel Blimp; yet there was something almost admirable in his rigidity, and it showed to best advantage in war. His phrases about the British lion were *clichés*, but his confidence was none the less genuine. His ministers, in the autumn of 1778, might be counting the probable size of a joint French and Spanish fleet in the Channel next summer, but the king only remarked, 'I doubt not whenever it shall please the Almighty to permit an English fleet fairly to engage any other, a most comfortable issue will arise.' Next summer came, and sixty-six French and Spanish ships of the line were daily expected off our coasts. All England was hoping that our own fleet, only forty strong, would somehow avoid meeting them; there was one man, however, whose wishes were very different. 'I own', said the king, 'I have not the smallest anxiety if the ships already under the command of Sir Charles Hardie, can bring the combined fleet of the enemies to a close action. I have the fullest confidence in Divine Providence; and that the officers and men of my fleet will act with the ardour the times require.'[3] If we consider how Nelson

---

[1] *Hist. MSS. Comm., Dropmore MSS.* iii. 170, 256, 327; *Diaries and Correspondence of Lord Malmesbury*, iii. 96. According to another story told by Malmesbury, George III's idea of diplomatic method were somewhat odd: instructing Malmesbury on his mission to the adulterous Frederick William II of Prussia, the king said, 'You must first represent to him, that if he allows his moral character the same latitude in his explanation of the force of treaties, as he has allowed it in other still more sacred ties, all good faith is at an end' (ibid. iii. 7).

[2] See his letter of 29 Jan. 1801 to Addington (Pellew, op. cit. i. 285–6), and the message he is said to have sent Pitt after his recovery (Stanhope, op. cit. iii. 303). I think he had the same thing in mind when he tried to exact a pledge from the Grenville ministry in 1807.

[3] *Correspondence of George III*, nos. 2434, 2717, 2719; see also his letters to Sandwich in *Sandwich Papers* (Navy Records Society), iii. 41, 49; in one of these he writes that he 'sighs for an action'.

and St. Vincent, less than twenty years later, cut through French and Spanish squadrons like butter, can we think his confidence altogether absurd? Lastly, Speaker Abbot tells a story, which I have not verified but should like to believe, about George III's demeanour in a later invasion scare: if the enemy had landed early in 1804, the queen and the princesses were to be packed off to Worcester, out of harm's way; the old king, however, would proceed *towards* the invading force—if it appeared in Kent, he would make his headquarters at Dartford, if in Essex at Chelmsford. He meant to have the invaders under his own eye.[1]

A man of such rigid and limited ideas can hardly be said to have understood the art of politics. Indeed he despised the art and most of its practitioners. Though he defended the legal claims of the House of Commons, as an established institution, against the electors of Middlesex or the American colonists, he sometimes spoke of it with some contempt as a mere talking-shop;[2] and this, perhaps, accounts for his refusal to take ministerial defeats there very seriously. Most of all did he despise the 'popular' politician, and the resolution devised to attract popularity. He once wrote that he could not suspect General Conway of 'so unfair a motive as the love of popularity',[3] and he never treated the public support for a measure, such as the Contractors' Bill or the Dissenters' Relief Bill, as a reason for allowing it to become law.[4] At best, politicians were, for the most part, ignorant declaimers, without professional training and obsessed by *arrière-pensées* which no sane man would respect; at their worst, they were corrupt and factious. He had imbibed from Bute (who knew no more about politicians than he knew himself) the idea that there was hardly a single honest man in the political class: if Fox and his 'mirmidons' did not attempt a *coup d'état*, at least the apostasy of Pitt, the enemy of continental entanglements, proved that there was no health in them.[5]

The political vice which George III came to denounce most strongly was that of faction, 'that hydra faction'. Here he was involved in a celebrated controversy over the place of party in British politics.

[1] *Diary and Correspondence of Lord Colchester*, i. 470.
[2] e.g. *Correspondence of George III*, no. 3450.
[3] Ibid., no. 693.   [4] Ibid., no. 2536.
[5] *Letters from George III to Lord Bute*, pp. 6, 11, 19, 43, 45–46; see my article in the *Transactions of the Royal Historical Society*, 5th series, i. 127–51, especially 129–33.

To talk of 'whig' and 'tory', or of 'party', as if these terms meant the same thing throughout the eighteenth century is to imply a fallacy which is now exploded. The parties of 1760 were certainly not the same as those of 1714. Even in the first classical age of the two-party system, as we know from Mr. Walcott's researches, the apparently homogeneous cohorts of whigs and tories were rather aggregations of personal groups, each a few dozen strong at most;[1] and since 1714 the two great parties had dissolved still further, their meaning was still more diluted. Bolingbroke had pointed this out. Because he was a deist and had been a public enemy, those elderly dukes who wished to perpetuate the relevance and the power of the whig party could easily discredit his remarks. But they were quite true; and when we read that George III's preceptors were accused of bringing him up on the commonplaces of the *Patriot King*, we feel surprised that anybody should have thought the charge worth making.[2] George III could have known, without reading a page of the *Patriot King* or, indeed, of any other book, that the distinction between whig and tory, which Newcastle in all sincerity exploited,[3] was now a trifling one, and that the different connexions into which the whig party was beginning to split were divided by personal interests rather than divergences of policy;[4] and he could likewise have formulated for himself the idea of trying to unite his people by ruling without regard to these illusory differences.

Though this ambition seemed so obviously right that hardly anybody, at first, thought it worth while to dispute it, yet it

---

[1] Robert Walcott, Jr., 'English Party Politics, 1688–1714', in *Essays in Modern English History in Honour of Wilbur Cortez Abbott* (Harvard University Press, 1941), pp. 81–131.

[2] See Mr. Sedgwick's very ingenious explanation of the origin of this charge in his Introduction to *Letters from George III to Lord Bute, 1756–1766*, pp. xxiv–xxxvii. In one respect, it is a mistake to underrate the seriousness of this accusation. The whigs had maintained themselves in power for a generation, not so much by convincing the public that the tories were Jacobites, as by convincing the king of it. If a king should come to the throne, who denied the distinction between whigs and tories, the whigs would suffer—provided that there were still any tories of any importance to whom he could appeal.

[3] Newcastle had dealings with tories, but I do not think he ever liked it. In 1746 it was Chesterfield who wanted to take some tories into the Ministry, Newcastle who preferred to make his bargain with opposition whigs (*Private Correspondence of Chesterfield and Newcastle*, ed. Lodge, pp. 108, 114, 117–18).

[4] See the long and clever description of the origins of the spoils system in the Rev. John Brown's *Estimate of the Manners and Principles of the Times*, i. 108.

was not realized, and in time even its respectability was questioned.

There were many good reasons for this. In the first place, it was useless to appeal from whigs to tories if there were no effective tories to answer the appeal. Horace Walpole once said, 'In truth all the sensible Tories I ever knew were either Jacobites or became Whigs; those that remained Tories remained fools'; and he spoke very truly.[1] A tory who was not a Jacobite had nothing left to be a tory about, and might just as well become a whig; if he did not, he was sacrificing not only his advantage but his political utility to a personal luxury of nomenclature. Such men were not of ministerial timber. Thus, though George III was willing to take loyal tories into his service, as he told Pitt in 1765,[2] few of them came; some of them coldshouldered him,[3] others were useless.

George III's failure to break down the distinctions between whigs was a more serious defeat, and harder to explain, for the idea of reuniting the whig party was one to which nearly everybody, at one time or another, paid service—Chatham, Rockingham, Grafton, perhaps even Charles Fox. What was there about these whig groups which made them so hard to reconcile? We can only understand this by considering how these groups arose and what kept them alive.

First of all, however, let us remember that by no means every politician belonged to them. Even the most expert political calculators of the time could not predict the behaviour of nearly every M.P. Newcastle's and Robinson's lists abound in doubts: the categories of 'probable' and 'possible'—or 'hopeful' and 'doubtful'—are not so numerous as the definite 'pro's and con's', but they account for nearly a third of the House. Thus in 1783 Robinson estimated the 'hopefuls' and 'doubtfuls' in the present House at 178 out of 558, and 182 in the House he hoped to see elected.[4] Charles Fox's arithmetic, twenty years later, tells the

---

[1] *Memoirs of the Reign of King George III*, ed. Russell Barker, i. 192.

[2] 'You can name no Whig familys that shall not have my countenance; but where Torys come to me on Whig principles let us take them' (*Correspondence of George III*, no. 100).

[3] The University of Oxford, the last home of the old toryism, showed little desire to welcome Lord Bute as Chancellor in 1762 or Charles Jenkinson as M.P. in 1766. 'Straight' tories were preferred on both occasions (*Jenkinson Papers*, ed. Jucker, pp. xxi, 47–60).

[4] *Parliamentary Papers of John Robinson*, ed. Laprade, pp. 66–105. In 1706

same story: the various known categories in his list only add up to 450 members out of a House which now numbered 658—the rest were doubtful.[1] He accounts for the remainder as 'such as vote whimsically or for from fear of their constituents', and those who seldom or never attend.[2] This last class was, indeed, numerous: a division of 450 was reckoned a very big one.[3] But Charles Fox was always inclined to underrate the men who belonged to no party;[4] they were numerous, respectable, and sometimes powerful. In the parliament of 1780–4 they were almost an organized body; it was their decision which brought about the fall of North,[5] and their efforts to reconcile Pitt and Fox, though

Godolphin professed to account for 450 out of 513 (*Hist. MSS. Comm., Portland MSS.* iv. 291). The reduction to 380 out of 558 in Robinson's time seems to show the weakening hold of party politics in the House. A calculation made in 1788 and quoted by Professor Donald G. Barnes (*George III and William Pitt*, p. 197), accounts for as many as 473 out of 558, but this result was only achieved by describing the 108 country gentlemen as a party; most people would have regarded them as unclassified.

[1] The addition of a hundred Irish M.P.s must have increased, for a time, the proportion of the House which was not affiliated to any English party, as the addition of the Scots had done a century earlier. This, incidentally, helps to account for the legend of the collective venality of the Scots: thinking the English factions made a lot of fuss about little or nothing, they could have no scruples about selling their votes to the Government of the day, in return for personal advantages for themselves or sectional advantages for Scotland. Exactly the same thing would happen today if Great Britain were to join the U.S.A.: knowing and caring nothing about the differences between Democrats and Republicans, the British members of Congress would be, for a time, a disturbing and demoralizing force, since they would feel free to bargain with either party for their own advantage or that of Great Britain.

[2] *Memorials and Correspondence of Charles James Fox*, iv. 98. Compare this with George Rose's more modest calculation in 1804 (*Diaries and Correspondence of George Rose*, ii. 119). In 1802 the first Lord Liverpool remarked to his son, 'The House was rather flat, but this I have observed is generally the case with a new Parliament; a great proportion of the members who attend being new members, who are unacquainted with the ways of the House, and who cannot be expected to give much encouragement to any party' (C. D. Yonge, *Life and Administration of Lord Liverpool* (London, 1868), i. 99). He thus assumed that the average M.P., like the average Deputy in the Third French Republic, chose his political affiliation after election, not before it.

[3] Speaker Abbot describes the division of 493 on the Army Bill, 18 June 1804, as the biggest for sixty-three years (*Diaries of Lord Colchester*, i. 520).

[4] See his remarks in *Parl. Hist.* xxiii. 1425, which were much resented by Powis (ibid. xxiv. 45).

[5] Lord North did not resign on the news of Yorktown; he only sent in his final, and effective, letter of resignation three months later, when he heard that Grosvenor, the spokesman of these country gentlemen, was going to announce their decision to withdraw their support from the Ministry (*Correspondence of George III*, no. 3566). Some country gentlemen believed that they, as an organized body, held the balance of power in the House (see Lord Fielding's speech, May 1781, *Parl. Hist.* xxii. 149),

fruitless, had to be attended to because they held the balance of power in the House.

Even of the M.P.s whose conduct was predictable, not all could be said to belong to any group, unless those who habitually supported the Government of the day could be described as a group. (This raises the question whether the so-called 'King's Friends' were a political party, which I shall discuss later.)[1] In Fox's calculation already quoted, 180 out of the 450 classifiable M.P.s were 'supporters of the Chancellor of the Exchequer for the time being'. This reduces the members of the factions, or parties, properly speaking, to a minority of the House—barely more than a third. Similar calculations for earlier times would probably have yielded similar results. But the factions contained a high proportion of the ostensible politicians, who furnished the candidates for office; that is the reason why George III had so much trouble with them.

What was it that kept the members of one of these groups together? In the first place, we should probably name friendship. Politicians of the eighteenth century attached high importance to political friendship; sometimes it made up their whole scheme of politics. The friendship of Hardwicke with the Pelhams is a respectable example; and when Horace Walpole interrogated the exasperating Conway as to his political views, all he could get out of him was 'that for his part he desired no place, and liked very well to act with a few', and that 'he preferred his character and the Cavendishes' to the country'. The Cavendishes themselves were just as clannish: Lord John 'wished the Opposition was reduced to six or seven, who could depend upon each other'.[2] The beauty of personal friendship in politics, without which there could be no political confidence or consistency,

and they tried to use this influence in order to reconcile Pitt and Fox in the early months of 1784. In 1788 they were reckoned as a separate party, numbering 108 members, by the author of the calculation quoted on p. 72, note 4.

[1] v. infra, pp. 107–8.

[2] Memoirs of the Reign of King George III, ed. Russell Barker, ii. 92, 96. Lord John Cavendish, like Burke, seldom missed an opportunity to testify in public his devotion to the principle of party connexion (Cavendish, Debates, i. 157; Parl. Hist. xxiii. 1404). The late Duke of Devonshire had left Conway £5,000; but, as Horace Walpole said, there was no reason why this should be 'a retaining fee to make him a servant to that family' (op. cit. ii. 249). Horace Walpole himself was a case in point: he was so much attached to Conway, his first cousin, that (apart from satisfying a few hereditary grudges arising out of his father's career and safeguarding his own sinecure) he may be said to have had no politics but Conway.

formed a part of Burke's argument for party connexions. Perhaps nobody ever rated friendship higher as a political virtue than Charles Fox, who is said to have had a genius for friendship (though he also harboured very ugly and vindictive enmities which his admirers have overlooked). As he once asked, 'is it possible to be happy in acting with people of whom one has the worst opinions, and being on a cold footing (which must be the case) with all those whom one loves best, and with whom one passes one's life?'[1] Nor was this only a young man's *schwärmerei*. In Charles Fox's circle the exclusive mutual admiration, which was always the besetting sin of the Opposition whigs, went to its absurdest lengths. They were all too much inclined to believe that the men of their own clique were fit for any post, however small their experience or qualifications; but perhaps nobody but Charles Fox would have imagined that Lord Fitzwilliam, who was nothing but Lord Rockingham's heir, could preside over the destinies of India in the crisis of 1783, or that Grey, who had never had an executive office in his life, was the best choice for First Lord of the Treasury in the year of Trafalgar and Austerlitz.[2]

Friendship alone would not make the wheels of party go round. Leadership was more important. But who were the party leaders, and how did they make or get their parties?

From such nicknames as 'Bedford whigs' or 'Rockingham whigs' one might suppose that the parties were proprietary groups formed and controlled by the electoral patronage of some great nobleman. This is only half true. Nobody in this age controlled, in his own right, more than twelve or fourteen parliamentary seats; very few more than five. (The same thing is true of the Government itself: people talked of the 'Treasury boroughs' as if they were legion, but the number of genuine Government boroughs—that is, constituencies of which the Government, as

---

[1] *Memorials and Correspondence of Charles James Fox*, i. 170, ii. 208; *Parl. Hist.* xxiii. 176. Very few politicians would have altogether denied the necessity of friendship among political colleagues. Lord Grenville did so in 1789 (*Courts and Cabinets of George III*, ii. 173); but his tastes, like his father's, were those of a 'man of business' intent upon dealing with particular situations as they arose, rather than a party politician. Even Lord Grenville showed, in his later career, an obstinate enough adherence to his political friends to entitle him to Charles Fox's praise as a 'good party man'.

[2] *Memorials and Correspondence of Charles James Fox*, iv. 115; *Parl. Hist.* xxiii. 1431.

such, was the direct electoral patron—was quite small).[1] Any
influence beyond this could only be obtained by arrangement.
It might be a simple alliance of borough patrons to make common cause: for instance, the Duke of Bedford and Lords Sandwich, Gower, and Weymouth, each one an independent
borough-owner with three or four seats at his disposal, joined
together in a durable group under the leadership of Bedford,
who gave his name to it. The Duke of Newcastle and Lord
Rockingham, in the same way, built up a part of their parliamentary followings by means of seats controlled (and sometimes
filled) by relations, friends, and like-minded politicians. But this
proprietary influence would not go very far. Seats for the party's
indispensable 'men of business' might have to be obtained in
the open market, or on what I might call the 'grey market', in
which love and money were blended. That is to say, a borough
patron who had a definite political allegiance but could not
afford to give his leaders the seat gratis, might offer it to them
somewhat below the market price, or a candidate who thought
of attempting a constituency not controllable without expenditure of money, might offer to try it if his leaders would help him
with part of the cost. In Treasury language this would be called
a 'friend, with money'; but the factions had their 'friends, with
money', as well as the Treasury.[2] Last of all, the factions promoted and financed candidatures in the 'open' seats with special
prestige, for the same reasons as the Government did so; and
they aimed, like the Government, at attracting into a permanent
allegiance as many as possible of the 'independent' M.P.s.

Money, connexions, and direct electoral influence were
evidently great recommendations in those who set up for party
leadership; but they were not indispensable, for many party

---

[1] Namier (*Structure of Politics*, i. 174) puts it at thirty-two seats in 1761. Robinson's
calculation of Dec. 1783 seems to put it at twelve: but he speaks of thirteen additional seats as being under Government influence but requiring money. Many of
these were among the Cinque Ports (*Parliamentary Papers of John Robinson*, ed. Laprade, pp. 105–8).

[2] See Burke's letters to Rockingham, 16 and 25 Sept. 1774 (*Works* (1852 edn.),
i. 237–9); Lord Verney was too hard up to give his seats at Wendover, as hereto-
fore, to his political friends; he had to sell. 'In this situation, as Lord Verney enter-
tains exactly his old principles and regards, we ought to wish to get some of our
monied friends for his seats, by which your lordship's force in parliament will not
be so much impaired as otherwise it might be.' The Secretary to the Treasury might
have used exactly the same words to the First Lord.

leaders possessed few or none of them. Neither the elder nor the younger Pitt had them; though the father had been a hanger-on of an extremely close-knit proprietary party, he did not owe his power to it, and it was only his own eminence which procured him a party of his own.[1] George Grenville had belonged to the same group as Pitt; but he, too, built up his own connexion without its help, when he was at variance with his brother who controlled it. North had no electoral influence of his own outside his family constituency of Banbury; Canning, again, had none; and even the Grenvilles of the second and third generations, the last independent group of the old type, probably owed more to Lord Grenville's eminence as a statesman than to Lord Buckingham's boroughs.

Some of these leaders recruited their followers from among the admirers of their genius and their policies. The two Pitts were unique in this respect. Neither of them set up for party leaders. Chatham had, indeed, a little group of colleagues—Camden, Shelburne, Bristol—whom he brought into office because he admired their talents or because they symbolized in his mind some doctrine which he wished to maintain or some episode in his past career which he wished to vindicate.[2] But his following was always small in bulk, and this is why Lord North advised George III at least once that a coalition with it would be less troublesome than one with Rockingham's party, as its claims to office would be smaller.[3] Chatham's lieutenant Shelburne and his son William Pitt aped this indifference to party, though both promoted their cliques of personal coadjutors to office. Shelburne lived in a cloud-cuckoo-land where parties

---

[1] One has only to look at Pitt's extremely artful letters during the formation of Newcastle's Ministry in 1754, to see that he had nothing to learn about the art of manœuvring a party for the advancement of its members' interests (*Grenville Papers*, i. 109–10, 112–13; R. J. Phillimore, *Memoirs and Correspondence of George, Lord Lyttelton* (London, 1845), pp. 449–74, *passim*). Pitt gave the impression, and perhaps believed, after 1762 that he had never been a party man. That was quite untrue; but it was true that he did not owe to party his final rise to power.

[2] Camden undoubtedly symbolized for Chatham the acceptance of his doctrines about political liberty and the meaning of the 1688 Revolution (*v. supra*, p. 56, note 3). Bristol and Hans Stanley had served under him in diplomatic posts, and probably symbolized for him his resentment at the conduct of our negotiations with France and Spain in 1761–2. What Shelburne meant to him, it is hard to see; Shelburne denied that there had been any personal intimacy between them, and obviously rather disliked him as a rhetorician (Fitzmaurice, op. cit. i. 57–65, 74–78). [3] *Correspondence of George III*, nos. 2193, 2255.

did not exist, and his fall in 1783 seems to have taken him completely by surprise.[1] The younger Pitt's party was always small: at the end of seventeen years' undisputed pre-eminence he commanded no more than fifty or sixty personal followers. This could only be because he took no trouble to attach men to himself— gave no dinners, wasted no time on the small change of politeness, and did not even answer letters (indeed, he could not have found them in the litter on his desk).[2] Almost alone among party leaders, he was so unworldly as to keep his promise not to go into opposition when he left office;[3] this piece of disinterestedness embarrassed his followers acutely. Yet the Pitts were party leaders, in spite of all this: so long as there was a chance that their genius and public reputation would render their return to office indispensable, some men in the House of Commons would follow them in spite of all discouragements.

[1] Fitzpatrick to Ossory, 2 Dec. 1782, in *Memorials and Correspondence of Charles James Fox*, ii. 10; *Politital Memoranda of Francis, Fifth Duke of Leeds*, pp. 82, 89. Historians have never explained why Shelburne gave up the struggle so quickly in Feb. 1783; he afterwards said that George III was playing him false, but there is no evidence of this; indeed, George III seems to have blamed Shelburne for deserting him (Fitzmaurice, op. cit. ii. 245). Probably his House of Commons colleagues regarded him as a liability and wanted to get rid of him (*Correspondence of George III*, no. 4130), but I suspect, also, that Shelburne suddenly woke up to the fact that one could do nothing without a party in the House of Commons, and had no idea what to do next. He does not seem to have rated the importance of the House of Commons so highly as his contemporaries: 'Governing by the House of Commons is in fact converting the legislature into a false executive, and lays the foundation of a succession of parties and factions' (Fitzmaurice, op. cit. i. 80; see also Shelburne's depreciation of the House of Commons, ibid. ii. 358). The truth is that Shelburne was not a politician at all but had the instincts of a subtle and far-sighted administrator: he would have shone as the Prime Minister of a benevolent despot, as a Tanucci or a Turgot.

[2] Wraxall and the Duke of Richmond commented on Pitt's unwillingness to take the trouble of cultivating the members of parliament (Stanhope, op. cit. i. 241, ii. 79), Lord Bulkeley and Canning on the bad impression he made by leaving letters unanswered (*Courts and Cabinets of George III*, ed. Buckingham, ii. 15– 16; *Private Correspondence of Lord Granville Leveson Gower*, i. 169). Woronzow, the Russian ambassador, described the litter on Pitt's desk in a letter to Grenville (*Hist. MSS. Comm., Dropmore MSS.* vi. 259). Pitt's omission to answer a letter is said to have turned Wolfe Tone into a revolutionary (Frank McDermott, *Theobald Wolfe Tone* (London, 1939), p. 20).

[3] Not in 1783, when he belied his promise of taking the Coalition Ministry's measures on their merits (*Parl. Hist.* xxiii. 554), but in 1801–4, when he had bound himself by a personal understanding with the king and Addington. Perhaps one should add that the elder Pitt had almost refrained from opposition for about a year in 1761–2, and might have continued to do so, had not the Peace of Paris and the Wilkes episode set him off.

No other party leader was quite like the Pitts; but many others collected a considerable following without any electoral influence of their own. In default of genius it was office that enabled them to do this. Any man who held the patronage, as first minister of the Crown, for any length of time, had the power not merely to reward those who followed him already, but to attach new adherents to himself. Those who received places or favours from the Crown, for themselves or their friends, through a minister, did not always ask themselves whether their allegiance was due to the Crown or to the minister. Many reckoned themselves the friends of the minister, especially if he remained so long in power that his personal and official characters became merged, and respect for the former could hardly be distinguished from gratitude for favours received by means of the latter. The dilemma only presented itself when he left office; only then would those who had long been accustomed to receive their meat in due season from the hand of Newcastle, Grenville, or North as First Lord of the Treasury, have to decide whether they adhered to the First Lord of the Treasury for the time being, or to Newcastle, Grenville, or North. They did not all make the same choice. Newcastle, for example, was much put out by the desertion, in 1762, of many whom he had reckoned his assured friends; but though he did not keep all that he expected, he kept rather more than a cynic would have foretold.[1] Other ministers fallen from power had the like experience: George Grenville had hardly one personal follower when he became First Lord of the Treasury, but he left office with a very useful connexion. North, again, commanded more than a hundred votes in the winter of 1782.[2] Addington, as Speaker, could not have had a single political follower before he stepped down to the Treasury Bench, yet he collected, in office, a party of men[3] who were not all, as his enemies supposed, his brothers or

[1] Sir Lewis Namier describes this disappointment, most entertainingly, in *England in the Age of the American Revolution*, pp. 417–83. George III believed that Newcastle would not have ten followers out of place (*Letters from George III to Lord Bute*, p. 91). This was an under-estimate. Fox told Rigby the Opposition would not divide sixty (*Bedford Correspondence*, iii. 161); this, too, was a slight under-estimate.

[2] George Selwyn put it at 120 in ?July 1782 (*Hist. MSS. Comm., Carlisle MSS.*, pp. 633–4). W. W. Grenville reported to his brother on 19 Feb. 1783 that of the 221 M.P.s who voted against Shelburne's peace treaty in a recent division, 160 to 170 belonged to Lord North (*Courts and Cabinets of George III*, i. 158).

[3] Charles Fox thought sixty in July 1805, but Charles Long spoke in Dec. 1806

brothers-in-law. Possibly Rockingham had not the same experience in 1766: Burke complained that 'as there are many rotten members belonging to the best connexions, it is not hard to persuade several to continue in office without their leaders. By this means the party goes out much thinner than it came in.' This was certainly not a general truth, though it may have held good for the Rockinghams.[1] As a rule, friends and political influence stuck to the fingers of every man who had ever handled any high office from which patronage depended.[2]

These parties were not inspired solely by friendship, gratitude, or admiration for their leaders. No doubt those things had a great deal to do with it; for the leader's death often brought the party to an end. In this respect the parties kept together by electoral patronage fared better than those whose leader's personality was their chief asset; for electoral influence is heritable

of the recent general election as having reduced it from somewhere about thirty to twelve or fourteen (*Hist. MSS. Comm., Lonsdale MSS.*, p. 230). Sidmouth may have lost followers in the interval, but I suspect that Charles Fox's figures were pretty slapdash.

[1] *Thoughts on the Cause of the Present Discontents* (*Works* (1852 edn.), iii. 127). It was a curious complaint to make, for Rockingham had allowed some of his followers to remain in office, for a time, under Chatham. No doubt it is meant for Conway, who did not resign when the others did in Dec., and was forever bickering with Burke in the House of Commons about the claims of party upon a politician's allegiance (e.g. Cavendish, *Debates*, i. 15, 277); the controversy was still going in 1782, when Charles Fox threw in Conway's teeth his behaviour in 1766–7, and described his whole career as a misfortune for his country (*Parl. Hist.* xxiii. 169–70). Incidentally, this complaint is a good example of Burke's habit of constructing a theory of politics out of generalizations (in this instance a false generalization) on every incident in the career of the Marquis of Rockingham.

[2] The use of public patronage for the creation of a private party in parliament was part of the general misappropriation of influence which took place at all levels of political society: it is well described by Sir Lewis Namier in *Structure of Politics*, especially vol. ii, pp. 441–93. A member of parliament, or a local election agent, put in to represent or manage a constituency on behalf of the Crown, or a minister, or a party leader, or a private borough patron, often found means to retain for himself the influence he was set to cultivate for others, so as to make himself independent of his employers, or even to substitute himself for them. No doubt it was for this reason that a patron with a precarious hold on his influence might return a candidate for a seat on condition that the latter would engage never to go near the borough. Palmerston is said to have been returned for Newport, Isle of Wight, on this condition in 1807 (Sir H. L. Bulwer, *Life of Palmerston* (London, 1870), i. 22–23). Or the holder of an office from which electoral influence depended (e.g. the Lord Warden of the Cinque Ports), might succeed in bequeathing it as private property to his heirs, who would defend it against the next holder of the office: this happened at Hythe, where the sons of the late Duke of Dorset contested a seat, ultimately without success, against his successor Lord Holdernesse (*Hist. MSS. Comm., Stopford-Sackville MSS.* i. 68, 118, 124).

and can be exercised even during a minority, as talent cannot. This, and the cohesive force of self-interest, explains why the Bedford whigs survived the fourth duke's death by more than a decade. Personality was more vulnerable: the Grenvillites were quickly merged among North's supporters after George Grenville died; Chatham's small party seems to have dwindled away to nothing in Shelburne's hands; only the party of the younger Pitt presented, for a year after his death, the curious spectacle of a connexion whom nothing connected but the leadership of a ghost,[1] and it is doubtful if they could have kept that up very long.[2]

Even while the leader lived, it was not only his virtues and his reputation that kept his following together; still more, it was his prospect of returning to office soon. Nothing exhibits this better than the contrast between Newcastle's fortunes in 1757 and 1762. The first time he left office, most of his followers rightly expected him to return, and stuck to him; the second time, they as rightly foresaw that he would stay out, and many of them left him. Perhaps this consideration explains North's decision to ally himself with Charles Fox in 1783: he could see that his followers would drop off before very long unless he took some definite step towards a return to office, and any action was better than none.[3] This was a fundamental rule of tactics: the party must

---

[1] It is hardly too much to say this: George Rose consulted Pitt's ghost in June 1806, and was still obtaining its approval for his actions in 1809 (*Hist. MSS. Comm., Lonsdale MSS.*, p. 191; *Diaries and Correspondence of George Rose*, ii. 247, 410). Malmesbury, too, made a resolution of the same sort after Pitt's death (*Diaries and Correspondence of Lord Malmesbury*, iv. 350). Pitt's ghost was, in some respects, a better party leader in Opposition than Pitt himself would have been, for the party could keep itself together by an occasional field-day against insults to his memory, which the living Pitt would never have allowed it to do.

[2] Canning had tried in vain to pick a quarrel with Castlereagh and Perceval, and was on the point of transferring himself to Grenville when Grenville's Ministry was suddenly thrown out of office (*Diaries and Correspondence of George Rose*, ii. 246–7, 262–3, 312; *Hist. MSS. Comm., Lonsdale MSS.*, pp. 164–5).

[3] *Journal and Correspondence of Lord Auckland*, i. 6–45, *passim*, especially Loughborough's letter on pp. 42–45: as Loughborough said, those Conservatives who followed North as a defender of the constitution would support, but would not oppose with him, and at any rate their numbers would soon disappear, 'for it is not the nature of such troops to keep the field long'. A leader whose followers suffered, like North's country gentlemen, from the belief that opposition was improper, must make especial haste to bring them back into the haven of office. Incidentally, Eden and Loughborough themselves played with the idea of detaching thirty or forty of North's men in order to form a third party of their own (ibid., pp. 28–29). A party leader surrounded by such counsellors needed to keep a good look-out.

keep in action, or it would cease to be a party; it would lose its alliance-value and its nuisance-value, and before long its followers would quit. Only a leader like the younger Pitt, who expected to be recalled to power by the voice of heaven or of the people could be so blind to the requirements of parliamentary warfare as genuinely to discountenance 'a teasing, harassing opposition'.[1] Others must keep in motion, even at the cost of commitments of which they might afterwards repent; and this is one reason why the Grenvilles, despairing at last of any active alliance with the inert Pitt, took up with Charles Fox whose politics did not suit them so well; at least he was a party man.[2]

It was the first business of a party leader to keep the party together.[3] A great figure in the House of Commons might do it by flying the flag in debate. A peer of parliament might speak in the House of Lords, though this was not necessary (Rockingham could hardly open his mouth, even as Prime Minister, and Portland was remarkable for his monumental silences).[4] But if

[1] See, for example, his letters to Grenville, 15 Nov. 1802 and 4 Feb. 1804, and Bishop Pretyman's letter to Carysfort, 13 Jan. 1804, in *Hist. MSS. Comm., Dropmore MSS.* vii. 126, 209, 231; and the lamentations of Canning and George Rose over his inaction in *Diaries and Correspondence of George Rose*, i. 456–92, *passim.*

[2] The Grenvilles twice warned Pitt, in 1802 and 1803, that if he would not move before the parliamentary session began, they should have to do something which would make it harder for them to co-operate with him. On the second occasion they fulfilled the threat (Lord Grenville to Pitt, 8 Nov. 1802, 31 Dec. 1803, 31 Jan. 1804, *Hist. MSS. Comm., Dropmore MSS.* vii. 123, 203, 211). See Fox's letter in *Memorials and Correspondence of Charles James Fox*, iii. 443–4.

[3] Some, however, were so temperamental, or so doubtful of the propriety of opposition, as to introduce resolutions without properly warning their followers or allies beforehand. The elder Pitt missed opportunities in both Houses, and George Grenville made a great merit of having disclosed to none of his followers the part he meant to take in the debate (2 Feb. 1769) nor asked them to attend. (I cannot understand why he should make a parade of this; perhaps he knew of the king's strong feelings on the subject.)

[4] Rockingham did not open his mouth in the debate on the Address, the first day of the session: he reported to George III, 'Lord Rockingham is ashamed to inform his Majesty that he did not attempt to speak upon this occasion', and a month later, when the Bedfords at last baited him into saying something, the king commented that he was glad they had forced him to hear his own voice (*Correspondence of George III*, nos. 163, 210, 212). In Dec. 1792 when two of Portland's followers called upon him to give him a good talking to, he was silent for ten minutes or a quarter of an hour at a time—the best way of leading the party, just then (*Diaries and Correspondence of Lord Malmesbury*, ii. 478). Yet Portland's leadership had been uncontested until the middle of that year—partly because Charles Fox, the genius of the party, was hardly a respectable character, but still more because it was, as Fitzwilliam said, 'a great aristocratical party' (*Hist. MSS. Comm., Carlisle MSS.*, p. 700).

he wanted to keep a following in the Commons, he must resort to other arts—above all to hospitality. Brougham, in 1816, thought that 'a house of rendezvous is more wanted than a leader', and perhaps he was right, for the whig party might have died altogether in the doldrums but for the hospitality of Devonshire House, Bedford House, Lansdowne House, and Holland House.[1] But it took more than dinners to keep a party together; and the Opposition whig leaders, who had few other talents to recommend them, partly deserved their position by the assiduity with which they fulfilled this task, by meeting or correspondence. They not only sacrificed time and money to the upkeep of their own borough influence. (Newcastle impoverished himself, and Rockingham remained drunk or elevated for eleven hours on end in the good cause at the height of the election of 1768.)[2] Newcastle's enormous correspondence, prompted by an insatiable desire for consultation or reassurance, must have had the effect (perhaps undesigned) of keeping his party together. Rockingham was not so active with his pen, and he disliked leaving Yorkshire, where he had everything his own way, for London, where he did not; but when he could be induced to do so, he regularly maintained a caucus, or shadow cabinet to which he seems to have attached peculiar importance, whether in office or in Opposition.[3] The confusion of this party caucus with the Cabinet may have led to changes in the Cabinet's functions;[4] and in Opposition, Rockingham tried to subject not only his own conduct but also that of his allies in Opposition, to the judgement of 'the lords who have usually

[1] Brougham to Creevey, 14 Jan. 1816, in *The Creevey Papers*, ed. Sir Herbert Maxwell (London, 1903), i. 247. Brougham's advice was, of course, not disinterested: he wanted a nominal leader in the Commons, that he might do all the talking and managing himself. Dinners were a recognized means of building up a political party as late as 1819, when Arbuthnot complained of Peel's assiduity in giving them (*Correspondence of Charles Arbuthnot*, ed. Aspinall, p. 17). These dinners, however, led to no results—perhaps because, as Mrs. Arbuthnot suggested, Peel would not be civil to his guests (see her *Journal*, ii. 345).

[2] *Hist. MSS. Comm., Savile-Foljambe MSS.*, p. 146.

[3] Perhaps this party caucus arose out of the club of young members of the Opposition, which started to meet for dinner or supper in 1763 (Grafton, *Autobiography*, p. 25). Newcastle held a meeting of eighteen leaders on 30 June 1765, which decided by a majority of twelve to six to take office without Pitt (Albemarle, *Memoirs of the Marquess of Rockingham*, pp. 218–20); see George III's comments on this leadership by sanhedrin, in G. Harris, *Life of Lord Chancellor Hardwicke*, iii. 448.

[4] *V. infra*, p. 167.

done me the honour to meet here in the course of this winter',
to the annoyance of Chatham, who certainly did not mean to
be taken under the wing of a 'gentle warbler of the grove'.[1]
When Edmund Burke, Rockingham's mouthpiece and some-
time his private secretary, had composed the *Thoughts on the
Cause of the Present Discontents*, it was handed round among the
party leaders for advice and perhaps expurgation;[2] and this
party manifesto, which is quite as likely to have expressed
Rockingham's opinions as Burke's own, did more than any other
publication to rescue strict party connexion from the stigma of
'faction' and to consecrate the opinion that it was the only permanent defence against executive tyranny, the only guarantee
of a consistent policy or an elevated political morality.[3]

For what purpose did these leaders so sedulously foster their
parties' will to survive? Were they only grasping at power and
office for their own sake, or trying to carry out policies to which
they were pledged, or both?

Undoubtedly office was an end in itself for many of them. I
have already[4] tried to explain that this was not quite as dis-
reputable as it looks, in an age when politics consisted almost
entirely of executive government, of whose contingencies few
could be defined beforehand by programmes. But some groups
were, no doubt, hungrier for office than others. The contrast
which the 'whig' historians have made between the Bedford

---

[1] *Chatham Correspondence*, iii. 445, iv. 79, 101–2, 391, 432, 450, 457. Rockingham
tried, several times, to rope Chatham into his caucus, but Chatham did not always
consent to go, or let his friends go, even when he was trying to co-operate with
Rockingham. On occasions he burst out into tirades against the very idea of 'old
corps connection' (ibid. iv. 167).

[2] I do not know how much of this advice Burke took: Portland, for example,
recommended that Burke should go for Bute and let Chatham off lightly (Albemarle, *Memoirs of the Marquess of Rockingham*, ii. 146), but the animus against
Chatham is at least as strong as the animus against Bute in the published version.
Leland, however, seems to have thought Burke had taken too much advice (see his
letter to Burke, 11 June 1770, in the latter's *Works* (1852 edn.), i. 113).

[3] Burke was a man of genius and Rockingham was not; but men of genius might
be expected, in those days, to take their tone from their employers. The prejudices
which Burke expressed were Rockingham's prejudices, and the incidents upon
which Burke founded his opinion were incidents in Rockingham's political career
(the disputes with George III over the discipline of the 'King's Friends', the
inspired recalcitrance of Northington and Egmont in Rockingham's cabinet, the
formation of Chatham's Ministry, and the Edgcumbe affair). Burke, no doubt,
believed what he wrote: he brought this shibboleth of connexion into parliamentary
debates where it had little or no relevance (Cavendish, *Debates*, i. 276, 441).

[4] *V. supra*, p. 5.

whigs and the Rockinghams is not wholly imaginary: in their negotiations the Bedfords always asked more and better places than they were offered, and they never made any stipulations about policy, though they occasionally gave it to be understood that they had their views on America.[1] Provided one paid their price, one knew where one had them. But it would be a great mistake to suppose that other parties—for instance, the Rockinghams—did not care a farthing about the disposition of offices. They did not even pretend to this: Burke might denounce the Bedfords (without naming them) as forming a cabal 'avowedly without any public principle, in order to sell their conjunct iniquity at the higher rate', but himself proclaimed that 'The due arrangement of men in the active part of a state, far from being foreign to the purposes of a wise government, ought to be among its very first and dearest objects.'[2] The Rockinghams did not strike observers as indifferent to office: George III complained in 1782 that they had insisted upon 'a more general removal of other persons than, I believe, ever was known before', and would 'rather see the country in a flame than not restore the late lieutenants of Wilts and East York to those county Honours'.[3] This preoccupation with patronage did

---

[1] *Bedford Correspondence*, iii. 342–3, 349–60; Grafton, op. cit., pp. 99–106, 172; *Grenville Papers*, iv. 76–84; *Duke of Newcastle's Narrative*, pp. 141–53. It seems pretty clear that in the abortive negotiations with Rockingham in July 1767 it was the Grenvilles who made trouble about American policy (the Bedfords, however, not dissenting from their views) but the Bedfords who broke off on the question of Conway, presumably because they wanted his post for one of themselves. It was for the same reason, no doubt, that they edged Shelburne out of half his department in 1767 and the other half next year (Grafton, op. cit., p. 215; Horace Walpole, *Memoirs of the Reign of King George III*, ed. Russell Barker, iii. 98).

[2] *Thoughts on the Cause of the Present Discontents* (*Works* (1852 edn.), iii. 133, 135).

[3] *Correspondence of George III*, nos. 3593, 3596. George III could hardly cast the first stone at Rockingham since, by his own admission, he had 'declared I would sooner let confusion follow than part with the late Governor of my sons, and so unexceptionable a man'. Moreover, since he had himself removed the noblemen in question from their Lieutenancies for political reasons, he could not wonder at the Rockinghams' wish to advertise their triumph by a symbolical restitution. This kind of symbolical restitution was not new: Pitt, for example, is said to have insisted (in his negotiation of Aug. 1763 with George III) on a restoration of Newcastle's 'martyrs' of the previous year, and a counter-proscription of all who had been responsible for making the Peace of Paris (G. F. S. Elliot, *The Border Elliots*, p. 377). Some of the 'martyrs' were, of course, restored when Newcastle and Rockingham returned to office in 1765; room could only be made for them by further removals, which Bedford thought he owed it to himself to reverse in their turn, in his negotiation with Chatham, Nov. 1766 (*Bedford Correspondence*, iii. 351, 356). Demands of this sort added greatly to the difficulty of forming an Administration, especially

not die out with Rockingham. No doubt Charles Fox was quite sincere when he told Lauderdale, in September 1805,

the re-establishing of old interests, and especially where the persons to whom they belong have been steady to us, is, without exception, my first and principal object in wishing for any degree, more or less, of personal power, and therefore in any arrangement, whether by means of coalition or otherwise, it is what I shall most anxiously look to.[1]

When Grenville and Fox formed their coalition, they were 'nearly inundated by the pretensions which poured in from their respective connexions',[2] and every vacancy or accidental shift of power in the short life of this Ministry was attended by bickerings over places and readjustments of pretensions.[3]

The struggle for office created a code of tactics. The important art was that of making oneself necessary. Many of the eighteenth-century Prime Ministers—Henry Pelham, Newcastle, Bute, Grafton, North—were men of weak nerves. They were proud of the goodwill of the House in which they sat; and those who did not sit in the House of Commons, knew that it must be kept quiet. An opposition group had only to show itself formidable in debate, or to run the Ministry close in a few divisions, and the minister would soon begin to think of buying it off or strengthening himself against it by buying off somebody else.[4] It was all very well for the king to say that a few defeats

where there had been frequent changes of Ministry in the recent past, for the candidates for restitution or compensation might be standing two or three deep before each office.

[1] *Memorials and Correspondence of Charles James Fox*, iv. 113.

[2] Pellew, *Life of Sidmouth*, ii. 413. Sidmouth was astonished at his own moderation; but he did quite well for himself and his friends.

[3] *Hist. MSS. Comm., Dropmore MSS.* viii. 197–200, 204, 337, 342, 345–9; Holland's letter to Lauderdale in his *Memoirs of the Whig Party* (London, 1852), ii. 53–58.

[4] The negotiations of 1767 are a good example of this: Grafton was so much intimidated by some narrow squeaks in his own House that he resolved to strengthen his Ministry by taking in somebody—but he did not much mind whom (*v. infra*, p. 90). The negotiations failed in the summer, but when the next parliamentary session approached, the Bedfords made it clear to him that they should make more trouble for him, and he took them into the Ministry (Grafton, *Autobiography*, pp. 132–55, 172; *Chatham Correspondence*, iii. 255–70; *Correspondence of George III*, nos. 542, 567–71). See also the discussion among the Pittites in 1806, especially Long's and Canning's letters of 24 Oct. and 23 Nov., in *Hist. MSS. Comm., Lonsdale MSS.*, pp. 214, 223: Canning wanted to induce Grenville to drop the Foxites from his Ministry and take the Pittites in their stead; he was convinced that the right

did no harm:[1] he did not have to bear the brunt of them. Moreover, when a Ministry was in obvious danger, things might go from bad to worse, for the 'rats' began to desert, and a small majority got smaller.[2] The minister might calm the waves by merely throwing his policy overboard, as Walpole threw over the excise and the younger Pitt threw over his foreign policy in 1791; but a run of small majorities on miscellaneous subjects nearly always produced, and was meant to produce, a reconstitution of the Ministry.

In the haggling which followed, the groups in possession aimed at buying off criticism as cheap as they could, preferably by detaching one or two of the most useful members of an Opposition group without taking that group in as a whole.[3] The other party to the bargain tried to maintain its unity, not only in the act of entering the Ministry but after it was in. Constant struggles went on, between the head of the Ministry, or its dominant party, trying to absorb the new recruits, and the new recruits trying to preserve their separate identity and the semblance of a coalition between two independent powers.[4] When

way to make him do it was to oppose briskly, and perhaps he was right, for he had almost made his bargain with Grenville when Grenville suddenly fell from power.

[1] *Correspondence of George III*, nos. 1405, 2295, 2536.

[2] Good examples were the diminishing majorities for North's Ministry in 1782 (on 16 Mar. Robinson complained that 'the Rats are very bad; I fear they will increase before Wednesday, when Mr. Fox has given notice they will again attack'), and for Addington's Ministry in 1804. In the Oczakoff crisis of 1791, Pitt's majorities were still large, but he thought he could hear the rats packing up to leave him, and abruptly changed his policy.

[3] Here again the Bedfords in 1766–8 and the Pittites in 1806–7 are the two best instances, but there are others: for instance, a few individual Opposition whigs could have got back to office in the summer of 1763, but they insisted on coming as a group (*Grenville Papers*, ii. 191; P. C. Yorke, op. cit. iii. 468–9, 512).

[4] Perhaps the best instance is the dispute between Pitt and Sidmouth in 1805. Sidmouth had made it clear, when he joined the Ministry, that he looked upon this as the junction of two independent forces, not merely an absorption of his party in Pitt's; on several occasions his followers exercised the privilege (natural enough, in view of their past commitments) of voting against Pitt on matters important to the Ministry's prestige; and they finally resigned because Pitt made inadequate excuses in order to avoid bestowing upon them the quota of Cabinet offices to which they were entitled (Pellew, *Life of Sidmouth*, ii. 327, 331, 357, 360, 363, 371). When a junction between Pitt's and Portland's parties was under consideration in Oct. 1792, Fitzwilliam claimed that if any of the latter were to be excluded from office it should be their own party that was to designate them, not Pitt (*Hist. MSS. Comm., Carlisle MSS.*, p. 700). That is to say that the party acceding to the Ministry was to choose its own representatives in the Cabinet. Yet in 1812 when the Prince Regent offered Grenville and Grey a fixed number of places in the

the king was an active force in politics these struggles between groups took on a constitutional aspect, for they interfered with his right to choose his Ministry: this will be discussed later.[1] But these conflicts for advantage would have taken place, and did take place, even when the king was politically inert: they were part of the political world in which he lived.

These negotiations usually resulted in a coalition, not in the total replacement of one group by another in power: only the Rockingham whigs ever succeeded in monopolizing office by themselves, even in appearance and for a short time.[2] In forming these coalitions there was much art.

The main presupposition of the art was this: that no leader of a coalition could ever hope to find, as Lord Chesterfield said,

Cabinet, to be filled by themselves, they were much affronted (*Annual Register*, 1812, supplement, pp. 286–9).

[1] *V. infra*, chapter iv, especially pp. 114–18.

[2] Even this is not quite true, for the first Rockingham Ministry contained two strangers—Northington and Egmont—and the second was a coalition in all but name—besides Lord Chancellor Thurlow, a wholly foreign body, it contained Shelburne and Ashburton who had only half put themselves under Rockingham, also Conway and Grafton, both men of somewhat doubtful allegiance. The Rockinghams, however, were committed (so far as Burke could commit them) to the opinion that the party must reserve all the 'capital offices of deliberation and execution', the 'great strongholds of government' in its own hands, leaving only the minor posts for members of other parties or of no party at all (*Observations on a late Publication intituled 'The Present State of the Nation'*; *Works* (1852 edn.), iii. 100; see also the passage quoted from Richmond's journal, June 1766, which recommends offering some posts to Bute's friends 'provided they are not places of ministers, and that we keep them out of the Cabinet' (Albemarle, op. cit. i. 350)). They tried once more to act on this principle when they made their coalition with North. Fox sent a message to North in Aug. 1782, in which he 'was so good as to allow Lord North to have a good office, but by no means in any superintending situations: this he said was quite impossible' (*Journal and Correspondence of Lord Auckland*, i. 28). Portland assured Lord Temple in Feb. 1783, after the negotiators for a coalition had come to close quarters, that all the 'responsible efficient offices' would be held by followers of Rockingham, though North 'may make part of such a new arrangement' (*Courts and Cabinets of George III*, i. 163). In fact, North himself told George III, a day or two later, that he could not hold any office though he was ready to sit in the Cabinet (*Correspondence of George III*, no. 4153). But he must soon have changed his mind, for the bargain was held up for some time by Portland's refusal to let North's party have a Secretaryship of State or to admit Stormont to the Cabinet. This besotted arrogance is hard to understand if, as W. W. Grenville reported, North contributed more than half the Coalition's voters in the House (*Courts and Cabinets of George III*, i. 158). Presumably Portland believed that North, saddled with the discredit of the American war and perhaps with the threat of some kind of impeachment hanging over him, was so completely down and out that he could not make use of his bargaining power. Shelburne and his friends made exactly the same mistake (ibid. i. 143; *Memorials and Correspondence of Charles James Fox*, ii. 32).

enough pasture for the beasts he had to feed. An all-embracing coalition was, therefore, out of the question. Newcastle, who feared even the most insignificant opposition and tried hard to accommodate the pretensions of a commanding majority of active politicians, could only do it by more than half promising the same object to two or three candidates, so that nobody believed him to be an honest man. Chatham's attempt to lay the foundation of an all-party coalition in 1766 cost an unusually large sum in pensions, and never completely succeeded even at that price. The right tactics, therefore, was to aim at an alliance with the smallest number of groups which would afford a sufficiency of votes, speakers, and administrative talent. A con-nexion like Chatham's, with a few very useful office-seekers, was a more convenient ally than one like Rockingham's, with great pretensions but few speakers or men of business. If an alliance with one group would suffice, it was a mistake to try for an alliance with two, for there would be more mouths to fill: thus in the unsuccessful cabinet-making of June 1757, Bedford posi-tively hoped that all the existing ministers would resign, 'for that every vacancy would either serve an old friend, or gain a new one'.[1] For the same reason it was generally thought better to negotiate for power with another Opposition group than with a Ministry in possession, for one could disregard in the former case, but not in the latter, the presumption in favour of the man in possession.[2] The choice of allies and enemies might be a matter of indifference. For instance, in the negotiations of

---

[1] Waldegrave, *Memoirs*, p. 127. Bedford evidently thought that if only Fox had a little spirit they could get through in the House of Commons, and, that being so, it was a pity to make assurance double sure by sharing office unnecessarily with men who were no friends of his.

[2] No doubt this is why the negotiation of July 1767, which was meant originally to take place between Grafton, the First Lord of the Treasury, and Rockingham, soon turned into a negotiation between Rockingham and the other Opposition groups. Charles Fox told Lauderdale in Sept. 1805 that if they had come to terms with Pitt eighteen months earlier, when he was still in Opposition, they would have got more out of him than they could get now, when he had all the existing office-holders (some of whom were no particular friends of his) to protect (*Memorials and Correspondence of Charles James Fox*, iv. 114; see also his letter of 9 Apr. 1804, ibid. iv. 40). See also James Oswald's letter to Henry Home, 1 Dec. 1744, in which he boasts of the disinterestedness of his political group: they could have negotiated with Carteret, who had everything to offer, being out of office, but preferred to deal with the Pelhams who, being in office and having all their colleagues to protect, could make very little room (*Memorials of the Life and Character of James Oswald of Dunnikier* (Edinburgh, 1825), p. 37).

July 1767, Grafton, the First Lord of the Treasury, seems to have wanted an alliance with Rockingham and Bedford but not with Grenville. Conway, the Secretary of State, preferred to negotiate with Rockingham alone. Rockingham does not seem to have known whether he wanted to ally himself with Bedford and Grenville or Bedford and Grafton, while his friend Richmond would rather have negotiated with Grafton alone, or even with Bute, than have anything to do with Grenville or Bedford. Grenville lent one ear to Bedford and the other to W. G. Hamilton who was asking him why 'To exclude the Court, you will submit to divide with Lord Rockingham, but to exclude Lord Rockingham, you won't condescend to participate with the Court?' Bedford negotiated with everybody except Grafton and ended, a few months later, by joining Grafton alone.[1]

In all these discussions, it is fair to say, the name of America was sometimes mentioned; but the Grenvilles were the only group who could claim that their attitude was determined by consideration of policy[2] in general. The programmes of the parties, were, to say the least, much less conspicuous than their views on patronage. Even the Rockinghams, who claimed that in their first Administration 'for the first time were seen men attached in office to every principle they had maintained in opposition',[3] would have been rather hard put to it to demonstrate this claim: for they had not a very noticeable past record

[1] Details of this highly elaborate negotiation are given by D. A. Winstanley in *Lord Chatham and the Whig Opposition* (Cambridge, 1912), pp. 152–84. It may be followed in the printed documents: Albemarle, op. cit. ii. 50–63; *Grenville Papers*, iv. 48–153, 228–31; *Bedford Correspondence*, iii. 365–87; Grafton, op. cit. pp. 139–54; *The Duke of Newcastle's Narrative*, ed. Bateson, pp. 104–66; *Correspondence of George III*, nos. 542–8; and Horace Walpole's *Memoirs of the Reign of King George III*, ed. Russell Barker, iii. 41–64. Horace Walpole, on this occasion, is a well-informed witness and played some part in the comedy himself; the artificiality and absurdity of his motives is almost unbelievable.

[2] Mansfield admitted to Whately that 'in the late negotiation you (George Grenville) were the only person who had rested at all upon a measure' (*Grenville Papers*, iv. 152). Perhaps this was because the Grenvilles were so far from the centre of the negotiation that it was premature for them to speak of places. But they were to have had something; it seems to have been Bedford who invented, on their behalf, the expedient (which so much revolted Rockingham) of reserving for them a block of offices to be divided by themselves (Albemarle, op. cit. ii. 52).

[3] *Thoughts on the Cause of the Present Discontents* (*Works* (1852 edn.), iii. 131). To do them justice, George III made exactly this criticism of them: that they stuck too much to the ideas they had adopted in Opposition (see his letter to Bute, in *Letters from George III to Lord Bute*, p. 242).

on the question of the Stamp Act, nor were their original intentions about it very distinct; presumably they must have been thinking rather of their resolution on General Warrants. By repealing the Stamp Act and passing the Declaratory Act, however, they committed themselves to an attitude which divided them from George Grenville and Bedford on the right hand and from Chatham on the left. Thereafter they seldom missed an opportunity of vindicating, in season and out of season, the appropriateness of this compromise; Chatham and Grenville missed very few opportunities of demonstrating its absurdity. Grenville had blundered into the Stamp Act,[1] just as the Rockinghams, one might almost say, had stumbled upon its repeal. But once the colours were nailed to the mast, there was no taking them down. Chatham, too, had his own formula on this question, from which he would not depart: as Grenville thought it lawful and expedient to tax the colonies, and Rockingham thought it lawful but not expedient, so Chatham thought it neither lawful nor expedient. This was the way policy was made in those days: men did not usually think it out for the future, but they defended very tenaciously the commitments, even the mistakes, of the past. Even at the end of the American War, when everybody must have known what had to be done, the Rockingham Ministry was broken up by Shelburne's efforts to find a way of making peace without violating the principle, which he had inherited from Chatham, that the sun of the British empire would set when the independence of America was recognized.

After two decades of fairly simple and intelligible politics, the same confusion broke out again. Pitt defended the conduct of Addington's Ministry in 1801 but not its conduct in 1803; Addington defended it all, Lord Grenville denounced it all, whereas Fox, while more or less sharing Pitt's views about Addington, wished to condemn the past actions of Pitt and Grenville themselves. In addition, Grenville and Fox thought that Catholic Emancipation should be granted now, Pitt that it should be granted later, Addington that it should not be granted at all. None of the parties was strong enough to form a Ministry by itself (as Pitt found after a few months of office), so each was

---

[1] He probably did not invent it, and the recent article of Professor E. S. Morgan in *William and Mary Quarterly*, 3rd series, vii. 353–92, makes it appear very doubtful if he knew what he was doing.

condemned to a coalition with some other group from which it had ostentatiously differed.

Perhaps, in default of any policy-making party organization, this rigid adherence to any attitude once taken up was the only way in which politicians could introduce any principles into politics or keep their followers together. Perhaps they had all eaten a great deal more meat than was good for them. Whatever the cause, these badges of difference, which assumed more and more importance in the opinion of those who wore them, did quite as much as patronage, in the long run, to hinder the co-operation of politicians. Probably George III did not understand this: in his young days, hardly a single genuine difference of opinion divided the factions within the amorphous whig party. But these new issues—some of them, like Wilkes and Catholic Emancipation, chiefly created by George III himself—made it harder and harder, as time went on, to form a government by a coalition of the wise and the good—or even the foolish and the bad—without scandal and recrimination.

IV

THE APPOINTMENT AND DISMISSAL OF MINISTRIES

THE controversies between George III and the factions centred on the appointment and dismissal of ministers. There were two reasons for this. In the first place, no Ministry could be formed without some reference to the dispute whether party allegiances were to be regarded or disregarded in its composition. In the second place, the king could not govern the country without ministers who could normally carry the two houses of parliament with them; and, if he wished to govern, not merely to sit on the throne, any opposition to his policy was likely to take the form of questioning his right to maintain his instruments, his ministers, in office.

This question of ministerial responsibility had never been completely settled; or perhaps it would be more true to say that a settlement had been implied, but the implication had never been conclusively established. The various impeachments—even the abortive impeachments—of unpopular or unsuccessful ministers had pretty clearly established the right of the House of Commons to criticize the king's instruments and to demand their removal; and when the quasi-criminal procedure of impeachment was replaced by the wieldier weapon of a vote of censure (or such other resolution as might drive the ministers out of office), the right of the House of Commons was not merely maintained but rendered more effective. From the right of removing the king's ministers to the right of controlling their appointment is not a very long step in theory. But this step was not taken in theory because it could not be taken in practice: a House of Commons which sat for less than half the year, and consisted largely of amateurs who attended irregularly and placemen who did not much mind who they served under, was not organized to dictate positively the composition of Ministries, except at occasional crises: those crises only took place at the height of unsuccessful wars, and even then, no right was ever affirmed in black and white, as the unpopular minister invariably bowed to the storm.[1] Thus the House of Commons had never yet formally passed over from the position of a check on the executive government and become, in effect, the executive government itself. The king was free to govern, and to choose the instruments of government. It was not a figure of speech to call the ministers his servants. But they knew, and he knew, that they served him at a risk.

The knowledge of this risk would give them power over him, if they chose to use it. A particular minister, afraid of the parliamentary consequences of an act which the king called upon him to do, might resign without putting the king to much inconvenience.[2] But if the ministers were all of a piece—if they refused collectively to take the parliamentary responsibility for any measures but those of their own choosing—they might put the king into great difficulty. Indeed they might go further and almost erect themselves into a new estate of the realm unknown to the constitution: by dispensing the king's patronage they might induce an effective majority of the House of Commons to follow them, and by threatening the king with the displeasure of that majority, they might coerce him into giving them yet more control over patronage and policy.[3] This could only be done if the king did not know his business, and if there was enough real or artificial solidarity among the politicians of the dominant group. George II, in his later years, seems to have been such a king; and, though it would be melodramatic to suppose that

[1] Walpole retired in 1742, Newcastle in 1756, and North in 1782 (all during wars which were going badly) without having been censured beforehand, though they knew they might be censured if they stayed. The most striking instance is a modern one: Neville Chamberlain retired in 1940 after obtaining a majority in the House of Commons which might, in other circumstances, have been regarded as handsome.

[2] Sir Robert Walpole resigned in 1717, without having any immediate effect on George I's policy.

[3] Evidently George II thought this a perversion of power. Chesterfield, advising Newcastle to coerce George II, said in 1745: 'Your strength is in Parliament, and you must use it while you have it. The unanimity you have procur'd there, far from recommending you in the Closet, is us'd as an argument against you there, and somebody is told *since they can do what they will there, make 'em do what you will*. It is, therefore, surely time to show the person who suggests that argument that, as you can do what you will there, you will do what he won't like' (*Private Correspondence between Chesterfield and Newcastle, 1744–6*, ed. Lodge, pp. 21–22). 'Somebody' is, of course, George II; it must have been Carteret who suggested the argument, which rested on the old-fashioned assumption that the ministers were to use their influence in parliament to do the king's business; Chesterfield could see that they were there to do their own.

Newcastle consciously thought out any scheme for enslaving the king, all his actions tended to create such a solidarity—as he supposed, in the interest of the king himself.

Newcastle's characteristic device was the collective resignation: he brought it off in 1746, was ready to try it again in 1757, and once more, with far less success, against George III in 1762. It would not be fair to say that these manœuvres had nothing at all to do with policy;[1] but their great object was to prevent the king from giving his confidence to anybody but Newcastle. On the first of these occasions, Newcastle evidently believed himself to be acting on an important constitutional principle:[2] namely, that only those who had an ostensible position as the king's official servants had a right to give him any advice. 'The King's servants must be his ministers, exclusive of all others, or they cannot remain his servants': the king must 'determine who shall be his ministers, either those who are now his servants, or to make those his servants who are now his favourite ministers'.[3] Or, as Harrington put it somewhat more intelligibly, 'they who dictate in private should be employed in public'.[4] Fair enough; but this was not mere self-protection, as Newcastle may have wished to think: it was also a parliamentary manœuvre. Chesterfield, who had been hounding Newcastle on to show his power without regard to 'little notions of frivolous decency or compliment'[5] had advised him to do it while parliament was sitting

[1] Newcastle had really differed from Carteret on questions of policy in 1744, and had, incidentally, been preparing to bring matters to a head on that occasion by a collective resignation (W. Coxe, *Pelham Administration* (London, 1829), i. 166, 168); but Newcastle's own policy shifted very soon afterwards (as he would have said, under pressure of circumstances), so that it is not easy to say what were the differences between them in February 1746, the date of the collective resignation.

[2] He had already annoyed George II by threatening to resort to the 'constitution', or, as he preferred to put it, arguing that though the king was free to choose between the different policies proposed by his ministers, those who disagreed with his choice had a constitutional right to resign rather than comply with it.

[3] *Private Correspondence of Chesterfield and Newcastle, 1744–6*, pp. 17, 41. Evidently Newcastle uses the term 'minister' in the sense of 'adviser'—even 'secret adviser'.

[4] P. C. Yorke, op. cit. i. 427. George II never forgave Harrington for his unexpected and uncalled-for participation in this manœuvre: probably he looked upon Harrington (who had been a career diplomat) as a civil servant rather than a politician like the Pelhams, or else he wreaked his revenge upon Harrington because he knew he could not indulge it upon the Pelhams (W. Coxe, *Pelham Administration*, ii. 381).

[5] Hardwicke, according to his son, entertained such scruples and afterwards looked upon the collective resignation as unjustifiable; Henry Pelham later told Newcastle 'I have promised the king, and I will keep my word, that I would never

because his strength lay there; and the collective resignation was, in fact, preceded by an agreement with one of the principal Opposition groups, which rendered the Pelhams' strength in the House of Commons unassailable.[1] Moreover, on the second and third occasions when Newcastle tried to arrange resignations, he had no constitutional warrant for doing so, since he was not a minister trying to prevent the king from taking unofficial advice, but a politician out of office trying to force his way in.[2] The same thing is true of the other concerted resignations which Rockingham and Chatham promoted from outside the Ministry in 1766 and 1770 respectively.[3] These were meant to demonstrate the parties' power to make the king or the minister uncomfortable by depriving him of votes in parliament or strength in debate.

These demonstrations twice deterred George II; none of

enter into any cabal again, to prevent his Majesty from either removing or bringing into his service any person he had either a prejudice to, or a predilection for' (ibid. ii. 389).

[1] *Private Correspondence between Chesterfield and Newcastle, 1744–6*, pp. 21, 45, 108. It was an understood thing that a Ministry which possessed any private strength of its own in parliament was stronger *vis-à-vis* the king in the session than in the recess: for instance, Horace Walpole claims to have advised the Rockinghams in 1766 to try and get through the recess, at the end of which 'they might surprise and distress the King by a sudden resignation, or force him to give them better terms' (*Memoirs of the Reign of King George III*, ed. Russell Barker, ii. 232). This explains why George III liked to have the Houses adjourned or prorogued while he was changing the Ministry, for fear his late ministers or their partisans should embarrass or frustrate him (*Grenville Papers*, iii. 171; *Correspondence of George III*, no. 76).

[2] Rockingham, Rutland, and others were ready to resign their posts (mostly quite minor ones) in order to show George II that he could not get support for a Fox ministry in June 1757 (P. C. Yorke, op. cit. ii. 399). Rockingham and others resigned in October and November 1762, ostensibly (for the most part) in order to protest against the dismissal of Devonshire, but the real reason, I think, was to convince George III that he could not do without Newcastle and his friends, whom Rockingham described as the persons who 'had hitherto deservedly had the greatest weight in this country' (Albemarle, op. cit. i. 143). The prominence of Rockingham in these collective resignations is to be noticed, for it may perhaps explain why his party chose him as a leader, and how Burke can have imagined him to be qualified under the general rule that 'Before men are put forward into the great trusts of the State, they ought by their conduct to have obtained such a degree of estimation in their country, as may be some sort of pledge and security to the public, that they will not abuse those trusts.' I cannot think of anything else that Rockingham had done.

[3] For the collective resignation of Rockingham's supporters over the Edgcumbe affair, see D. A. Winstanley, *Lord Chatham and the Whig Opposition*, pp. 75–85; for Chatham's attempt to bring down Grafton's Ministry by getting Camden and Granby to resign, see *Chatham Correspondence*, iii. 388–9, 392, 394, 398.

them had the slightest effect on George III. He called the bluff.
In October 1762, believing that the Duke of Devonshire was
coming to court to resign his office, he dismissed him first, in order
to show that resignations cut no ice with him.[1] George II ought
to have done the same thing; indeed if he had taken Carteret's
advice he would have done it, for it was reported that when
Carteret heard the Duke of Grafton was going to resign on the
morrow, 'he bravely replied, "If it is so, turn him out tonight." '[2]
But George II was not made of that stuff: as Carteret lamented
long afterwards to Shelburne, the king 'had not sufficient courage or activity or sufficient knowledge of the country or perhaps
of mankind'.[3]

The strength of this, or any other, threat to the king's control
of his administration depended on two things: the lengths to
which opposition could properly go, and the king's ultimate control over the membership of the House of Commons.

Very few politicians admitted that it was right to oppose the
measures of His Majesty's Government systematically. (Charles
Fox did so in 1783; but Charles Fox was always saying what
everybody else was content with thinking and doing).[4] The
generality of politicians would at least profess to be ready to
look at the Ministry's measures on their merits. But it was no
more than a profession. Every group which left office in
George III's reign went into Opposition, sooner or later, with
the sole exception of the younger Pitt after 1801. As I have tried
to explain already, they could not have kept their parties
together otherwise, still less would they have had any chance of
returning to office. Some of them opposed not merely systematically but unfairly. It was quite obvious, for example, that

[1] See his two letters to Bute, 28 Oct. 1762, in *Letters from George III to Lord Bute*,
p. 152. George III showed himself sensitive, on other occasions, to anything that
looked like an obstructive resignation. For instance, he resented that of Shelburne
in 1763, thinking it had been meant to force him to recall Pitt against his will
(Fitzmaurice, op. cit. i. 209–10). Hillsborough related that the king was once so
angry with him because he suspected him of trying to put pressure by resigning,
that he cut him dead (*Hist. MSS. Comm., Various Collections*, vi. 263).

[2] *Private Correspondence of Chesterfield and Newcastle, 1744–6*, p. 117. Chatham
showed a similar spirit in 1766, when he countered the argument that the best way
to keep Rockingham quiet was to leave Dowdeswell in office as Chancellor of the
Exchequer, by saying that this was a reason for immediately dismissing Dowdeswell
(*Correspondence of George III*, no. 364).

[3] Fitzmaurice, *Life of William, Earl of Shelburne* (2nd edn., 1912), i. 37.

[4] *Parl. Hist.* xxiii. 1427.

Newcastle opposed in 1762 a peace which he would have been only too glad to make himself; George Grenville went through some amusing contortions in order to explain why he had persecuted Wilkes in the first stage of his career and defended him in the second; still more did his son Lord Grenville tie himself into knots in order to show why he opposed in 1810 a Regency Bill so remarkably like that which he had helped to pass in 1788. The king, therefore, could not rely much on any respect for decency or consistency which might restrain the politicians from pushing their opposition to all lengths. Yet there must have been, at any rate sometimes, a strong feeling that certain kinds of opposition were not respectable. Nothing is more remarkable, in the sparring between Pitt and Fox during the early months of 1784, than the obstinacy with which Pitt drove Fox towards the violent courses of withholding the supplies and moving an impeachment, and the ingenuity with which Fox tried to avoid them. Other reasons have been suggested for this long and obscure struggle, but it is at least probable that Pitt wanted to take advantage of a general feeling that extremities of opposition were wrong.[1]

The king, then, could not hope for the co-operation or even the neutrality of the party politicians unattached to his Ministry, though he could usually rely on the patriotism and the good sense of the House of Commons as a whole to restrain the partisans from bringing on a conflict between the House as an institution and himself.

In 1762, when the party politicians, lately in power, tried to make him take them back, they were easily broken and discredited. Their claim to serve him on their own terms, not his,

[1] Other explanations are, indeed, possible: for instance, Pitt may have been waiting for Robinson to rig the general election, but this is not very likely, for Robinson seems to have been ready (Donald G. Barnes, *George III and William Pitt*, p. 102). The Duke of Leeds suggests a more likely explanation in his *Memoranda* (pp. 94–96), viz. that the House of Commons resolutions of 12 Jan. (for which, see *Parl. Hist.* xxiv. 299–303) had made it impossible to dissolve parliament at once without incurring financial difficulties. Professor Barnes prefers to believe that Pitt delayed because he still hoped to come to terms with Fox (op. cit., pp. 78–104). It is hard to see how he can have seriously expected to do so, except on terms which George III would flatly refuse to accept; and there is no reason to think that he meant to let George III down, for he repeatedly argued that he could not resign (which he must have done if he wanted Fox's goodwill), as no other administration could be formed—this can only mean that he knew the king would refuse to form one (*Parl. Hist.* xxiv. 433, 470, 590).

was too recent and too unofficial to be sustained. Bute was able to rally a great majority of interested and disinterested men to resist this attempt 'to give the law to the best of princes'. Henry Fox was not a popular or a pleasant man, but he probably expressed a very general feeling when he said 'The H. of Commons has a right, & has sometimes exerted it, to accuse a Minister, & make it very unadvisable for a Prince to retain him in his favour. But I do not remember they ever undertook to say who should succeed him.'[1] Pitt, whose opinion counted for more than Fox's, maintained just as strongly that nobody ought to force himself, or be forced, on the king.[2] Even politicians, like George Grenville, who had forced themselves on the king and would have done it again if they could, paid lip-service to this principle.[3] Only the clan of Newcastle, Devonshire, and Rockingham aimed at limiting the king's choice from the first. 'You may fancy what you please about the power of the Crown', Devonshire wrote to Fox, 'but believe me you will find yourself mistaken. If a King of England employs those people that the nation have a good opinion of, he will make a great figure; but if he chuses them merely thro' personal favour, it will never do, and he will be unhappy.'[4]

If Devonshire had only meant that George III ought to appoint ministers from the narrow circle of Cavendishes and

[1] Memoir, in *Life and Letters of Lady Sarah Lennox*, i. 76. George Selwyn, an old friend of Henry Fox, continued to express this opinion as late as 1782 (*Hist. MSS. Comm., Carlisle MSS.*, p. 581). He even held that if George III had shown a proper firmness, he need never, at any time of his reign, have allowed a minister to be forced upon him by parliamentary pressure (ibid., pp. 582–3).

[2] Pitt's behaviour was very ambiguous. He said repeatedly that he acquiesced in George II's rejection of his services (*Chatham Correspondence*, i. 100, 103; Dodington, *Diary*, p. 367), and yet he was obviously annoyed with Newcastle and Hardwicke because they did not force him in. Perhaps he may have suspected that they never tried to do it but used the king as a Jorkins (a very reasonable suspicion). Perhaps, however, he was a consummate hypocrite (a view which, like Hardwicke and Shelburne, I have often been tempted to take of him), or an extraordinarily muddle-headed man who wanted the impossible to happen of its own accord, whose left hand took instinctive care not to know what his right hand was doing. Horace Walpole says that Pitt in 1764 'at once talked of an Administration to be composed of great Whig Lords, and of his own resolution not to force himself upon the King; that is, he wished the great Lords should force him on the King without his concurrence, that he might have the merit of disavowing them and of profiting by their weight' (*Memoirs of the Reign of King George III*, ed. Russell Barker, i. 328). I must admit that Pitt's behaviour looks very like that.

[3] *Grenville Papers*, iv. 125.

[4] Ilchester, *Henry Fox, first Lord Holland*, ii. 203.

Pelhams, this would have been a laughable piece of social prejudice. But he meant something more. George III had used, in
a somewhat unacceptable way, the liberty of choice which most
of the politicians accorded him. Not content with choosing
between the leading politicians of the day, he had made a
minister of his personal confidant Lord Bute, who was not yet a
politician at all, for he was not a member of either House of
Parliament.[1] The king had a constitutional right to do it, and
nearly everybody must have expected him to do it; but it was
an affront to the political class, and so badly did George III
think of that class that it must probably have been meant as
such. Not only Cavendishes and Pelhams were affronted: Pitt
was more affronted still, for he could see that Bute, claiming to
prevail by court favour alone, slighted not only the so-called
'Revolution families' and their cliques but also the House of
Commons and the broader public which had lifted him to
power. It was one thing to defend the king's liberty of choice;
quite another thing, to acquiesce in a choice which meant that
court favour alone was enough to make a minister.[2] For that is
what the new king and his new minister believed, and some
others with them. Bute himself said that it was a question whether
His Majesty was to exercise 'the liberty that his poorest subject
enjoys, of choosing his own menial servants'.[3] That was no
longer a sensible thing to say about a ministerial appointment;
it would have been already somewhat out of date in the reign
of Charles II, and in that of George III it betrayed complete
ignorance of political life. For that ignorance Bute cannot altogether be blamed: he had been kept out of politics, and had

[1] He was a member of that curious little disfranchised class, the Scottish peers
who have not been elected to represent their fellows in the British House of Lords.

[2] This I take to be the meaning of Pitt's remarks printed by Namier in *England
in the Age of the American Revolution*, pp. 119–21.

[3] *Hist. MSS. Comm., Lonsdale MSS.*, p. 131; also printed in *Jenkinson Papers*, ed.
N. Jucker, p. 87. It is not quite clear whether Bute was thinking primarily of the
king's right to choose a First Lord of the Treasury or to dismiss a Lord Chamberlain; the former is more probable, though it would have been somewhat less of an
anachronism to describe a Lord Chamberlain as a 'menial servant'. These opinions
were caricatured by Burke when he said (in the *Thoughts on the Cause of the Present
Discontents*) that 'it was to be avowed, as a constitutional maxim, that the king might
appoint one of his footmen, or one of your footmen, for minister'. This sounds, to
my ear, like Henry Fox, who, according to Horace Walpole, ranted for an hour on
this subject in 1767, saying 'the King might make a page first minister, and could
maintain him so' (*Memoirs of the Reign of King George III*, ed. Russell Barker, iii. 49).

spent too many years waiting for 'D-day' as the head of the heir apparent's shadow-cabinet.[1] As a courtier, and nothing more than a courtier, he had never understood the limits of court favour; the whole history of his estrangement from Pitt shows it.[2] No doubt he had the virtues of a courtier as well as the limitations: he was disinterested, and seems to have returned, without exploiting, the maudlin devotion which George III felt for him. He knew there would be difficulties, and was vaguely

---

[1] The importance of the heir apparent, or the 'reversionary element' in eighteenth-century politics has been rightly stressed by recent historians. Every Hanoverian heir apparent from George II to George IV had a party of his own, which he used for his own purposes (such as getting more money from parliament than the king wished him to have) and may even be said to have figured as leader of the Opposition. The 'reversionary element' was only lacking between 1760 and 1782, when the heir apparent was a minor (and, incidentally, the king controlled the electoral influence of the Duchy of Cornwall). One might be tempted to suggest that if George III's opponents had been able to attach themselves to an heir-apparent in these years, they might not have thought it worth while to develop their anti-monarchical constitutional doctrines; but I believe this would be to over-rate the importance of the heir apparent. The prejudices of people like Devonshire and Newcastle, and some of their practices (such as collective resignation) originated before 1760. Moreover, they were not confined to professed adversaries of the king like Rockingham: Bedford and Grenville made very much the same claims in office, and that was what George III disliked about them (see the discussion of this subject in chapter v, below). Further, professional politicians who frequented the heir apparent's court would be likely to give him the same sort of constitutional advice that they would have given to the king (see the advice which Dodington claims to have given the Princess of Wales on 25 Jan. 1753 (*Diary*, pp. 205–6), and Lord Holland's account (in *Further Memoirs of the Whig Party*, ed. Stavordale (London, 1905), p. 84) of Grey and Grenville's quarrel with the Prince of Wales because he had altered their drafts of his messages to parliament. This, as Sheridan pointed out, was the language of ministerial responsibility although the prince was not king and they were not ministers, and Grey and Grenville seem to have withdrawn their claim.

[2] Pitt had made his bargain with Leicester House in 1755, and Bute seems to have supposed that when the great coalition of 1757 was formed, Pitt and Temple entered it as the prince's men. This belief was, perhaps, natural, since Bute had been invited to a meeting with Pitt, Hardwicke and Newcastle on 6 June (P. C. Yorke, op. cit. ii. 398), and other people shared it; for example, Fox's sister-in-law, writing from his house, spoke of the king as 'resigning himself his grandson's prisoner' (*Correspondence of Emily, Duchess of Leinster*, ed. B. Fitzgerald (Dublin, 1949), i. 47). This misunderstanding accounts for the prince's and Bute's constant exclamations against Pitt's and Temple's 'ingratitude' (*Letters from George III to Lord Bute*, pp. 19, 34, 35, 45). Pitt, on the other hand, did not admit that the obligation had been on his side; he objected to Bute's jealousy and his monopoly of the prince's confidence; he claimed to have fulfilled his part of the bargain by keeping out Fox, and did not think himself obliged to transmit all his information to Leicester House or to wait for orders from thence before taking decisions (see his letter printed by G. F. S. Elliot, *The Border Elliots*, pp. 363–4, and L. B. Namier, *England in the Age of the American Revolution*, pp. 119–21).

aware of his insufficiency (it seems to have been his own weak nerves, and nothing else, that restrained him from accepting the Treasury on the first day of the new reign).[1] But this well-intentioned greenhorn—or, rather, pair of greenhorns—proved to have relied a little too much on their *savoir faire* and on the subservience and the divisions of the despised politicians.[2]

The experiment in governing England by a 'menial servant' did not turn out well. From the first, the politicians made a dead set at Bute. Within the Cabinet, he had a little success at playing off Newcastle against Pitt,[3] and fortune favoured him, even more than he liked, by getting rid of Pitt for him a few months later.[4] But as soon as he came up against a serious parliamentary difficulty, he was nonplussed, and had to make the king 'call in bad men to govern bad men'. His bargain with Henry Fox was easily made, and yielded all the success that Bute could have desired, for both Houses approved the preliminaries of peace by large majorities.

Bute might now, perhaps, have established a parliamentary system not unlike that of Lord Sunderland. From inaugurating a reign of religion and virtue to keeping the House of Commons quiet by means of Henry Fox was, admittedly, a come-down; moreover, though Fox was in some ways an ideal partner, since he had no shame and no interest in policy, and so many shady

---

[1] G. F. S. Elliot, op. cit., p. 376; *Letters from George III to Lord Bute*, pp. 19–21.

[2] Ibid., pp. 18, 45.

[3] Pitt never forgave Newcastle for this: one of the incompatible vengeances between which his mind was torn, was his grudge against Newcastle for his disloyalty in the first six months of the reign, which did indeed contrast with his own loyalty (D. A. Winstanley, *Personal and Party Government* (Cambridge, 1910), pp. 35–37). This grudge was in Pitt's mind in the winter of 1762 (P. C. Yorke, op. cit. iii. 430, 447) and more violently in Dec. 1765, when he refused to have anything to do with the Rockingham Ministry unless Newcastle resigned (*Chatham Correspondence*, ii. 345) but not in Aug. 1763.

[4] It is quite untrue that Bute made Pitt resign, or even wanted him to do so at that time. He and the king had talked big about getting rid of Pitt (*Letters from George III to Lord Bute*, pp. 45, 49) and Bute had genuinely differed in opinion from Pitt about the peace terms and the proposals to make war upon Spain (Pares, *War and Trade in the West Indies*, pp. 576–7, 580), but when Pitt resigned of his own free will in Oct. 1761, Bute was frightened (see his letter to Dodington, 8 Oct. 1761, in John Adolphus, *History of England from the Accession to the Decease of George III* (London, 1840), i. 572). He must have communicated his alarm to the king, who wrote to him, at some time in Sept. 1761, 'Were any of the other Ministers as spirited as you are my Dearest Friend, I would say let that mad Pitt be dismissed, but as matters are very different from that we must get rid of him in a happier moment than the present one' (*Letters from George III to Lord Bute*, p. 63).

personal interests that the king had a hold on him, yet he could not be a permanent one, since he was in a hurry to get into the House of Lords. But Fox believed that the thing could have been done: brought up in the school of Sir Robert Walpole, and thinking almost as ill of his fellow politicians as Bute or the king could do, he trusted in a system of rigid parliamentary discipline exercised through the medium of rewards and punishments.[1] The king or Bute, in his opinion, could easily conduct such a system through a mere mouthpiece like Oswald; they had only to make it clear they would not depart from their plans, once settled, and this appearance of firmness would be enough.[2] Fox was undoubtedly exasperated by the thought that when, for once, a minister had the full force of the Crown behind him, he was not man enough to use it; the combination of full royal confidence and a man who knew how to use it without scruple, would have brought a return of the good old days of Fox's first master Sir Robert Walpole. But Sir Robert Walpole had sat in the House of Commons; and Fox did not explain how any agent of Bute's and the king's, other than himself, was to face a House of Commons in which Pitt was still at large, without renewing the paralysis of 1754 and 1755. Moreover, Bute was no Sir

[1] There is one remarkable fact about the 'proscription' of the opponents of the peace in 1761: most of it was done, not before but after the crucial votes in the House of Commons. Fox had always attached great importance to the fortunes of the first day's debate in a new session: for instance, in 1755 he only agreed to take the Secretaryship of State the day after the debate on the Address; and that, no doubt, explains why, in his circular letter of that year, he so particularly asked the attendance of his friends on the first day (Ilchester, op. cit. i. 272, 280). Still earlier, he had said of the new parliament of 1742, 'Attendance for the first part of the sessions is . . . the whole matter, and full or thin will either lessen or encrease the opposition exceedingly' (ibid. i. 93). In 1761 he prophesied that Bute would be sure of a majority and 'Let that appear, & the majority will be great' (*Life and Letters of Lady Sarah Lennox*, i. 77). At the beginning of Nov. Fox was still annoying the king by crying out for mildness (*Letters from George III to Lord Bute*, p. 156). He only started to propose the proscriptions after the Opposition had shown their weakness by not challenging a division on the Address, and most of them took place after the debate on the Preliminaries (Ilchester, op. cit. ii. 214). It is clear, then, that the object of the proscriptions was not to convert a minority into a majority but to punish an enemy already beaten, to answer Newcastle's campaign of resignations, and to establish a permanent Ministerial majority in the House of Commons (see his letter to Bute, end of Nov. 1762, in Ilchester, op. cit. ii. 214; and Rigby's letter to Bedford, 13 Dec., in *Bedford Correspondence*, iii. 171).

[2] Ilchester, op. cit. ii. 226. He would have been glad to see any Ministry try to put this scheme into effect, for he made similar remarks in Sept. 1763 and Nov. 1765 (ibid. ii. 269, 297).

Robert Walpole. The timorousness of which he had already given signs by his reluctance to grasp the Treasury, he now showed by running away from it. Either he had not foreseen the dead set which the politicians made at him, or he had not known how much he would dislike it. Brought down from his dreams of leading the country by an example of virtue and patriotism[1] to the mere distribution of loaves and fishes, he found this business neither edifying nor interesting, nor was he very good at it. He began to say that he had never meant to remain in office after the peace was made (of which there is no earlier evidence).[2] In short, he ran. One may say that it served George III right for choosing a minister from outside the political class: for even Newcastle and North, neurotic as they were, had at least enough stomach for politics to stay in office. But the poor young man is to be pitied. It was a bitter disappointment—the end of a dream, even though a silly dream. Henceforth he was living in the world of second-best.[3]

The world, however, had not yet done with Lord Bute. It would, in any case, have been difficult to believe in his complete disappearance from politics, for everybody could remember earlier instances of 'ministers behind the curtain'—Sir Robert Walpole for a few years after 1741 and Carteret after 1744.[4] Moreover, it is still doubtful whether Bute originally meant to renounce, and how soon he did renounce, all influence over the king's mind. On this matter, the king seems, from the first, to have shown common sense and respect for the constitution. Before he ever came to the throne, he warned Bute that if he did

[1] George III wrote to Bute, towards the end of Nov. 1762, 'I own I had flattered myself when peace was once established that my D. Friend would have assisted me in purging out corruption, and in those measures that no man but he that hath the Prince's real affection can go through; then when we were both dead our memories would have been respected and esteemed to the end of time' (*Letters from George III to Lord Bute*, p. 165).

[2] See his letter to Dr. Campbell, 30 Jan. 1763, quoted by Mr. Sedgwick, ibid., Introduction, p. lxii; his remark to Henry Fox, 2 Mar., in Ilchester, op. cit. ii. 225; and his own and Gilbert Elliot's letters to Baron Mure, in *Caldwell Papers*, II. i. 175–6.

[3] 'I shall never meet with a friend in business again' . . . 'tho' young I see but too much that there are few very few honest men in the world; as my D. Friend has quitted Ministry I don't expect to meet with it there again' (*Letters from George III to Lord Bute*, pp. 208, 220).

[4] One might almost say that the object of the collective resignation of 1746 was to get rid of Carteret from 'behind the curtain'.

not take office, 'the voice of envy would call him the Favourite'.[1] When he found that he could not prevent Bute from retiring, he seems to have tried to distinguish friendship from politics: he did not pretend to like any of his new ministers, whom he called his 'tools', and he made no secret of his intention to indulge his friendship with Bute for many years.[2] At the same time he reserved a small piece of political power—the recommendation to Scottish offices—for Bute or, rather, for his brother Stuart Mackenzie.[3]

Whether he meant to ask or take Bute's advice on politics is much less certain. Their published correspondence contains hardly anything, after April 1763, which looks like day-to-day consultation on politics. But the turn of a letter of November 1764 shows that the two were still meeting almost daily and another of May 1766 looks as if they corresponded secretly too.[4] Probably, as Mr. Sedgwick has suggested, the king later destroyed many letters from Bute. Whether those letters, and the daily conversations, touched on politics, we shall never know.[5] But if we may assume (as I think we may) that George III was an honest man, then the conclusion seems to be this: that when Bute first retired there was no definite understanding that he should keep out of politics, but his successors very soon began to wish for one;[6] that when one of the triumvirs died, and it seemed

[1] *Letters from George III to Lord Bute*, p. 21. It might be argued that this is contradicted by a later letter (ibid., p. 45) in which he assures Bute that he will be 'Minister' even though he does not take the Treasury; this, however, is consistent with the supposition that Bute might be going to take another ostensible office. (He did, in fact, begin with a Secretaryship of State.)

[2] Ibid., pp. 210, 233.

[3] This, too, he claimed to have told Grenville from the first (ibid., p. 210). But Grenville did not like this reservation, and quarrelled with Stuart Mackenzie; when he thought he had George III at the foot of the wall, in the summer of 1765, he insisted on driving Stuart Mackenzie from office (ibid., p. 238; *Grenville Papers*, iii. 41, 124).

[4] *Letters from George III to Lord Bute*, pp. 239–40, 249. On the other hand, Charles Yorke noticed in July 1765 that the king was particularly annoyed with Bedford for making him promise not to see Bute, because it implied that he had not kept the promise he had made already. This looks as though the king wished to give the impression that he had kept it (G. Harris, *Life of Lord Chancellor Hardwicke*, iii. 447).

[5] According to Gilbert Elliot, the king told Grenville in 1765 that he had not talked politics with Bute since Aug. 1763 (G. F. S. Elliot, op. cit., p. 393). I do not think Grenville himself reports this, but it is not incredible; there is no strictly political letter dating from this period in Mr. Sedgwick's edition.

[6] George III says in a memorandum of Nov. or Dec. 1765 that the triumvirs

unlikely that the two survivors could stand alone, everybody considered that a fresh situation had arisen and George III took the liberty of consulting Bute on this new situation, or Bute took the liberty of advising him. Bute's intervention turned out badly, for Pitt, whom he recommended the king to bring back to office, asked too high terms, and George III had no choice but to retain Grenville and Halifax, and bring in Bedford. All these, for their various reasons, had grudges against Bute,[1] and after their triumph they contrived to hustle him out of politics and, indeed, out of London, and to make a personal grievance against George III of every sign of correspondence with the 'minister behind the curtain'. Some conversation and correspondence, however, there must have been.

So things went on until Grenville was dismissed in 1765. The Rockingham whigs, who replaced him, had joined in the hue and cry against Bute as much as anybody, for Newcastle, the godfather of this group, had been virtually turned out by Bute three years earlier. They too, therefore, stipulated for the removal of his brother and some of his friends from office.[2] George III thought this unreasonable; but Bute himself, in order to avoid injuring the king's relations with his ministers, offered to abstain from seeing George III during the parliamentary session. Probably George III had already recovered from his puerile admiration; for he accepted the offer, and when Bute tried to retract it a few months later, the king would not see him.[3] But he wrote Bute three more letters, and the second of these made a crisis in their relations: treating Bute this time

still wanted to consult Bute during his holiday at Harrogate, May 1763, but soon turned against him (*Correspondence of George III*, no. 139, p. 163).

[1] Grenville's grudge is easy to see: he did not consider his Ministry at an end, and regarded Bute as having stabbed him in the back; the more so because it was clear that Bute had been treating with Pitt *before* Egremont died (*Grenville Papers*, ii. 90, 193–204; G. F. S. Elliot, op. cit., pp. 377–9). Bedford's grudge is harder to see: Bute had advised the king to send for Pitt (who had then insulted Bedford) but Bedford had given the same advice himself. More likely Bedford remembered a quarrel with Bute over the peace treaty, in which he had been made to look foolish (*Bedford Correspondence*, iii. 116–17, 125–30, 137–9). Moreover Bedford was, in many respects, a typical whig duke, though some of the other whig dukes did not think his politics quite reputable; and he probably shared, in some degree, the opinion that Bute had no business in politics. For Grenville's relations with Bute, see Charles Jenkinson's memorandum in *Jenkinson Papers*, pp. 393–400.

[2] *The Duke of Newcastle's Narrative*, ed. Bateson, p. 28.

[3] *Letters from George III to Lord Bute*, p. 245.

as the head of a party, he offered him power—and Bute, timorous as ever, declined it. After that, the king left Bute out of his calculations.[1] Chatham, who alone of the political leaders had now come to see that this intimacy was no longer dangerous, would have made no objection to a renewal of private intercourse. But it was too late: Bute looked upon himself, at this time, as a party leader and would not be satisfied with private friendship; whereas the king, whom he had failed once too often, no longer desired any friendship at all.[2]

The legend of the 'minister behind the curtain' died hard: Junius was still saying spiteful things about Bute in 1771.[3] It was confirmed, and diversified, by Bute's actions as a party leader. There was a party which went sometimes under the name of 'King's Friends', sometimes under the name of 'Lord Bute's Friends' in 1765 and 1766. These men, of whom Gilbert Elliot, James Oswald, and Charles Jenkinson were the most important, had not come into politics under Bute's auspices but had attached themselves to him while he was in power and remained attached, in some degree, after his retirement.[4] It is not quite clear how soon these men were recognized as a separate party; but this must have happened by the summer of 1765, for Elliot then lamented 'Lord Bute's conduct in transferring his friends backwards and forwards from one man to another'. Rockingham demanded, before he would take office, that the king should agree to dismiss some of these friends and warn the rest that they must loyally support the ministers of the day. The king gave this warning, indirectly, and thus gave colour to the belief that these men were as much his friends as Bute's.[5] (In an interview with Pitt he actually called them his

[1] Ibid., pp. 246–54. [2] Ibid., pp. 255–8.

[3] See his letter of 9 July 1771 to Grafton.

[4] I have already discussed (*supra*, pp. 79–80) the way in which politicians in office picked up followers of whom some adhered to them after their retirement. Perhaps the Scottish members of this party were particularly attached to Bute by the fact that his brother was still the minister for Scottish patronage; hence Grenville's and Rockingham's vindictive attacks on Stuart Mackenzie.

[5] *Grenville Papers*, iii. 196; G. F. S. Elliot, op. cit., p. 394 (from this document it appears that Grenville and Bedford, a month or two before their dismissal, had tried to bring Bute's followers to heel in very much the same way); *The Duke of Newcastle's Narrative*, p. 28; *Correspondence of George III*, no. 120. Egmont, however, said in May 1766, that Bute's friends had become an organized body 'this winter' (*Duke of Newcastle's Narrative*, p. 61). That seems to be putting it rather late; but their solidarity in the debates over the Stamp Act may have been conspicuous.

friends).[1] It is not certain, however, that they all recognized any obligation to follow the king's directions against their own opinions, especially on the question of American taxation.[2] The king, having accepted Rockingham as his minister, agreed, somewhat against his own judgement, to support the repeal of the Stamp Act. His private opinions were known and shared by his friends and Bute's and, indeed, by Bute himself, who even seems to have been ready to concert with Bedford and Grenville a common resistance to the repeal.[3] Naturally Newcastle asked the king once more to tell his 'friends' to support the Ministry; George III replied that he had done so, 'But what can I say, when they tell me they can't in conscience vote for the repeal?'[4] Newcastle brushed this aside; and the legend became established, that George III had encouraged his 'friends' under hand to vote against his ministers' measures. In all probability these 'friends' really thought—as many other people thought, and George III himself came to think—that the repeal was a disaster, and would have voted against it whatever George III had told them.

George III's relations with Rockingham were complicated by another dispute, in which George III was undoubtedly on Bute's side and even corresponded with him: he wanted to take Bute's party into the Ministry as equal partners in a coalition, whereas Rockingham would have preferred some other alliance such as Pitt's, and resolved that Bute's men were to be treated not as equal partners but as underlings to be disciplined into obedience.[5] Thus Rockingham was already claiming, by impli-

---

[1] *Correspondence of George III*, no. 100. They also gave themselves this name: Northumberland spoke of 'the king's friends connecting themselves together closely and acting in a body as occurrences shall happen' (*Jenkinson Papers*, p. 380).

[2] See Gilbert Elliot's account of a conversation with Charles Townshend, Dec. 1765, from which it appears that Townshend was afraid to vote against the king's wishes but Elliot was not (G. F. S. Elliot, op. cit., p. 397).

[3] It is not clear who took the initiative in this negotiation. Bedford and Grenville thought that Bute had done so, but this may have been a misunderstanding (*Bedford Correspondence*, iii. 326–9; *Grenville Papers*, iii. 350–5, 360–3). Nor is it clear whether Bute was thinking only of defeating the bill for the repeal or of forming a new Ministry as well: but it is clear that Bedford and Grenville had no thought of sharing political power with him.

[4] *The Duke of Newcastle's Narrative*, p. 50. Newcastle's reply is interesting: 'Conscience, Sir, is too often influenced by prejudice in favour of persons and things, and that courts have ways of letting their opinion be known.' A pretty ancestor for Lord Rockingham's knot of spotless friends!

[5] This difference of opinion is more clearly visible in May 1766; see Egmont's

cation, that the king was to put his personal influence and connexions unreservedly at the disposal of his official servants, who
would make their own political alliances but would never treat
him as a political ally. George III wriggled in order to avoid this
situation, which was calculated to deprive him of personal control over politics. Thus it was not without some reason that Bute,
and the king's relations with him, symbolized something quite
repugnant to the conception of ministerial responsibility which
Newcastle and Rockingham were trying to build up; and this
is the best justification, though an indirect one, for the disproportionate attention which the politicians and the public paid
to Bute for nearly a decade.

The whole episode of Bute was an abnormal one—though a
very important abnormality, for it gave George III a bad reputa-
tation with a certain kind of politician. Having given up the idea
of governing through a friend, George III had now to govern
through politicians or, as he originally called them, 'tools'. Ministries of politicians could not be formed without some negotiation.

George III never liked negotiating in person: he always preferred to have the Ministry formed for him by some disinterested
agent. Thus in 1763 Bute, the outgoing Prime Minister, arranged
the Ministry which was to succeed him. In 1765 it was the king's
uncle, the Duke of Cumberland, who did the business; in 1766,
March 1782, 1804, (and 1828) it was the Lord Chancellor who,
at least, prepared the ground, and the unsuccessful negotiations of 1778–9 were also conducted by the Lord Chancellor.[1]

letters to George III (*Correspondence of George III*, nos. 303, 304, 307) and George III's
letter to Bute (*Letters from George III to Lord Bute*, pp. 247–9). But it is already visible
in Jan., when George III told Bute that if the ministers were allowed to make a
coalition with any other set without including Bute's and his own friends, he and
Bute would be 'irretrievably capotted' (*Letters from George III to Lord Bute*, p. 242).
Bute had tried for a similar alliance with Grenville two years earlier, and had
been rebuffed (*Grenville Papers*, ii. 493, 496). Why would these whig politicians not
share power with Bute? Presumably because they feared that a partner so much
dearer to the king's heart would always prevail against them in the closet, if he had
any official excuse for access to it—a view expressed much later in a similar connexion by George Rose, who tried to persuade Pitt for the same reason that it would
not be safe to sit in a Cabinet with Addington (*Diaries and Correspondence of George
Rose*, i. 492). Addington himself must have thought this a reasonable suspicion, for
he chose in 1806 a post in which he would have little personal intercourse with the
king, so as to avoid giving jealousy to his colleagues in the 'Talents' Ministry
(Pellew, *Life of Sidmouth*, ii. 416).

[1] George III must have considered a Lord Chancellor as an exceptionally suitable intermediary for this purpose, for he insisted on giving the Great Seal to

In 1782 the king insisted on conducting the final stages of the negotiation with Rockingham through the medium of Shelburne, and in December 1783 Richmond and Gower are said to have been joined with Pitt in the formation of the Ministry, although only Pitt was to be Prime Minister.[1] At one stage in the negotiations of 1812, Lord Wellesley was to have formed the Ministry but not necessarily to have had the first or, indeed, any place in it.[2] As late as 1827 there seems to have been some doubt whether a Ministry need be formed by the prospective Prime Minister himself, and this doubt accounted for a celebrated misunderstanding between Wellington and Canning.[3] In fact it was the exception, not the rule, when the king personally commissioned a politician to form and head a Ministry; one might say that Chatham in 1766, Portland in 1783, the younger Pitt possibly in 1783 and certainly in 1804, Addington in 1800, and Lord Grenville in 1806 were the only clear instances of this.[4] Thus, although the Opposition whigs may have believed that it was the proper way to do the business, they had no warrant for speaking, as Lord Buckingham spoke in 1803, of 'forming an administration in the usual way, that is, with *carte blanche* from the king'.[5]

Thurlow as a preliminary to any attempt at reconstructing the Ministry (see his letters to North, *Correspondence of George III*, nos. 2310, 2336, 2347). I do not know the reason for this; but presumably the Lord Chancellor was regarded (and usually regarded himself) as standing somewhat outside the parties, and as a semi-professional officer he might hope to serve in the new Ministry as well as the old, and so to represent the element of continuity.

[1] *Correspondence of George III*, nos. 3575, 3581–2; Fitzpatrick's narrative in *Memorials and Correspondence of Charles James Fox*, i. 291–2. According to Fitzpatrick, Rockingham wanted to insist on a direct negotiation with George III, as he had also tried to do in 1767, but was overruled by Charles Fox and Richmond, who did not think it necessary to insist on this punctilio; on this, see also Rev. Walker King to William Burke, 24 Apr. 1782, in Burke's *Works* (1852 edn.), i. 498; Grafton, *Autobiography*, p. 329.

[2] So he said in his communication to Grey and Grenville, 23 May 1812, printed in *Annual Register*, 1812, p. *275. According to Lord Bathurst, the Prince Regent had a similar arrangement in mind in Feb. of the same year: Wellesley was to form a Ministry in which Moira was to be Prime Minister (*Hist. MSS. Comm., Bathurst MSS.*, p. 166).

[3] Neither Wellington nor Westmorland understood that the person who formed the Cabinet was necessarily the Prime Minister (*The Formation of Canning's Ministry*, ed. Aspinall, pp. 70, 167; *Wellington, Despatches (Continuation)*, iii. 629, iv. 11, 18).

[4] I exclude Grafton (1768), North (1770) and, with more hesitation, Shelburne in July 1782 and Perceval in 1809, on the ground that they were only chosen to take command of a Ministry already in being.

[5] *Hist. MSS. Comm., Dropmore MSS.* vii. 118.

It is not quite clear why George III so much disliked a direct negotiation. Perhaps the reason is indicated by a remark of Chesterfield on the failure of one of the king's interviews with the elder Pitt: 'The King's dignity was not, in my mind, much consulted, by their making him sole plenipotentiary of a treaty, which they were not, in all events, determined to conclude. It ought surely to have been begun by some inferior agent, and His Majesty should only have appeared in rejecting or ratifying it. Louis XIV never sat down before a town in person, that was not sure to be taken.'[1] A Prime Minister in office who negotiated with other parties about the reconstruction of the Ministry put himself in danger if he allowed it to be known which of his friends he would have sacrificed, for they might desert him, thinking themselves disobliged;[2] much more ought a king to avoid such a situation. The difference between a negotiation and a commission was not always a very easy one to maintain:[3] a political leader who had the appearance of being already commissioned to form a Ministry might receive so many offers of support that the king might not be able to break the negotiation off. Whatever the reason, George III tried to avoid any direct interviews which might impair his control of the situation; he had to negotiate with the Pitts, for they would deal with nobody else, but he soon learnt the wisdom of having the ground

[1] *Letters of Philip Dormer Stanhope, Fourth Earl of Chesterfield*, ed. Dobree, no. 2254. Since Chesterfield had shown so little consideration for George II's feelings in 1746 (*v. supra*, p. 94, n. 3) I somewhat distrust the sincerity, or rather the meaning, of his concern for George III's dignity in 1763. Probably he was one of those whigs who thought the king most dignified when he was not trying to exert a personal influence in politics (*v. infra*, p. 124).

[2] According to Lord John Russell (who may be quoting a family tradition) the king himself once played this trick: he inflamed Bedford's anger against Pitt by letting him know which of his friends Pitt had proposed to expel from office (*Life and Times of Charles James Fox*, ii. 2). I am not sure that there is very much in this story: Bedford was certainly offended, but the whole town knew that Pitt had asked too much. In the negotiations of July 1767 Rockingham reported that Grafton had shown much caution 'by way of preventing at this moment it being said, that His Majesty gave up A, B, or C, etc.' (*Duke of Newcastle's Narrative*, p. 111). George Rose reported in 1812 that Grenville and Grey were particularly annoyed when the Prince Regent decided not to call them to office, as they had disobliged some of their friends by letting them know they would have been left out (*Diaries and Correspondence of George Rose*, ii. 479).

[3] Especially in the form prescribed by Portland in 1783 and 1784: he wanted George III to commit himself by placing him at the Treasury before he committed himself by telling the king whom he should include in his Ministry or whether he could form one at all (*v. infra*, p. 123).

prepared, if possible, by the Lord Chancellor or some other intermediary.[1]

This might be a mere punctilio; but two more substantial differences arose between king and politicians when Ministries were formed or reconstructed. The politicians might make stipulations about policy, or they might try to remove from the king to themselves the ultimate control over the Ministry's composition.

In our days it may seem to be self-evident that a set of politicians assuming office must do so on certain definite understandings as to the policy they will pursue; but this practice can hardly be traced back beyond the middle of the eighteenth century. Perhaps whigs and tories may have obtained office in the reigns of William III and Anne with the intention of reversing each other's policies in foreign affairs and the conduct of war; but I know of no deliberate attempts to make acceptance of office conditional upon stipulations as to policy earlier than the beginning of George III's reign.

In 1765 the elder Pitt, not content (as in earlier negotiations) with symbolizing his policy and his vengeances by appointments and dismissals, insisted that the king must agree to try for an alliance with Prussia and Russia, though he admitted that he ought not to make any demand which 'sounds like capitulating'.[2] This was an unpleasant dose for George III to swallow, for he considered Frederick II as a personal enemy and by no means an equal, to whom he should not like suing for an alliance. He would not commit himself to it unless Pitt would undertake to come into office, for the very good reason that nobody but Pitt had a chance of softening Frederick's heart. Even so, he did not wish to hurry. 'The King'—so Albemarle told Grafton—'wishes to employ Mr. Pitt, will submit to him as far as possible; he does not object to the system, but to the precipitate mode of

[1] Evidently George III thought afterwards that he had made a mistake in dealing directly with the elder Pitt on various occasions in 1763 to 1766, for in Mar. 1778 he refused to play 'the old game over again' or to have Chatham as 'Dictator . . . planning the new Administration'. He would only deal with Chatham through North, and would not even see him at all till his followers had already accepted office, when there could be no suspicion of conditional accession (*Correspondence of George III*, nos. 2221, 2223, 2224).

[2] See Lord Charles Fitzroy's and Albemarle's letters to Grafton, in his *Autobiography*, pp. 51, 83. I need hardly say that 'capitulating' is not used in its modern sense of 'surrendering' but in its original sense of 'making conditions'.

doing it'—an opinion which the result of the experiment, when it was tried a year later, proved to have been very sensible.

The negotiation failed, chiefly for personal reasons which it would be difficult to define. But other people besides Pitt could 'capitulate' even while they denied, as he had denied, that they were 'capitulating'. When George Grenville knew that the king had tried and failed to replace him, he too presented certain conditions—all personal—as the price of his service. According to a story related at third hand by Newcastle, the king asked whether these were 'conditions', and Grenville disclaimed such an impropriety; but George III smelt it in spite of the disclaimer, and asked whether they were *sine quâ nons*. Grenville admitted that they were. The king was much flustered—indeed, nearly out of his mind—and resented this coercion which made him break a personal promise: when one of the beneficiaries conveyed through Grenville his thanks for the king's goodness, George III replied bitterly, 'It's your goodness Mr. Grenville, not mine.'[1]

A few weeks later, he could bear Grenville no longer, and, since he could not get Pitt, he resorted to Newcastle, Rockingham, and their friends. This party, which afterwards boasted that it was the first to follow in office the principles it had proclaimed in Opposition, did not make any conditions about policy upon its entry into office; its only stipulations were the usual ones about the ostracism of Bute, which were almost common form. Indeed, it appears that Newcastle only thought it safe to come into office at all because Pitt and the king had already agreed upon the one important question of policy— namely, the Triple Alliance—so that he and his friends were hardly likely to get into trouble if they pursued it.[2] Here Newcastle reckoned without the chapter of accidents: the course of events in America brought forward another question of policy—

---

[1] *Correspondence of George III*, nos. 82, 139–42; *Grenville Papers*, iii. 41, 180–9; *The Duke of Newcastle's Narrative*, ed. Bateson, pp. 17–18. There is something to be said for Grenville: his credit as a minister had been much impaired by the king's obvious attempt to get rid of him, and he could only restore it by some public demonstration of the king's confidence (or rather, of his control over the king), without which, in the conditions of those days, his Ministry would not be worth a month's purchase. It was the same motive which made Sir Robert Peel so exacting about the Ladies of the Bedchamber in 1839.

[2] *The Duke of Newcastle's Narrative*, ed. Bateson, p. 27.

the Stamp Act—which was not already cut and dried for them by the king and Pitt; and on this subject they were lucky, or clever, to escape disaster in the House of Commons.

When Chatham replaced Rockingham next year, he and the king already knew each other's sentiments so well that no stipulations were necessary;[1] but it was understood that the Triple Alliance would be pursued. It was pursued—in vain, because Chatham executed a good idea with maladroit precipitation and, above all, because the idea itself was an anachronism, for Frederick and Catherine had other fish to fry. In America, too, the continued recalcitrance of the colonists gave the lie to Chatham's belief that his name—which he had unfortunately changed—was a talisman to cure all discontents. Only the psychologists can tell whether this discovery that all his ideas were inapplicable hastened his mental collapse; but at least it seems to show that while government consisted of executive action rather than legislation, stipulations as to future policy were not a very appropriate way of carrying it on.

Nothing more was heard of stipulations about policy for the time being; but George III had also to deal with another threat to his freedom of action. The politicians of his grandfather's reign had been used to making their own arrangements about offices and having them ratified by the king; when the king himself began to make the arrangements once more, they felt that there was something wrong.[2]

George III's earliest ministries after Bute's retirement were usually in no position to bargain with him: the triumvirs owed their places to Bute,[3] and the Rockinghams theirs to the Duke of

[1] The king claimed to know Pitt's sentiments through a speech in the House of Commons (*Chatham Correspondence*, ii. 436). Indeed this speech, which puzzled and intrigued contemporaries, may have been intended as a signal to the king (see Rigby's description of it in *Bedford Correspondence*, iii. 333).

[2] Newcastle, discussing certain law promotions with Pitt in Aug. 1763, told him 'upon what he said of the preference to be given by the King, that I did not apprehend that our consideration was which of the two would be preferred by His Majesty—that would entirely depend upon the person who had His Majesty's confidence. Our business was to form such a plan of administration as should be most for His Majesty's service' (P. C. Yorke, op. cit. iii. 518).

[3] Here again, we should distinguish the terms on which Grenville and his colleagues originally obtained their places in April 1763, from those on which they held them in June 1765 after George III had tried in vain to replace them. They evidently had some hope of making alliances for themselves which would enable them to dictate still further conditions to the king. Sandwich, discussing with Gren-

Cumberland. But although the Rockinghams entered office as a court party, they began to change very soon after their patron died. Everybody knew that Rockingham and his colleagues were too weak to stand long alone. The king would have liked Rockingham to take in the friends of Bute as partners on equal terms, but Rockingham would rather have reunited the whig party by an alliance with Pitt. With the king's reluctant permission he approached Pitt; but the king could hardly have approved the spirit in which Rockingham conducted the discussions, for he made it quite clear to Pitt, as Newcastle would have done, that they ought to come to terms with each other and impose them on the king, rather than leave it to the king to play them off against each other and so to introduce other elements into the Ministry.[1] This was exactly what the king wanted to do, and he particularly feared a coalition of the politicians with each other at his expense; as he told them, 'I should not permit them to form me a Ministry, but should do that myself.'[2] It was Pitt, however, who put an end to the scheme. He neither intended to put himself under Lord Rockingham's protection for the sake of whig reunion, nor needed to do so for the sake of access to the king, who, as he knew very well, looked upon Rockingham as little more than a *locum tenens* for himself.[3] Perhaps, moreover, he was really shocked by the proposal to bind the king's hands in the matter of appointments to office. He therefore held out for a direct negotiation with the king; and a few months later George III, finding Rockingham neither efficient nor obliging, resolved to come to terms with Pitt and to found a great Ministry

ville whether to confirm or contradict the rumour that they were not raising their terms, said 'I am aware that if you have acquired any additional strength it may be saying too much' (*Grenville Papers*, iii. 57).

[1] See Shelburne's report of Rockingham's conversation, 24 Feb. 1766 (*Chatham Correspondence*, iii. 7): '. . . that *he was certain*, when they came to go in to the King, if nothing previous was settled, it would give his Majesty such advantage, that everything would be given up, without anything certain, and a convulsion would follow, which might bring in the late ministry, or no one knew what; while, if they went in united, and in good humour with each other, the King was so hampered by many things that had passed, that without entering into any consideration of the interior of the court, he must certainly agree to it'.

[2] George III to Bute, 10 Jan. 1766 (*Letters from George III to Lord Bute*, p. 244). This letter makes it clear that George III was trying to edge Rockingham into a partnership with Bute and was afraid that he and Bute would be 'irretrievably capotted' if Rockingham was allowed to make an effective alliance of his own with some other group.

[3] Rockingham had begun by doing so himself, but his pretensions rose.

by combining the legitimate authority of the Crown and the genius of a great demagogue. The parties of Grenville, Rockingham, and Bedford, which had all annoyed or insulted him, were to be not merely disregarded but pulverized. Their members might serve as individuals, but were not to be negotiated with *en bloc*.[1]

This celebrated experiment did much to determine the development of orthodox 'whig' doctrine. It explains, for example, Burke's venomous hatred of Chatham. When Burke said that 'the least peep' into the king's closet 'intoxicated' Chatham, he only exaggerated: Chatham's offence, like that of his son, was that of not holding constitutional progress and liberty to depend on depriving the king of his freedom to choose his ministers; of believing that the ability to govern, to dominate the House of Commons by oratory, and to impress the imagination of the general public, were more valuable than connexion. Perhaps he was wrong: his own experience showed how vulnerable and transitory were such gifts, compared with the humbler qualifications of the pedestrian Rockingham. But so long as parliamentary and administrative talent could hold its own unsupported by connexion, the king had a possible resource for carrying on the government without capitulating to the cliques; talent held the balance between monarchy and aristocracy, whose mutual contest it regarded as more and more irrelevant to the real purposes of government.

Chatham's experiment in non-party or all-party government figured in whig legend as an unscrupulous attempt to destroy the sacred principle of party. It was the only serious attempt that George III ever made or countenanced; but it was he, rather than Chatham, who bore the blame; and not unnaturally, for he had always considered 'faction' wicked, and the

---

[1] See the king's letters to Pitt, 29 July, 28 Nov., and 2 Dec. 1766 (*Chatham Correspondence*, iii. 21, 134, 137). The attempt to obtain Gower without the other Bedfords shows Chatham's wish to obtain individual recruits by detaching them from their connexions, and the refusal to compromise with the Rockinghams on the Edgcumbe affair shows his determination not to allow any separate 'caves' within his Ministry (see his big words in Grafton, op. cit., p. 107). In criticizing the failure of this experiment it is fair to say that Chatham only had time to make a beginning, because the personal arrangements were so hard to make. But, for the same reason, it is hard to see how he could have gone much further towards a complete coalition, even if he had not himself virtually proscribed parties, e.g. the Grenvilles on account of their American policy.

whole tendency of his reign had been to pulverize parties.[1] Probably Burke's charges did him very little harm; for it was still common form, many years later, to speak as though a coalition of all parties were obviously desirable—those who, like Eldon, came bluntly into the open and dismissed it as absurd or impossible were a minority. Only the consecration of party by the success of the two-party system in Victoria's day has deceived posterity into thinking that Burke had the better of the argument in his own generation.

In one respect, however, Burke triumphed over Chatham: the experiment of 1766 failed, and Rockingham's party not only saved its identity but could be found at its old work again within a year. When Grafton tried to strengthen his Administration by taking in Rockingham, he very nearly found the negotiation taken out of his own hands. Rockingham insisted, as a preliminary, on considering Grafton's Ministry at an end; this was a favourite gambit, for it deprived the existing ministers of any excuse for protecting their followers and, consequently, of most of those followers' loyalty.[2] Rockingham then did what he could

---

[1] George III did not like the constant changes of Administration in the first ten years of his reign (see his letter to Northington, 9 Jan. 1766, *Correspondence of George III*, no. 179, and his remarks to General Irwin, reported in *Grenville Papers*, iv. 184), although some of his enemies, such as Junius, accused him of bringing them about deliberately (see Junius's letter of 21 Jan. 1769). Nor were they all his doing. But in one respect they must have helped him to keep his hands free. Although a party might go out of office stronger than it came in (*v. supra*, pp. 79–80), the incessant alternations of ins and outs detached from it some useful members who gravitated towards the ranks of permanent placemen or 'King's Friends' and, still more, the contrast between the king's permanence and the impermanence of his administrations must have taught those who wanted continuous employment the quarter where they were most likely to obtain it. Hence the jargon (so much disliked by Burke) of those placemen who claimed 'that they are under no obligations whatsoever to Administration; that they have received their office from another quarter'. These men were not altogether creatures of Burke's imagination: for instance, there was Lord Hillsborough who 'never means to ask a favour but from your Majesty immediately' as well as one or two others (*Correspondence of George III*, nos. 41, 894). Hillsborough once told William Knox that 'His object was to fall in with what he knew to be the King's plan, that each of his ministers should hold of him and not of one another or of the first' (*Hist. MSS. Comm., Various Collections*, vi. 263).

[2] Horace Walpole criticized the king and Cumberland for dismissing Grenville in May 1765 before they were sure of Pitt (which, incidentally, is not exactly what they did), saying that the king had thus 'exposed himself to the extravagant demands of all who saw the dilemma to which he had reduced himself, and the necessity he was under of submitting to some disagreeable set of men or other, who were sure to make him purchase dearly a support that they knew he wished not to accept at all' (*Memoirs of the Reign of King George III*, ed. Russell Barker, ii. 116). The

to turn a negotiation between Grafton and himself into a negotiation between himself, as Prime Minister designate, and other
faction leaders to the probable exclusion of Grafton; and if he
had not quarrelled with them over the terms, he would have
presented the king with the same kind of commanding coalition
at which he had been working in January 1766.[1] A Cabinet so
constructed would have contained nobody who preferred his
allegiance to the king above his allegiance to Rockingham; even
Horace Walpole, no friend to the prerogative, was moved to
ask 'if they expected that every man should depend on King
Rockingham, and nobody on King George'. Nor was this exi-
gence peculiar to Rockingham: it was Rigby, a Bedford whig,
who 'swore a great oath' on a similar occasion two years earlier
'that the King should not have power to appoint one of his own
footmen'.[2]

Thus Rockingham had twice failed to enclose the king in a
coalition of his own making, and these failures restored the
king's freedom of action for the time being—perhaps they also
strengthened his hold over his ministers.[3] But for a few days of
great danger in 1770, when the Chathamites' desertion nearly
left him without a Ministry, George III could believe that he
had triumphed over faction: that the politicians could no longer
hope to haggle with him over policy or to take from him the
control over the composition of his own Ministry.

He was undone by his own success. Unchallenged in the control of the political machine, he persevered for years in a war
which, however popular in its beginning, not even all his own

king was, indeed, at a great disadvantage when the old Ministry went out before he
had made his bargain with the new—as in Mar. 1782, Feb. 1783, and Jan. 1806;
this explains why he was so angry with North for declaring his resignation in a
hurry (*Correspondence of George III*, no. 3567).

[1] For this negotiation see Horace Walpole, *Memoirs of the Reign of George III*, ed.
Russell Barker, iii. 46–65; *The Duke of Newcastle's Narrative*, ed. Bateson, pp. 104–66;
Grafton, op. cit., pp. 143–55; *Grenville Papers*, iv. 48–153, 228–30; Winstanley,
Lord Chatham and the Whig Opposition, pp. 152–83. Grafton said afterwards that
Rockingham's principle was 'not to trust that they shall have his Majesty's support,
but to make it impossible for the king not to give it to them'.

[2] Horace Walpole, *Memoirs of the Reign of King George III*, ed. Russell Barker, ii.
126; iii. 47.

[3] I shall discuss George III's so-called 'personal rule' in the next chapter; in the
main, it resulted from other causes, but perhaps it was rendered easier by the
knowledge that the factions had repeatedly tried and failed to come to terms with
each other for the purpose of coercing him.

ministers now wished to wage or hoped to win.[1] His political enemies were now opposing one policy to another; and a difference of opinion on so vital a question as the independence of America increased the divergences which already existed about the right way to form a Ministry. George III believed that it was the duty of men of goodwill first to accept office and only then to discuss the policy to be pursued;[2] but how could he expect the Opposition leaders who demanded the reversal of his policy to accept such terms?[3] Indeed, he himself rendered it impossible by saying 'before I enter into any consideration as to particular offices I must have an assurance that it is intended to strain every nerve to keep the empire entire, to persecute the war with vigour in all its branches, and that past measures shall be treated with respect'.[4] This was just what the Opposition did not mean to give.

The negotiations for a coalition in 1778 and 1779 were bound to fail, for this reason, and the war had almost brought about, for a short time, something resembling the two-party system of the nineteenth century. Change of Ministry became inseparable from reversal of policy; and the policy to be reversed was the king's. George III's person and behaviour now became an issue in politics, even more than they had been at the time of the Middlesex election. The politicians did their best to conceal their hostility to the king behind the fiction of denouncing his 'secret advisers'.[5] But, as the king knew very well, there was no mistaking the sense of Dunning's famous resolution, in April

[1] North's mind fluctuated according to the course of the war; but he normally desponded from the end of 1778 or the beginning of 1779.

[2] Thurlow told Rockingham, 14 Mar. 1782, that the king considered his four points as 'rather the objects to be pursued by an Administration when formed, than a basis to form it on', to which Rockingham replied, 'I do not think it an advisable measure, first to attempt to form a Ministry by arrangement of office—afterwards to decide upon what principles or measures they are to act' (Albemarle, *Memoirs of the Marquess of Rockingham*, ii. 456, 459).

[3] See Richmond's letter to Charles Fox, 7 Feb. 1779, in *Memorials and Correspondence of Charles James Fox*, i. 213–23, which explains, better than any other printed document, why the Opposition leaders thought they had to insist on *carte blanche*, or at least a clear understanding with the king before they entered office.

[4] *Correspondence of George III*, no. 2797. See also no. 2674, where he expressed similar opinions and, above all, no. 3099, in which he demanded that 'those who come into office must give assurance that they do not mean to be hampered by the tenets they have held during their opposition'.

[5] It was not all fiction: many politicians really believed that such persons existed. I shall discuss this in the next chapter, pp. 171–3.

1780: 'That the influence of the Crown has increased, is increasing, and ought to be diminished.'[1] The hostility became personal; for George III never had a greater personal enemy than Charles Fox, who was now becoming the real leader of the Opposition.[2] The king was approaching the crisis of his reign. Parliament was resolved to end the American war; and it became a question, how much of his authority would be permanently forfeited by the failure of his policy?

Nobody seriously thought of deposing him, but he seriously thought of abdicating, because he could not endure the loss of national prestige.[3] Nobody had time for impeaching Lord North; but if he had not resigned, there would certainly have been a motion for removing him.[4] His only possible successor was Rockingham, who now obtained the reward of his devotion to his party.[5] The question was, what terms would Rockingham impose? About ending the war, there could be no dispute; but Rockingham took the opportunity of tacking on, as an additional condition, three measures which were designed to reduce the king's power permanently by limiting the rewards he could offer to members of parliament and their constituents.[6] Such

---

[1] North tried to pretend that the resolutions were directed against him, but the king knew better (*Correspondence of George III*, nos. 2986, 2987).

[2] Charles Fox generally contrived to speak with respect of George III's private character; the nearest he ever came to disparaging him in public was when he appeared to draw a distinction between the king's domestic virtues and the political virtues which (Fox implied) he did not share with his ancestors (*Parl. Hist.* xxiv. 223-4). But in fact he hated the king (see his outburst of 9 Sept. 1781, in *Memorials and Correspondence of Charles James Fox*, i. 267). According to George Selwyn, he 'talked of the King' in Mar. 1782 'under the description of Satan, a comparison which he seems fond of, and has used to others' (*Hist. MSS. Comm., Carlisle MSS.*, p. 599). The Duke of Leeds reports, about the same time, that he said 'certainly things look very well, but he, meaning the K., will dye soon, and that will be best of all' (*Political Memoranda*, ed. Browning, p. 66). The king was justified in saying of Fox, a few months later, 'the contest is become personal and he indeed sees it also in that point of view' (*Correspondence of George III*, no. 3872).

[3] The draft message of abdication is in *Correspondence of George III*, no. 3601. It does not complain of any invasion of his constitutional rights; indeed, it could not.

[4] North himself was afraid of this (ibid., no. 3568).

[5] Shelburne and Rockingham differed about the American war, for Shelburne had inherited from Chatham the opinion that the British Empire would be ruined if America was allowed complete separation, whereas Rockingham was embarrassed by no such scruple. Shelburne must have felt, from 1780, that his was an unrealistic doctrine, and he allowed Richmond to reconcile him to Rockingham. He was therefore pledged to serve under Rockingham, and would not accept the Treasury from George III in March 1782 (Fitzmaurice, *Life of William, Earl of Shelburne* (2nd edn., 1912), ii. 87-92).

[6] I shall discuss this in chapter vi, p. 197.

conditions were not quite unprecedented, but they had a new feature: by making the king agree beforehand to the introduction of bills into parliament, they implied a restriction upon his use of the veto. He had to accept them, after some resistance, for fear a worse thing befall;[1] for Rockingham would not have consented to form a Ministry without them, and he alone could form one.[2] Thus the failure of the American war enabled Rockingham, as the one acknowledged leader of the Opposition, to impose terms on the king which the generality of politicians would never have supported in ordinary circumstances.

Rockingham's Ministry was short and unhappy, for George III treated him with less candour than he showed to any other Prime Minister, however unwelcome.[3] It ended in a fresh dispute, in which the politicians put forward yet another new constitutional claim. Rockingham's death having vacated the post of First Lord of the Treasury, Charles Fox pretended that a Cabinet in office had a right to elect its own head, and proposed the Duke of Portland, a blameless nobleman of the Rockingham school. There was a precedent, for George II had asked the Cabinet to suggest a new First Lord of the Treasury after Henry Pelham's death. But the Lord Chancellor, on that occasion, had not thought it very seemly to 'poll in Cabinet' for a Prime Minister; and it was one thing for the Cabinet to perform this duty at the king's request, quite another thing to claim the right to do it against his will.[4] Everybody knew that this claim (which has not even yet been recognized as constitutional) was only put forward in order to keep out Charles Fox's enemy Shelburne, and not all, even of Fox's own followers, approved of his resigning when it was rejected.[5] But it symbolized the persistent efforts

---

[1] He wriggled afterwards about one of them—Burke's Economical Reform Bill—by trying to get the less unfriendly members of the Cabinet to limit it, and to make some, at least, of the reforms by regulation instead of Act of Parliament. Rockingham, however, was determined to bind him fast (*Correspondence of George III*, nos. 3646, 3648, 3660, 3665).   [2] Albemarle, op. cit. ii. 459.

[3] As George III's relations with Rockingham and Shelburne concerned the internal working of the Administration, I shall discuss them in the next chapter, pp. 154, 158, 171.

[4] P. C. Yorke, op. cit. ii. 191, 211. In effect, the Cabinet did not make proposals of its own, but approved those put forward in the king's name. George IV would have liked to save himself embarrassment in 1827 by asking the Cabinet to suggest a new Prime Minister, but Peel convinced him that they could not do this.

[5] *Memorials and Correspondence of Charles James Fox*, i. 435; *Parl. Hist.* xxiii. 142–96, *passim*. Fox, indeed, claimed that he would have resigned even if Rockingham had

of the Opposition whigs to impose a Ministry upon the king, and that, presumably, is why Fitzpatrick exclaimed that if the king was suffered to appoint Shelburne, 'there is certainly a total end of Whig principles'.[1] Shelburne replied that if the Cabinet was to fill up all vacancies, 'the King must then resemble the King of the Mahrattas who had nothing of sovereignty but the name'; monarchy would be absorbed in aristocracy, and 'the famed Constitution of England would be no more'.[2]

The issue now joined was fought out in the House of Commons next year. George III's chosen minister was defeated not, as in 1782, by a spontaneous revulsion of the House of Commons against an impossible policy, but by a parliamentary manœuvre between two groups—the 'infamous coalition' of Fox and North.[3] Opinions differed on the question, whether this fact affected the validity of the action. Pitt, and some others, claimed that it did;[4] but Fox was technically correct in saying that the votes against Shelburne's Ministry were acts of the House of Commons, and had the authority which all its acts must have.[5] Unluckily for him, this was generally regarded, out of doors, as no more than a technicality. Still less did George III himself accept the implication that he had no right to question how an arrangement was arrived at in the House of Commons to his disadvantage.

The birth pangs of the Coalition Ministry were unusually painful. Fox's friends refused, from the first, to serve under anybody but Portland,[6] who put forward, on their behalf, yet an-

lived, because he had been outvoted in the Cabinet on a question arising out of the peace negotiation; this is not certain, though there is no doubt of his difference with Shelburne on this question.

[1] *Memorials and Correspondence of Charles James Fox*, i. 459.

[2] *Parl. Hist.* xxiii. 192.

[3] Much has been written for and against this coalition. I think its critics might have admitted more candidly that some coalition, more or less unnatural, was necessary to the carrying on of government; that the alliance of the pure virgin Pitt with Dundas, Thurlow, and Gower was likewise a coalition, and just as odd a coalition as Fox's with North; and that Fox and North did not disagree about questions before them when they made the coalition—at least, no more than Pitt and his allies, for parliamentary reform was to be an open question in both camps. Fox's offence was that of forgiving North for his past sins, which Pitt would not do (see Fox's speech in *Parl. Hist.* xxiv. 367 and North's, ibid. 254).

[4] *Parl. Hist.* xxiii. 794–5.

[5] *Parl Hist.* xxiii. 794. When Pitt criticized the coalition, Fox asked whether he was denying the right of the House of Commons 'to interfere with ministers, or to say who ought or ought not to govern the country'. See also Erskine, ibid. xxiv. 274.

[6] *Correspondence of George III*, no. 4158.

other new constitutional claim. There were no stipulations about policy this time; but the incoming Prime Minister not only insisted, as Rockingham had sometimes done,[1] on a personal interview with the king and a direct commission from him,[2] but demanded *carte blanche*, especially as to the appointment of junior ministers. He obstinately refused to show the king any names but those of the Cabinet, and when George III demanded the right to see and discuss the full detail of the Administration,

he . . . said this was a want of confidence in him for that the Cabinet once laid before me, he expected that on his coming to the head of the Treasury, I should rely on his making no propositions but such as he thought necessary for my affairs and consequently that I should acquiesce in them.[3]

Historically (for the Rockingham whigs never forgot their own history) this stipulation probably dates from their unpleasant experience of 1766, when the king refused to discipline the ministerial underlings into voting for the repeal of the Stamp Tax: they resolved to prevent the recurrence of such a situation by keeping the nomination of underlings in their own hands. But the demand signifies something more: it marks an advance towards the assumption that (as the Marquis of Buckingham said in 1803) an Administration should normally be formed by giving *carte blanche* to some principal contractor for power, who would then make his own arrangements and offer them to the king to take them or leave them as a whole.[4]

Indeed, it signifies even more than that. Portland's last words imply an intention to eliminate the king's personal will from politics altogether. There is no doubt that Charles Fox had formed the intention of de-personalizing the monarchy (if I may use so disagreeable a term). Not content with saying that the House of Commons had governed the country from time immemorial,[5] he began openly to imply, or to say, that the

---

[1] In 1767, but not in 1782, when Richmond and others had dissuaded him from stickling for it (*Memorials and Correspondence of Charles James Fox*, i. 291). He must have regretted his compliance, for George III treated the fact that Shelburne had technically formed the Ministry (though Rockingham was to be at the head of it) as an excuse for behaving as though Shelburne were joint Prime Minister, to share equally with Rockingham in patronage (*Correspondence of George III*, nos. 3627, 3628, 3632, 3637, 3639).

[2] Ibid., nos. 4209, 4236.   [3] Ibid., no. 4268, p. 326.

[4] *Hist. MSS. Comm., Dropmore MSS.* vii. 118.   [5] *Parl. Hist.* xxiv. 597.

king's powers could only be exercised by the ministers,[1] and that the question whether the king had any personal confidence in ministers was immaterial.[2] The king must be presumed to wish what the majority of the House of Commons or the general public wished. As for the prerogative, Fox said, 'it was his idea, that the rights of the Crown, as well as the rights of parliament, were not always to be exercised merely because they were rights'.[3] In short, the Crown 'was endowed with no faculty whatever of a private nature'.[4] If he was accused of trying to reduce the king to insignificance and royalty to an empty pageantry he answered (or North answered for him) that when the king used his prerogative without the support of parliament, it was only a 'scare-crow of prerogative' and the king was a nobody[5]—a view which George III could not have begun to understand.

[1] On 15 Nov. 1783 he is reported as 'combatting a little the witty, but at the same time invidious distinction that had been made between ministerial power and crown power; for his part, he could discover no ground for the distinction; he had always considered, that whatever conferred power on the ministry conferred, at the same time, an equal share of power on the crown, and vice versa' (ibid. xxiii. 1241).

[2] 'To confound personal and political confidence is a common error. That his Majesty may repose a personal confidence in his present ministers [Pitt, Jan. 1784], separately and individually, I have no doubt; but that he should repose a confidence in their political character, under the opprobrium which rested on them, is too gross an idea to be admitted or entertained' for it would mean that the favour of the court was more necessary to a political career than that of parliament (ibid. xxiv. 368).

[3] Ibid. xxiv. 287. The reminder that parliament too had rights was only fair: if the king insisted on his right to choose ministers, parliament might equally insist on its right to stop supplies. But Fox evidently came to dislike kings so much as to believe that they ought not to exercise their legal prerogatives just because they were kings. In Oct. 1792 he thus expostulated with his nephew: 'If you admit that the Jacobins, having the confidence of the Assembly and country, ought to be Ministers, what can be said for the Feuillans, who encouraged and supported the King, in maintaining an Administration of an adverse faction, and in using his veto, and other prerogatives in opposition to the Assembly and the nation?' (*Memorials and Correspondence of Charles James Fox*, ii. 373). He might have asked himself why the constitution had given Louis XVI a veto, less than two years ago, if he was never to use it.

[4] *Parl. Hist.* xxiv. 460. I have taken these quotations from the debates of the next winter, but I see no reason to doubt that Fox already entertained these opinions in Mar. 1783, when the Coalition was formed.

[5] Ibid. xxiv. 290–1. This resembles the opinions expressed by Burke in his later writings, when he tried to explain the sense in which he was (and, he claimed, always had been) a supporter of monarchy—e.g. the passage in *A Letter to a Member of a National Assembly* (*Works* (1852 edn.), iv. 388–9) in which he tries to explain that the king of Great Britain is 'a real king', although he 'will not trouble himself with contemptible details' and has to 'combine his public interest with his personal satisfaction'.

George III must have known what Fox was about, for he resisted Portland's pretensions as long as he could. Resistance, however, was vain when every politician who could have championed him in the House of Commons was convinced that the game was hopeless for the time being.[1] He played once more with the thought of abdicating, or of going down to parliament and appealing to both Houses against 'the obstinacy of a powerful combination that has long publicly manifested a resolution of not entering into the public service, unless the whole executive management of affairs is thrown actively into their hands'.[2] He must have known that this would be useless, and at last he submitted abjectly—signing blank warrants of appointment for the leaders of the Coalition to fill up as they would.[3] For the next few months he behaved as if he had no further interest in public business, and would sign almost anything that his ministers put before him.[4] But if they believed that they were overcoming his aversion, they made a great mistake.[5] He had made it very clear, in certain quarters, that he had accepted the Coalition under duress, owed it no loyalty, and would welcome anybody who would rescue him from it;[6] and, in order to signify this to the world at large, he steadfastly refused to create any peerages at his ministers' request. This was a prerogative which they could hardly claim to put in commission;[7] and his refusal to exercise it in their favour was so obvious a signal to their enemies that they were half afraid it might do them grave political damage.[8] They need not have taken it so seriously: in the

---

[1] He did not finally surrender to Portland until he had given up all hope of Pitt (*Correspondence of George III*, nos. 4244–6, 4249, 4250).

[2] Ibid., nos. 4259, 4260.   [3] Ibid., no. 4283.

[4] Ibid., nos. 4316, 4422; *Memorials and Correspondence of Charles James Fox*, ii. 154.

[5] They seem to have done so (ibid. ii. 118, 199). To do Fox justice, he seems to have wanted to behave like a gentleman in his personal relations with George III; it is a pity that George III had not the dignity to reciprocate this treatment (ibid. ii. 118; *Correspondence of George III*, nos. 4308, 4338).

[6] See his letter to Temple, 1 Apr. 1783 in *Correspondence of George III*, no. 4272.

[7] See Fox's letter to Ossory, in *Memorials and Correspondence of Charles James Fox*, ii. 200. For all that, Fox was much exasperated, next year, by the facility with which Pitt was allowed to create peers in order to show his master's confidence and to attach borough-mongers to himself: he described Pitt as using the patronage of the Crown 'with all the licentiousness and partiality of private property' (*Parl. Hist.* xxiv. 439). This was really a charge against George III who ought not, according to Fox's theory, to have discriminated between the facilities shown to ministers whom he liked and to those whom he disliked.

[8] Fox affected (in his letter to Ossory, quoted in the previous note) to make light

rather thin House of Commons sessions before Christmas 1783, they had a majority of nearly two to one. But George III was preparing a surprise for them.

He needed three things before he could shake off the servants whom he hated: he must have preparations ready for a general election in order to dislodge their supporters from the House; he must have an issue on which he could advantageously dismiss them; and he must have a new minister who was man enough to stand up for him in the House of Commons and convince the wavering politicians that his was the winning side. All these he had by Christmas.

The preparation for the elections (whose nature I shall discuss later)[1] seems to have been complete by the second week of December. By that time, too, Fox had given George III a handle against him in the East India Bill. Much has been written about the arrangements proposed in that bill for the control of Indian patronage; perhaps Fox has been somewhat unfairly treated from that day to this. Those arrangements were not the most important part of the bill; they were designed to deal with a new kind of problem, and, above all, to provide for some continuity of Indian policy in a political world which had seen three changes of Ministry in two years.[2] The proposal that parliament should appoint commissioners with executive power was not quite unprecedented, though the precedents were not good.[3] To suggest that these seven irremovable commissioners (if they really were irremovable)[4] could, by controlling Indian patronage, protect Fox and North against displacement by king, par-

of it; but he appears to have taken it more seriously than that, for Loughborough alluded to a scheme for restoring the Great Seal to Thurlow on condition that he should induce the king to make some peers (*Memorials and Correspondence of Charles James Fox*, ii. 204–5). Pitt too thought the question of peerages all-important (*Hist. MSS. Comm., Dropmore MSS.* i. 219).

[1] *V. infra* pp. 196–7.

[2] Fox emphasized this (*Parl. Hist.* xxiii. 1411, xxiv. 336, 396) and he may have been sincere.

[3] In 1696 parliament nearly appointed a similar body to deal with trade, but King William III forestalled this invasion of executive authority by creating a Board of Trade himself.

[4] The king could not remove them, but it was suggested that parliament might do so by resolution (*Parl. Hist.* xxiii. 1230, 1382, 1411). This, however, was begging the question, for the adversaries of the bill argued that so long as the commissioners controlled Indian patronage, they and their friends would always have a majority in parliament itself.

liament, or people was, perhaps, to exaggerate the value of India, or of patronage altogether. Yet Fox was not quite the injured innocent he seemed. He understood quite well that having forced himself into power, he had now to prevent George III from turning him out, for he had already begun to interpret his programme of reducing the power of the Crown in a new and peculiar sense: the king need not be restrained from appointing politicians to offices so long as he appointed them for life, so that he lost the power of removing them.[1] It is very unlikely that he devised the bill for the sake of party advantage, but he meant to have it incidentally, and at least to perpetuate his friends' hold on India, whatever might befall his Ministry.

George III, then, had his plans and his battle-cry ready for the election campaign; but, above all, he needed a man. Nothing but the want of a man to defend him in the House of Commons had obliged him to pass under the yoke of the Coalition; and as soon as this want was supplied, the Coalition could be dismissed. Such a man needed courage rather than skill. It is the fashion to extol Pitt's skill in debate during the session of 1783–4; this must always be a matter of opinion, but I do not consider that he was

---

[1] In the debates on the Custom House Reform Bill and still more explicitly on the Exchequer Regulation Bill, 21 May and 5 July 1783 (*Parl. Hist.* xxiii. 929, 1065). On the latter occasion he said: 'It was impossible for the government of a great Kingdom to go on, unless it had certain lucrative and honourable situations to bestow on its officers in a peculiar line, as a provision for their families, and a reward for their eminent and distinguished services. . . . As a bill of influence the present, undoubtedly, gave the Crown some influence; but he believed it would be admitted to be a sort of influence the least dangerous of any that could possibly exist. To put a man in such a situation, as that the Crown should never be able to be useful to him, was, in his opinion, a very foolish and unwise thing; but to put a man into such a situation, as that it should be out of the power of the Crown to be hurtful to him, might, in a variety of instances, be necessary and useful. He knew of no way of doing this more effectually than by giving a man an independent situation for life.' These remarks should be compared with Burke's on Economical Reform, 11 Feb. 1780 (*Works* (1852 edn.), iii. 385): 'I would, therefore, leave to the Crown the possibility of conferring some favours, which, whilst they are received as a reward, do not operate as corruption. When men receive obligations from the Crown, through the pious hands of fathers, or of connexions as venerable as the paternal, the dependencies which arise from thence, are the obligations of gratitude, and not the fetters of servility. Such ties originate in virtue, and they promote it. They continue men in those habitudes of friendship, those political principles, in which they began life. They are antidotes against a corrupt levity, instead of causes of it.' Since Burke was in Opposition in Feb. 1780, one cannot say that these are merely the excuses of politicians in office who do not want to be turned out. They exhibit a far graver disease: that of treating waste and inefficiency as venial, indeed salutary, provided the politicians and their children have a freehold in them.

the equal of Fox in debate at this time. His business was, above all, to show that he was there to stay, right or wrong; that was what heartened the wavering politicians to support him, and even the celebrated self-denial of bestowing the Clerkship of the Pells on Barré instead of taking it himself exhibited to the experts something more important than disinterestedness—it showed that he did not consider his attempt upon office as a mere smash-and-grab raid.

Everybody had known, for some time past, that Pitt commanded the situation; both Fox and George III knew that he alone could save the king from the politicians if he would.[1] If Fox could have roped Pitt into the Coalition, as he was still trying to do in November 1783,[2] he would have controlled a perfect monopoly of political talent. The king believed that Pitt could already have saved him in March, and that it was only Pitt's own hesitation that had put a stop to the attempt.[3]

Thus courted on all sides, Pitt remained enigmatic, and still remains so to this day. Fox believed that Pitt shared his own prepossessions against monarchy and only deserted the good cause for personal ambition.[4] There was some truth in this: for Pitt does seem (like Shelburne) to have suspected the influence of the Crown even while he served the Crown as its minister. He was also ambitious: in 1782 he had openly refused to begin his political life at the bottom of the ladder, or even half-way up, as many other great men, including Fox himself, had done; and that sanguine temper which so many of his contemporaries—Addington, Huskisson, Wellington, Tom Grenville—noticed, produced in him a mood of self-sufficiency which is almost incredible. Never in twenty years would he think of taking any post but the first; not for nothing was he the son of the man who said, 'I am sure that I can save this country, and that nobody else can.'

Yet it was a mistake to treat Pitt as a mere lost leader, who

---

[1] *Memorials and Correspondence of Charles James Fox*, i. 323–5, 446.
[2] See his letter to Ossory, 9 Sept. 1783 (ibid. ii. 208), and Temple's report to George III, 15 Nov., in *Correspondence of George III*, no. 4520.
[3] Ibid., nos. 4242–50.
[4] He foretold it in May 1782 (*Memorials and Correspondence of Charles James Fox*, i. 326; Lord John Russell was probably right in assuming that this passage refers to Pitt), and he and his followers declaimed against Pitt's 'unguided ambition' in 1784 (e.g. *Parl. Hist.* xxiv. 276).

sold his soul early for ambition. He must have known how much his father had despised the 'night caps', the 'gentle warblers of the grove' whose friendship Charles Fox now boasted as his chief political support. He must have known that Chatham had thought of himself as the arbiter between king and factions, and had (at least, in some moods) treated the vendetta of the aristocratic cliques against George III as a futile irrelevance. For him too, the son, it was neither here nor there: he could not treat the cause of liberty and progress as bound up with mere anti-monarchism. He had, indeed, joined in the campaign against George III from 1780 to 1782; but many other people who were no real enemies to monarchy had done so too, and for the same reason—there was no other way of getting rid of George III's American war. The abatement of this emergency was beginning to reveal the members of this grand alliance in their true colours: some, like Burke and Rockingham's clique, as high and dry anti-monarchists; others, like Fox, popular anti-monarchists; others, like the Grenvilles, conservatives; others again, like Pitt, reformers who believed that they could take service under the monarchy in order to reform the better.

Perhaps Pitt's expectations were excessive. He failed to achieve some of the most spectacular reforms that he attempted.[1] But he did achieve most of what he thought important; for he had inherited, along with the eloquence and the uneven self-confidence of a Pitt, the tastes of a Grenville—above all the passion for administrative and financial reform. Often, perhaps, these tastes misled him;[2] but they inspired him to immense labours in fields of which Burke had done no more than talk.[3] Charles Fox never understood or cared about these things: he preferred Homer and Demosthenes to the economists, whom he persistently

---

[1] I shall discuss in the next chapter Pitt's relations with the king and his colleagues over bills which he supported unsuccessfully as Prime Minister.

[2] For example, his speech against the second reading of Fox's India Bill misfired, because he concentrated on financial technicalities (*Parl. Hist.* xxiii. 1280–3). In 1801–2 it was very hard to rouse him against Addington's mistakes in foreign policy, but he immediately pricked up his ears when he thought he saw Addington making mistakes on finance (*Diaries and Correspondence of George Rose*, i. 442, 512–14). Diplomats, such as Malmesbury, complained of Pitt's excessive attention to finance (*Diaries and Correspondence of Lord Malmesbury*, ii. 258, iv. 53).

[3] See A. S. Foord, 'The Waning of the Influence of the Crown', *English Historical Review*, lxii. 495–7, and George Rose, *Observations respecting the Public Expenditure and the Influence of the Crown* (London, 1810), *passim*.

accused of talking rubbish,[1] and even his own followers, in the next generation, could not help lamenting his love of a job and his indifference to the waste of public money.[2] When Fox and Burke reformed administration or expenditure, they did so (as they were careful to point out) without any desire to increase efficiency or to save money, but solely to reduce the political influence of the Crown.[3] Pitt, on the other hand, seems to have had some idea of the political and financial machinery which a modern state requires. Shelburne had had it too, but as he did not know how to behave like a politician, he could not defend himself against those who did.[4] Pitt was free of this disability: Pitt, therefore, was the man, not only to save George III from Fox but to turn the opportunity to some constructive account, though to less than he had intended.

It took him some time to shake himself free from the prepossessions and the associates of his youth. His father had not died in charity with George III, and he himself had entered parliament at the height of the campaign against royal influence. He was still reported to be very shy of it in the summer of 1783, and if he came into office, he did not intend to become the king's dupe, as many people assured him he would.[5] Still less did he mean to sacrifice his projects of reform: when Thurlow tried to persuade him that he needed the king more than the king needed him, so that he had better give up parliamentary and administrative reform for the sake of office, he flatly refused to do it.[6] Moreover, his temperament, like his father's, was uncommonly

[1] See, for example, his letter to Holland, 23 Feb. 1803, in *Memorials and Correspondence of Charles James Fox*, iii. 215.

[2] *The Creevey Papers*, ed. Maxwell, i. 35, 37.

[3] See the answer of the seven peers, 9 Feb. 1780, in Wyvill, op. cit. i. 44; Burke's *Speech on Economical Reform*, 11 Feb. 1780, in *Works* (1852 edn.), iii. 400. In the debate on the Exchequer Regulation Bill, 4 July 1783, Courtenay, a supporter of the Coalition, contrasted the 'illiberal parsimony' of Pitt and Shelburne, who tried to save money, with the reforms of Burke, which merely aimed at reducing the influence of the Crown (*Parl. Hist.* xxiii. 1069). This sentence alone is enough to explain why the middle class preferred Pitt to Fox.

[4] Shelburne made a great parade of the administrative reforms he had in hand when he was turned out of office (*Parl. Hist.* xxiii. 824; see also Fitzmaurice, op. cit. ii. 224–9).

[5] Fox, in *Parl. Hist.* xxiv. 219, 222, 251. Shelburne and his friends obviously thought so (Fitzmaurice, op. cit. ii. 285–7, 290).

[6] *Hist. MSS. Comm., Dropmore MSS.* i. 215–18. The sense in which, when in office, he interpreted this reservation of his freedom will be discussed in the next chapter, pp. 164–5.

mercurial—'always in the cellar or in the garret'—and he oscillated between sublime disregard of difficulties and helpless abasement before them. This instability, which possibly helps to explain many of his later legislative failures, had caused him to draw back at the very last moment in March, after he had encouraged George III to break off the negotiations with Portland. He can hardly have been taken by surprise when George III struck his blow in December[1] but, a month later, he was very near giving up the game, had not his colleagues (very few of whom had to face the music in the House of Commons) protested against it.[2]

George III's way of getting rid of a Ministry he disliked was not quite orthodox: when the India Bill came to the House of Lords he admitted Lord Temple to an audience and allowed him to take away a piece of paper giving him authority to say that the king would regard as his enemy anybody who voted for the bill. That killed the bill in the House of Lords. The Commons, led by the ministers, resolved that 'to report any opinion, or pretended opinion, of his Majesty, upon any bill, or other proceeding, depending in either House of Parliament, with a view to influence the votes of the members, is a high crime and misdemeanor'. The ministers did not resign; but the king dismissed them next day. Pitt accepted office, and the great debate began.

On the face of it, the chief offence was not the dismissal of ministers but the interview with Temple. It was a mere technicality to say that any peer had the right of audience as an hereditary counsellor of the Crown;[3] if the doctrine of responsibility meant anything, this right was obsolete, for the king's servants could not be expected to protect him by their responsibility if he received and followed the advice of others who were

---

[1] Atkinson reported to Robinson that everything was ready for the blow, and Pitt had a secret meeting with him and Dundas on 15 Dec.; a few days earlier, the king was reported to have had 'a direct communication' with somebody—probably Pitt—and made all his arrangements with Pitt's cousin Temple (*Hist. MSS. Comm., Abergavenny MSS.*, p. 62).

[2] *Political Memoranda of Francis, Fifth Duke of Leeds*, p. 94.

[3] Temple himself used this argument (*Parl. Hist.* xxiv. 154). This was not the first incident of the kind in the Grenville family: Temple's uncle was said to have asked for an interview with the king in 1766, in order to obtain an opinion which he could use against the bill for repealing the Stamp Act (*Correspondence of George III*, no. 253).

not responsible.[1] Moreover—though the point had not been argued before—it was hardly consistent with ministerial responsibility for the king to persuade members of the House of Lords to vote against a bill promoted by his servants.[2] Fox, indeed, called it treachery;[3] it was only that, if the king had consented beforehand to the introduction of the bill, which we do not know.[4] It may be argued that if the king retained the right of veto, *a fortiori* he might properly dissuade people from voting for a bill he disliked; and George III defended himself by saying that Fox had intended to deny him this right.[5] Fox did indeed deny it by implication, for he argued that the king's veto upon legislation, like all his other prerogatives, should only be exercised upon the advice of his responsible servants—which amounted to saying, in these circumstances, that he should not exercise it at all.[6] But I doubt if the existence of the veto in the

[1] This was recognized later: the convention was established that if a peer insisted on exercising this right, the sovereign should avoid anything like a political discussion (*Letters of Queen Victoria*, ed. Benson, 1st series (London, 1907), i. 117, 421–2, 431–2).

[2] So Fitzwilliam argued in the House of Lords (*Parl Hist.* xxiv. 158) and Fox in the House of Commons (ibid., p. 216). Richmond tried to make a curious distinction: he contended that though the King's official servants had the right of advising him about all executive business,' it was as unconstitutional for a minister to advise the Crown, and endeavour to influence his Majesty in regard to any bill depending in parliament, as for any other person' (*Parl. Hist.* xxiv. 155). It is not easy to see what Richmond had in mind—whether he thought that such advice would prejudge the use of the veto, or that it was a breach of privilege even for a minister to report parliamentary proceedings to the king or to comment on them, or that bills ought not, strictly, to be considered as Government bills. (As to this, *v. infra*, pp. 164–6.) In any case, his remarks were completely at variance with the accepted practice and may, I think, be dismissed as a piece of his usual wrong-headedness.

[3] *Memorials and Correspondence of Charles James Fox*, ii. 221.

[4] A newspaper which supported the Coalition claimed that the king had expressed his assent to the bill 'a thousand times' in the closet (*Parl. Hist.* xxiv. 153), but Fox never said so, and it is possible that George III's consent had never been formally asked (*v. infra*, pp. 154–5).

[5] Stanhope, *Life of Pitt*, i, Appendix, p. vi.

[6] *Parl. Hist.* xxiv. 218. The question whether the king could still, in practice, exercise his right of veto was not much discussed. In 1825, or thereabouts, even Lord Eldon had to admit that though the legal right existed, yet 'considering how materially though gradually the exercise of the direct legal prerogatives of the Crown has been in many instances supplanted by its influence, how expedient if not necessary it is become to give undue, nay excessive attention to the public opinion', the veto could only have been used in 1807 after very careful tactical preparation. He had no doubt, however, that George III would have used it (*Correspondence of George IV*, ed. Aspinall, no. 1209).

background justified the indirect methods which the king had used; indeed, Fox had some justification for saying, as he once did, that he would have minded an honest veto less.[1]

Naturally the debate turned at first on the circumstances in which Pitt had come into office, and the Opposition refused to treat with him until he had purged the vice of his origin by resignation.[2] It was thus, I think, implied that by accepting office he had made himself responsible for those circumstances; but he was slow to admit this, and the Portland Ministry of 1807 seem to have been the first to proclaim, even half-heartedly, that those who accept office assume the responsibility for the dismissal of their predecessors though they were not privy to it.[3]

More, however, was at stake in the debate than the merits of this peculiar incident. Fox repeatedly claimed that the confidence of the House of Commons, however obtained, should be enough by itself to place and keep a Ministry in power regardless of the House of Lords and the king's personal wishes.[4] Pitt tried to avoid setting himself against the House; but he denied that it had any legal right to choose ministers—this right resided in the king—and his supporters insisted that a House of Commons would act factiously—indeed, unconstitutionally—if it condemned *a limine* a minister appointed by the king without giving him the chance to stand or fall by his measures and his legislative proposals.[5]

Behind the House of Commons stood the people. Robinson's negotiations behind the scenes were daily detaching from Fox the undecided members of parliament who were beginning to believe that Pitt could stand up for himself and the king; and Pitt's propaganda was meeting with a response, not only in addresses whose authenticity and representativeness Fox might dispute, but in a visible though indefinable tide of public opinion. Pitt and his supporters never afterwards forgot the buoyancy with which they felt themselves floated upon this

[1] *Parl. Hist.* xxiv. 366.

[2] Ibid. 466; *Memorials and Correspondence of Charles James Fox*, ii. 235, 239–40. There was some dispute whether Pitt must actually resign or it would be enough for the king to set him aside by sending for Portland and asking him to form a new Ministry in which Pitt should serve, though not as Portland's equal. Since Pitt insisted on equality, this discussion was unimportant.

[3] *V. infra*, pp. 139–40.

[4] *Parl. Hist.* xxiv. 222, 286, 365, 381, 387, 690, 736.

[5] Ibid. 310, 371, 442, 663, 677, 706, 709–10, 717, 740–2.

tide: many years later, when Malmesbury was questioning whether such a movement ever 'rose of itself, *quite alone and unaided*', Pitt replied, 'Yes, often in a way not only unknown, but in a manner as if it had no concerted beginning.'[1] Fox, too, must have known which way this tide was setting; and the knowledge led him to the tactical imprudence—one may even say the constitutional impropriety—of denying the king's right to dissolve and trying—though not quite whole-heartedly—to prevent him from exercising it.[2] It was a tactical imprudence, for a party which founded its claim to power upon the public confidence, to forbid any attempt to test the justice of that claim, even though the verdict of the electorate was not necessarily, in those days, the verdict of the people. It was a constitutional impropriety to deny the right of an executive, however constituted, to appeal to the electorate against an adverse House of Commons,[3] for this right is still, to this day, a highly valuable means of breaking political deadlocks. But Fox and Burke were so much convinced that the House of Commons was, by definition, the people's check upon royal tyranny, that they refused to admit that its operations, in this capacity, should be conditional on the approval of the people itself.[4]

[1] *Diaries and Correspondence of Lord Malmesbury*, iv. 112–13, 290; see also W. W. Grenville's remarks in 1788 (Buckingham, *Courts and Cabinets of George III*, i. 453, ii. 24): Grenville evidently expected this tide would flow again in Pitt's favour, and so strongly that even if the Prince of Wales should assume the regency, he would not be able to help readmitting Pitt to power. Professor A. Aspinall has suggested in *Politics and the Press* (London, 1949), p. 68, that this movement of opinion in Pitt's favour in 1784 was not quite so spontaneous as it appeared.

[2] A motion was passed to this effect, 18 Dec. (*Parl. Hist.* xxiv. 226) and on 12 Jan. two more resolutions were passed, of which one, at least (the resolution postponing the second reading of the Mutiny Bill) could only be meant to put difficulties in the way of a dissolution (ibid. 299, 303). They had this effect, according to the Duke of Leeds (see his *Political Memoranda*, ed. Browning, pp. 95–96).

[3] 'Is not this separating the House of Commons from its constituents, annihilating our importance, and avowedly erecting a monarchy on the basis of an affected popularity, independent of and uncontrolable by parliament?' (Charles Fox in *Parl. Hist.* xxiv. 476.)

[4] Ibid. 474. Burke, even after the event, wished to deny the right of ministers to set up the constituencies as arbiters between themselves and the House of Commons. 'If there must be another mode of conveying the collective sense of the people to the throne, than that by the House of Commons, it ought to be fixed and defined' (*A Representation to His Majesty* (1784) in *Works* (1852 edn.), iii. 525). Not until many years later (in the *Observations on the Conduct of the Minority*) did Burke admit that the decision of the electorate, though unwise and intemperate, was one against which he could not appeal.

The methods by which George III and Pitt won their election in 1784 have been much discussed, and I shall have something to say about them later.[1] It was, for that generation, a decisive battle. Starting with every disadvantage—for almost the whole nation, after Yorktown, repudiated his policy—George III had come through the two years' crisis of his reign. Historians rightly insist upon the mistakes of his enemies; but I think that when the lapse of a year or two had dissociated his reputation and his authority from the memory of the American disaster, he was sure of winning in the end: he held the *ultima ratio* of a general election in his hand, and the nation was not yet ripe to receive Charles Fox's doctrine that kings should reign but should not govern.

Fox himself never fully accepted the verdict. In his eyes, the illegitimate origin of Pitt's Ministry, no matter how often ratified by the choice of the electorate, constituted a permanent taint which could only be wiped out by resignation. It was chiefly for this reason that even at the rare moments when other considerations inclined him to a coalition with Pitt, he insisted that Pitt's Ministry must, as a preliminary, be considered at an end, and that in the completely new Administration which should replace it, Pitt should have no more than parity with himself.[2] This principle overrode, in his mind, the requirement of any emergency. He spent the last twenty years of his life as a sad example of arrested development, obsessed by his hatred of monarchy. Even wars and revolutions hardly interested him except as incidents in his struggles against it.[3] His fatal reverse of 1784, and his

[1] *V. infra*, pp. 197 n., 206 n.

[2] See Fox's, Loughborough's and Fitzwilliam's letters to Carlisle in *Hist. MSS. Comm., Carlisle MSS.*, pp. 696–700. (Fitzwilliam seems to have doubted whether Fox could be admitted to office, but he too expected Pitt to resign his post to Portland.) Other evidence of Fox's attitude to the reconstruction of the Ministry in 1792 is to be found in *Political Memoranda of Francis, Fifth Duke of Leeds*, ed. Browning, pp. 175–95, especially p. 180; *Diaries and Correspondence of Lord Malmesbury*, ii. 454–72, especially p. 462; and H. Butterfield, 'Charles James Fox and the Whig Opposition', in *Cambridge Historical Journal*, ix. 293–330. For a moment, Fox must have lost his bearings and felt his dislike of Pitt even more strongly than his dislike of the king; for he thought of approaching the king through Thurlow, Pitt's discarded rival and a 'King's Friend' of twenty years' standing, in order to form a ministry without Pitt (*Diaries and Correspondence of Lord Malmesbury*, ii. 462).

[3] He believed that Pitt, in resisting France, was fighting a war for monarchy; that he was trying to reintroduce absolute monarchy into Great Britain (*Memorials and Correspondence of Charles James Fox*, iii. 125). Although he denounced the war, he

continued exclusion from power, confirmed in his eyes the exaggerated estimate which he had always made of the influence of the Crown: in 1804 he rebuked his nephew for saying '*such things would not go down*, the *public* this, and the *public* that', arguing that even public opinion was regulated from above. Perhaps this explains why he came to place all his hopes in the favour of the heir apparent (hence the significance of the Regency crisis of 1788) and so little in his own exertions in parliament: he could afford to be seen lolling in the shade at St. Anne's Hill, with a harper playing soft music and books of botany lying open on the table, or even to secede from parliament altogether, if he was relying upon the king's death or his madness (about which he eagerly swallowed every piece of gossip) to waft him back to office without any effort of his own.[1]

It was a long time before George III changed his Ministry again; and when he did so, it cost him no effort to get rid of a minister whose seventeen years of uninterrupted power had almost made him look like a permanent part of the political landscape. The king's easy success is, indeed, mainly explained by the curious circumstance of Pitt's acquiescence; but it is quite probable that he could have got his way even if Pitt had resisted.[2] When Pitt forced his way back to office in 1804 there was some repetition of the usual struggles for a direct interview and *carte blanche*:[3] but it would be fair to describe these as struggles between Pitt and Addington, not between Pitt and the king; indeed, Pitt's parliamentary tactics in the preceding months can only be understood as signals emitted in order to attract the

wished in 1796 that Pitt might not be able to make peace, as the question of war or peace was less important than the maintenance of a bad régime or Ministry (ibid. iii. 132–3). His chief concern about Catholic Emancipation seems to have been the fact that 'it is the only question that can be started to make what can be called a *cause* against the Court' (ibid. iii. 442). He was glad when George III refused to admit him to the Ministry, because it 'lowered the cause of Royalism' (ibid. iv. 57).

[1] We do not know whether Fox had any reason for thinking that the Prince of Wales would behave as a constitutional monarch ought to do, or any understanding to that effect. He cannot have thought very well of the Prince's character (see his letter to Grey, ibid. iii. 341), but weakness of character would not necessarily have made the Prince the worse an instrument. When it came to the point (after Fox's death) the Prince disappointed the hopes of the Opposition, who forthwith began to place them on his daughter Princess Charlotte. Even in the reign of William IV the political proclivities of the heir apparent were an object of interest to the whigs.

[2] I shall deal with this incident more fully in chapter v, p. 164.

[3] Pellew, *Life of Sidmouth*, ii. 119–28; Barnes, *George III and William Pitt*, pp. 404–9, 421–44.

king's attention, for they were singularly ill contrived to procure success in the House of Commons itself.[1] When George III agreed at last to let Addington go, Pitt deferred to his prejudices in the composition of the new Ministry; for, though he strongly urged the king, more than once, to allow a real coalition of the political leaders, he would not make it a condition of his own acceptance of office, and acquiesced too readily in the king's refusal.[2] No doubt he thought, as sanguinely as ever, that he could stand alone. But he also showed how whole-heartedly he believed that the king must have the last word on the choice of ministers. He made a terrible mistake: his last Ministry was pitiably weak, and if he had not killed himself in the effort to maintain it, an adverse majority of the House of Commons would probably have driven him from office in a few days. Pitt must be held to have sacrificed the public good unjustifiably to the king's personal wishes. But those were his principles; he stuck to them and he died for them.[3]

In these last years of his political life George III's scruples of conscience against Catholic Emancipation had raised a new question about his right to choose ministers and to affix conditions to his choice. It was no longer a question of his freedom to choose or to reject persons, nor (as in 1782) of the politicians'

[1] This is particularly true of his behaviour on Patten's motion, 3 June 1803, when he was left in a humiliating minority. He had promised not to oppose Addington, and he did not believe that the House of Commons ought to drive ministers out of office; but he would have liked to frighten them out of it, and above all to show the king that he was ready to return. The king, however, was slow to take the hint.

[2] Barnes, op. cit., pp. 440, 462; Stanhope, *Life of Pitt*, iv. 162–80, 334. Pitt had resolved from the first to take this line (*Hist. MSS. Comm., Dropmore MSS.* vii. 213). When some of his supporters wanted to hold a meeting for the purpose of pressing him to be more peremptory with the king, he declared that he should not consider as his friend anybody who attended it (*Hist. MSS. Comm., Bathurst MSS.*, p. 39). The coalition proposed by Pitt was not a complete one, for he insisted on leaving out Addington. Perhaps this was unavoidable, for Pitt had just forced himself into office because he thought Addington incompetent and meant to reverse his policy. It is far from certain that Pitt could have come to terms with Grenville and Fox even if the king had allowed him to do so. Catholic Emancipation might not have been an obstacle, but Fox's distrust of Pitt probably would (*Memorials and Correspondence of Charles James Fox*, iv. 44–47).

[3] It is particularly difficult to separate principle from expediency in Pitt's conduct after 1801, because he knew that George III was liable to go mad, if seriously perturbed, and that would throw the power into the hands of the Prince of Wales and Fox. One cannot be sure whether he believed that he ought not to resist the king's wishes, or that he would be defeating his own ends if he did so. Probably both these things were in his mind.

freedom to stipulate for a policy before they took office; but of the king's right to demand, before admitting them to office or retaining them in it, that they should abstain from making proposals to which he could not in conscience agree. When Addington was driven to resign, George III might have got into difficulties, for all the other political leaders believed, for one reason or another, that Catholic Emancipation ought to be granted. The difficulties, however, were less than they seemed; for all those leaders were content, more or less, to postpone it while the king lived: they considered the difficulty as a temporary one, for they did not expect him to live long, nor did they then foresee that his son would follow his line about the Catholic question. Pitt had given a positive pledge that he would even resist Catholic Emancipation if anybody else proposed it during George III's lifetime.[1] Grenville and Fox were quite disgusted when they heard of this pledge,[2] and they took the opportunity of embarrassing Pitt by bringing on a motion in parliament. But they had themselves been willing to consider a postponement if they could keep Ireland quiet;[3] and in 1806 they did, in effect, what they had criticized Pitt for doing in 1804—they came into office without intending to pass Catholic Emancipation at once or stipulating for the right to do so. They were not, however, pledged to refrain;[4] perhaps the king regarded Sidmouth's and Ellenborough's presence in the Cabinet as a sufficient guarantee. It was only on another subject that the king tried to make conditions, and there he ended by agreeing that the ministers might make such proposals as seemed good to them, provided that they were not to assume his previous consent and he was to reserve his liberty of action.[5]

[1] Stanhope, *Life of Pitt*, iii. 304; Barnes, op. cit., p. 381; *Diaries and Correspondence of George Rose*, i. 360.

[2] Grenville heard about it from Carysfort in Oct. 1803 (*Hist. MSS. Comm., Dropmore MSS.* vii. 192). Fox does not seem to have been sure of it before Jan. 1804 (see his *Memorials and Correspondence*, iv. 20). It is surprising that they should not have learnt of it much earlier; Malmesbury claims to have known of it in Mar. 1801 (*Diaries and Correspondence*, iv. 31). Malmesbury has been suspected of giving false dates to the entries in his diary; but in this instance he would have had to misdate a whole series of entries.

[3] *Memorials and Correspondence of Charles James Fox*, iv. 44–47.

[4] They emphasized this in their controversy with George III, e.g. in the Cabinet minute of 17 Mar. 1807, printed in Holland's *Memoirs of the Whig Party*, ii. 319.

[5] This was the question of army reform (*Hist. MSS. Comm., Dropmore MSS.* viii. 2, 7–9).

But the Ministry of All the Talents came to grief on the Catholic question after all. Lord Grenville, whose mind, like his father's, was that of an administrator rather than a politician, convinced himself that the war could not be won without removing the hindrances which certain English laws offered to the recruitment of Irish Catholics.[1] George III regarded this as the thin end of the Catholic wedge, and a long and excruciating misunderstanding[2] ended by raising a constitutional issue. The ministers withdrew their bill, but reserved the right to offer the king any advice which they might in future think it for his service to give him, and the king retaliated by demanding a pledge that they would never, so long as he lived, renew the present proposal in any form. When they refused it, he dismissed them.[3]

In the uproar which followed this action, the dispossessed ministers raised the old cry against secret, unofficial advisers, who had persuaded the king to resist or dismiss his responsible servants.[4] This complaint was plausible, but does not appear to have been well founded. They did not content themselves with castigating this mythical secret cabal; they also argued that the new ministers, by the mere acceptance of office, had made themselves responsible for the circumstances which led to their doing so. Perceval admitted this responsibility but then denied it;

---

[1] There is every reason to think that Grenville really believed this, and was not merely trying to placate the Catholic demagogues or to overreach the king (see his letters to Bedford and Elliot, *Hist. MSS. Comm., Dropmore MSS.* viii. 261, 486, 492–3).

[2] Which I shall discuss elsewhere, p. 156.

[3] Most of the documents are printed in Lord Holland's *Memoirs of the Whig Party*, ii. 270–320, and in *Hist. MSS. Comm., Dropmore MSS.* ix. 100–20.

[4] Lord Eldon had just paid a visit to Windsor; but he always maintained that he had only gone to discuss the king's private affairs, and had talked no politics. (Cobbett's *Parl. Debates*, ix. 339, 343; Twiss, *Life of Lord Chancellor Eldon*, ii. 38.) Hawkesbury was also accused; but his father circumstantially denied the charge (see his letter to Auckland, in *Journal and Correspondence of Lord Auckland*, iv. 308). But Malmesbury drafted, and Portland seems to have sent, a very extraordinary letter to the king, offering to defeat the bill in the House of Lords, provided the king would signify that he had not consented to it. This the king could not do, for he had consented to it; but he sent a message to Malmesbury, that his intentions about Catholic Relief were what they had always been. As the bill was dropped before the final crisis, the incident had no effect, but the letter is a curiosity, for it would be impossible to tell (without certain accidental references) whether it was written by Temple against Portland's Ministry in 1783 or by Portland against the Ministry of Temple's brother in 1807 (*Diaries and Correspondence of Lord Malmesbury*, iv. 360–5, 370; see also Michael Roberts, in *English Historical Review*, l. 72 n).

Canning tried to dodge it by pointing out that, historically, the posts which he and his colleagues had assumed had been vacant; finally, however, he said he should be proud to assume the responsibility.[1] Whitbread insisted on the point, with some reason; for he wished, like all Fox's followers, to claim that the king could not do any purely private action for which no other person was responsible.[2] He and his friends declaimed with still more force against the demand for a pledge, as inconsistent with the idea of ministerial responsibility.

The king's right to dissolve a parliament which did not suit him was questioned as in 1784, and with more reason, for this House of Commons was only a few months old and never passed an adverse vote on the new Ministry. Finally, the debate—especially out of doors—went into still larger issues. The substantial grievance was the king's refusal to do what a Ministry possessing the confidence of the House of Commons had recommended; that he had opposed to their wishes, and to the interests of his empire, his personal interpretation of his coronation oath.[3] The majority, however, believed that the king's conscience was his own property and should have been respected. He was old; he was pathetic; he was the symbol of the nation's will to

[1] *Parl. Debates*, ix. 316–17, 342, 473. Eldon seems to have repudiated this responsibility (Twiss, *Life of Eldon*, ii. 45); but perhaps he was thinking of the historical facts, rather than the constitutional law.

[2] *Parl. Debates*, ix. 335.

[3] Lord Kenyon had, in effect, advised the king that the person who had taken the coronation oath must decide whether a particular proposal would violate it (G. T. Kenyon, *Life of Lord Kenyon* (London, 1873), pp. 308 seqq.) but Dundas had tried to suggest that an Act of Parliament could not be deemed contrary to the coronation oath. George III had dismissed this as 'Scotch metaphysics'; but it was a serious question whether, according to the constitution, even the king's conscience was his own property. The Foxite whigs contended that, like everything else about him, it had been turned into an institution controlled by his responsible advisers (see Erskine's speech, *Parl. Debates*, ix. 362: 'The king, as chief magistrate, can have no conscience which is not in the trust of responsible subjects'). Eldon denied this doctrine in 1825 (*Correspondence of George IV*, ed. Aspinall, no. 1209). George III knew that in 1689 the parliament which passed the Coronation Oath Act had considered and rejected an amendment which would have provided 'that no clause in the Act shall be understood, so to bind the Kings and Queens of this Realm, as to prevent their giving their royal assent to any bill, which shall at any time be offered by the Lords and Commons assembled in Parliament, for the taking away or altering any form or ceremony in the established Church, so as the doctrines of the said Church, and public liturgy, and episcopal government be preserved'. If he thought that the rejection of this clause implied an intentional reservation of the king's right to put his personal interpretation on the coronation oath, he was probably making a historical mistake (see Barnes, *George III and William Pitt*, p. 349).

survive the terrible struggle with France. It was easy for his supporters to raise the cry of coercing the king, and to charge Lord Holland with denying him the right even to think; and that probably comes near enough to what Holland, who was Charles Fox's favourite nephew, really believed. Once more the doctrine of the Foxes was, to say the least of it, in advance of their time; more people would have agreed with Melville when he said:

> If men in office held opinions different from those of their sovereign, he did not say they ought to give their opinions up; but if the sovereign could find other servants who would undertake to conduct the government without requiring this sacrifice, he had certainly the right to appoint and make use of them.[1]

Once more the 'whigs' forgot the actual opinions of the people. They spoke as though George III alone were obstructing something that everybody else wanted to do. But it is questionable whether George III could have forced Catholic Emancipation through both houses of parliament even if he had wanted to do it. The superior persons—Pitt, Fox, Canning, Grenville, Grey, even Castlereagh—were all for it, but the great mass of people in the electorate, the House of Lords and (though this is more doubtful) the House of Commons were against it. In this they were faithfully reflected by the second-rate political leaders—Addington, Perceval, Abbot, Hawkesbury—who owed much of their popularity to the very fact that they were second-rate.[2] A bad churchgoer like Pitt and a bad Christian like Fox were probably less representative of the nation than Perceval, who spent his labour and ingenuity in applying Daniel xi. 36–45 to the career of Napoleon Bonaparte. It is doubtful if Catholic Emancipation could ever have been forced through the British political machine except by the expedient, which was finally adopted in 1828, of bringing Ireland to the brink of civil war. It might have been better policy to grant it without such a

---

[1] *Parl. Debates*, ix. 256.

[2] Lord Holland, in his *Memoirs of the Whig Party* (ii. 213) quotes an acquaintance who said about Addington's Ministry: 'He was glad that Mr. Pitt and Mr. Fox should know that in spite of their speaking and fine talents, the business of the country could be conducted in a plain way by a man who had no pretensions to genius.' When Sir James Mackintosh, Holland House's tame man of genius, made his first speech in the House of Commons, John Ward could hear the country gentlemen all round him 'damning him for a Scotch lawyer' (*Letters to 'Ivy' from the first Earl of Dudley*, ed. S. H. Romilly, p. 228).

convulsion in 1807, just as it might have been better policy to grant dominion status to the American colonies in 1776. But George III almost certainly had the support of the majority of his subjects in refusing to make either of these concessions before it was demonstrably necessary.

These controversies left a mark upon the doctrines of the constitution. The whigs, who believed that they had been tricked in all their dealings with George III, were more set than ever on their own interpretation of ministerial responsibility, and on refusing to take office without *carte blanche*. In the negotiations of 1812 they threw away their chances (as the Prince Regent meant them to do)[1] by stiffly refusing to have anything to do with him unless he left to them complete liberty as to measures, and complete control of every branch of the administration, including the court.[2] They sacrificed too much for their consistency. But perhaps this may be counted unto them for righteousness—that the usages for which they contended have become—after their time and for reasons which they could only half foresee—the accepted conventions of the constitution.

[1] See Michael Roberts, 'The Ministerial Crisis of May–June 1812', in *English Historical Review*, li. 466–87.

[2] See the minutes in *Annual Register, 1812*, pp. *293–4.

V

THE KING AND THE CABINET

THE controversies over the appointment and dismissal of ministers were more than half the battle of politics, in the eyes of George III and of his conscious adversaries. But the king also had to determine his relations with his ministers during their tenure of office. These relations were regulated by custom and, upon occasions, by definition; though they were less public than those other controversies, they led to constitutional results of more permanent importance. When the king had to accept ministers who neither trusted him nor were trusted by him, naturally his relations with them were defined more sharply than was usual, and innovations were made or, at least, attempted; but it did not always happen, conversely, that his dealings with the ministers of his own choice were free from difficulty—indeed, he had more trouble with George Grenville than with Rockingham, and lost more power, at least in matters of every-day importance, to the younger Pitt than to Charles Fox.

The maxim that 'the king can do no wrong', and its implication that his ministers are responsible for all his actions, were discussed at length in the great debates of 1784 and 1807. This maxim necessarily had its effect in the closet and the Cabinet. It was manifested, above all, in the claim that the king was obliged to accept the collective advice of his servants in the form of a Cabinet minute, and that he could not use his veto upon the bills which his servants collectively promoted in parliament. I shall discuss these questions in their place; but I wish to point out first that any doctrine founded upon the collective responsibility of the ministers, made certain assumptions as to their individual responsibility. Even if there had been no Cabinet and no collective responsibility, there might still have been a debate whether the king must accept the advice of an individual minister or could act without, or even against, that advice.

In the reign of George III the Cabinet was so well formed, that this question of individual responsibility could not often arise in the sphere of policy; but it frequently came up over appointments, for many of these were the business of the individual minister, not of the Cabinet as a whole. George III claimed and exercised the right to make appointments of his own mere motion, but mainly in certain departments—the Church, the army, the royal household, and, to a rather less degree, the peerage. Several of his letters to Lord North announce his intention to promote or translate bishops, in circumstances which seem to prove that he cannot have received any advice.[1] Later in his career, he made an Archbishop of Canterbury in a ministerial interregnum, and another against the advice of the younger Pitt. He gave his instructions likewise upon promotions in the army, and Lord Barrington, the Secretary-at-War, was so used to this procedure that he did not even trouble to come to town upon news of an important vacancy, 'recollecting', he said, 'that when you are pleased to give anything immediately away, your Majesty commonly sends your directions in writing'.[2] He seems to have reserved for his own decision all military promotions above the rank of colonel upon the Irish establishment—a very salutary precaution, for the Irish were too much given to jobbery—and he even interfered, from time to time, in the junior appointments too.[3] On one of these occasions he came into conflict with the insufferable Marquis of Buckingham, whose more prudent brother tried to explain to him that even the most absolute minister who ever governed the country could not exclude all personal interference of the king in the nomination to offices—certainly Pitt did

[1] On 31 Oct. 1776 George III instructed North, using the word 'must', upon a whole scheme of ecclesiastical promotions arising out of the Archbishop of York's death, of which he had only just heard (*Correspondence of George III*, no. 1923). In Apr. 1781 he did not even wait for the Bishop of Winchester to die before giving North his instructions (ibid., no. 3313). He may have known North's opinion already; on the second occasion, at least, it nearly coincided with his own (*Hist. MSS. Comm., Abergavenny MSS.*, p. 42), and he had a special motive for precipitation, for he wished to promote North's own brother, a thing which North might feel some embarrassment in recommending. (George III was always particularly imperious when conferring favours upon his Prime Ministers.)

[2] *Correspondence of George III*, nos. 818–21. Barrington, it is true, was unusual among politicians in the humility with which he treated himself as a mere *commis*.

[3] It seems to have been the etiquette, when the king wished to make a junior officer or an A.D.C., for the Secretary of State to transmit his 'wishes', not his 'commands' to the Lord Lieutenant (Buckingham, *Courts and Cabinets of George III*, i. 405).

not profess to do so. But, Grenville added rather significantly, if the king's recommendations 'cease to be the casual exertions of private favour, and begin to be systematic interferences with the power entrusted to his servants' that would be another matter.[1]

George III also watched jealously over the promotion and creation of peers. He only once had any political motive for his resistance, when he displayed his dislike of the Coalition Ministry by refusing to create any English peers at their recommendation.[2] He was rather concerned, on other occasions, to prevent his ministers from making the peerage too cheap—an attitude which most of his successors have maintained and needs no explaining. His ministers never presumed to dictate to him about the peerage or the orders of knighthood, though they might put some pressure on him when an important political object was at stake, as Cornwallis insisted on keeping the promises he had been allowed to make in order to bring about the Union with Ireland.[3] There was somewhat more controversy, however, about another of the spheres which George III reserved for himself—the royal Household. He would not let George Grenville meddle with the Keepership of the Privy Purse in 1763, alleging that Bute had held this office as a personal friend, not as First Lord of the Treasury; and when he invited North's opinion on the Household of his eldest son, he

[1] Ibid. See also the further controversy about this and similar grievances, op. cit. i. 408–10, 134–45, and *Hist. MSS. Comm., Dropmore MSS.* i. 336, 339, 343, 344, 345, 354, 355, 437, 442–57, 473. In the course of this rumpus, Lord Buckingham not only threatened to resign at a very awkward moment, but nearly caused his brother to resign the Speakership of the House of Commons; and he spoke of the king in tones of personal enmity which are almost unique in the history of the reign. This seems to have been a hereditary characteristic of the Grenvilles. His uncle, Lord Temple (according to Shelburne) 'entertained a most sovereign contempt for the Royal closet without any exception, which he never wished to conceal, even at his table' (Fitzmaurice, op. cit. ii. 27). His father, George Grenville, irritated George III more than any other Prime Minister he ever had, and managed to give him the impression that he did not think him an honest man. As for Lord Buckingham himself, Lord Sheffield told a story which, if not true, was exceedingly well invented. George III had gone mad in the middle of this rumpus about the Irish military promotions. 'In one of his soliloquies he said, "I hate nobody, why should anybody hate me?"—recollecting a little, he added, "I beg pardon, I do hate the Marquis of Buckingham" ' (*Journal and Correspondence of Lord Auckland*, ii. 244).

[2] *V. supra*, p. 125.

[3] *Memoirs and Correspondence of Viscount Castlereagh*, ed. Londonderry (London, 1848), iii. 320–46, *passim*.

took care to make it clear that he was consulting him 'as a friend, not a minister'.[1] Even Portland offered to let the Bedchamber alone in 1783;[2] but the Lords of the Bedchamber voted too conspicuously against the East India Bill of that year, so that the whig purists began to think they owed it to the constitution to demand control of all the Household appointments. There was more than whig pedantry in the fiasco of 1812, when Moira's negotiations with Grey and Grenville broke down over their claim to include these offices in the political arrangements made on a change of Administration;[3] but the principle was promulgated. George IV, profiting by his success in resisting it upon this occasion, continued to claim very large exceptions under this heading,[4] and sharply reproved Lord Liverpool for suggesting the nominations of Household officers or even transmitting their resignations.[5] William IV showed more facility as to their appointment and dismissal, and all parties seem to have assumed, in the Bedchamber affair of 1839, that had the queen been a king and her Ladies of the Bedchamber lords, their offices would have been at the Prime Minister's disposal just like any others.[6]

Even outside these fields of patronage reserved for the king's special control, it was by no means an understood thing that he must give up his opinion to that of ministers. Sometimes he might do so, and make a merit of it.[7] But they had no right to expect it; and it is most unlikely that any of them (Charles Fox excepted) would have dared to address to George III such language as the so-called 'tory' ministers of the Prince Regent

---

[1] *Grenville Papers*, ii. 209–10; *Correspondence of George III*, no. 3201.

[2] Fitzmaurice, op. cit. ii. 260.

[3] *Annual Register, 1812*, pp. *293–4; Professor Michael Roberts in his article in *English Historical Review*, li. 466–87, makes it clear that neither the Prince Regent nor Moira intended the negotiation to succeed at this stage.

[4] It was even alleged that he considered the Chancellor of the Duchy of Lancaster as a sort of Household official (*The Formation of Canning's Ministry*, ed. Aspinall, pp. 59, 70). But he accepted Liverpool's recommendation to the Mastership of the Buckhounds, which was supported by the argument that 'in other instances when the offices of the Household have been generally kept distinct from the political arrangements, this principle has not been applied to the office now vacant' (*Correspondence of George IV*, ed. Aspinall, no. 1079).

[5] Ibid., nos. 661, 942, 946.

[6] *Letters of Queen Victoria*, 1st series (London, 1907), i. 198–217, especially 208–9.

[7] In Nov. 1778 George III claimed to have often yielded his opinion to North's on appointments and measures (*Correspondence of George III*, no. 2451).

thought fit to use.[1] Perceval virtually refused to recommend a peerage which the prince had promised long ago in writing, with the argument that 'by the Constitution of the country, H.R.H. cannot, either as Regent or as King, exercise any of the prerogatives of the Crown but under the advice of some responsible Minister'.[2] In the controversies over Sumner and Berkeley Paget in the summer of 1821, George IV posed in vain the question 'whether the King's word is to be held sacred or of no avail'. Castlereagh hinted that he would not defend in parliament the king's letting Sumner kiss hands for the preferment before the Prime Minister's consent was obtained, and Liverpool offered to

recal to your Majesty's recollection cases in which it could not but be distinctly admitted that the expectation which might have been personally held out by the sovereign was subject to the responsibility of his ministers, and that it must be a sufficient answer on such an occasion that the appointment has been obstructed in a quarter which cannot by the laws of the country be passed by.[3]

These claims implied that the king must submit his action to the judgement of his responsible ministers; but it did not follow that the responsibility was collective, though the Prime Minister often exerted the strength which the latent or avowed solidarity of his colleagues conferred upon him. The principle of collective responsibility was rather dimly and uncertainly apprehended in 1760. The collective action of ministers in the closet and the Cabinet, and their collective discipline in the houses of parliament, were much more elaborate and better defined when George III closed his political life in 1810.

[1] One of the few occasions upon which George III's ministers tried to coerce him into making an appointment was May 1765, when Grenville and Bedford tried to force him to make Weymouth Lord Lieutenant of Ireland. Even so, they disclaimed any attempt to coerce (*Bedford Correspondence*, iii. 309), and it cost them their places; for this seems to have been the king's chief reason for dismissing them (see the account of his conversation with Charles Yorke in Harris, *Life of Lord Chancellor Hardwicke*, iii. 446: he says that 'upon this', i.e. the Weymouth affair, 'thought it right to adopt some other persons').

[2] *Correspondence of George IV*, ed. Aspinall, i. 245, note. The promise was claimed again in the time of Liverpool, who not only held the same opinion as Perceval, but persuaded the Prince Regent himself (who did not want to fulfil the promise) to express it too.

[3] Ibid., nos. 910, 914, 916–21; C. D. Yonge, *Life and Administration of Lord Liverpool*, iii. 153–4. Eldon expressed a similar opinion about another of the king's promises (Twiss, *Life of Lord Chancellor Eldon*, ii. 381). I do not know what were the precedents upon which Liverpool relied; but I have never come across one in the reign of George III.

The king did nearly all business with the ministers in the room called his closet. He normally saw them one by one. (The Secretaries of State, before 1783—at any rate before 1760—were an exception, for their diplomatic responsibilities were divided geographically, so that a general question of foreign policy could best be discussed with the Secretaries for the northern and southern department together.)[1] Only certain officers had the entrée to the closet. For instance, the Secretary-at-War had it, but the Chancellor of the Exchequer had not,[2] nor had the President of the Board of Trade.[3] A minister had no strict right to discuss anything in the closet but the business of his own department;[4] but a senior minister—especially if he were leader of the House of Commons or had pretensions to consider himself as Prime Minister, could range more freely.[5] Moreover George III himself, in his prime, habitually talked so much, hopping from subject to subject in a desultory way, that the rule confining ministers to the business of their own departments cannot have been very strictly observed.[6]

[1] This seems to have been usual in George II's time. Newcastle complained of the scenes in the closet at his joint audiences with Carteret, whom the king much preferred (W. Coxe, *Pelham Administration*, i. 166). We hear of a set debate between the two Secretaries in the King's presence, 1746 (*Correspondence of Newcastle and Chesterfield*, ed. Lodge, p. 143), and when Newcastle was trying to calm his own jealous fears about the promotion of Henry Fox to be Secretary of State, he argued (among other things) that 'He can seldom see the King without my Lord Holdernesse' (Ilchester, *Henry Fox, First Lord Holland* (London, 1920), i. 269). There are some traces of this practice in George III's reign, but not very many.

[2] Henry Fox assumed that the Chancellor of the Exchequer, even if also leader of the House of Commons, would only get into the closet three or four times in a year with a report of the proceedings of the House (ibid. i. 267). This was one of Pitt's reasons for wishing to be Secretary of State, that the leader of the House might have his own access to the king (Dodington's *Diary*, p. 371).

[3] Shelburne refused to take this post unless he could have as much access to the king as any other Cabinet minister (Fitzmaurice, op. cit. i. 175). It is clear from this claim and from Bute's rejection of it that access to the closet was not normally a privilege of this office (see also Turner and Megaro, *American Historical Review*, xlv. 767-8).

[4] George III commented on George Grenville's attempt to discuss a negotiation which was out of his province, and described him as turning a piece of departmental business into an excuse for a more general discussion (*Letters from George III to Lord Bute*, pp. 87, 99-100). Grenville was leader of the House at this time.

[5] The variety of Newcastle's memoranda for his interviews with the king proves this.

[6] See W. W. Grenville's account of a characteristic audience in which the king touched 'with inconceivable quickness' on all sorts of things (*Courts and Cabinets of*

The business of the closet does not appear, at first sight, to have afforded the ministers much opportunity for collective action. But they knew how to counteract the tendency to separate and confine them. On any question of general political importance, they would agree beforehand what to say, and then go into the closet, one by one, and repeat the identical story. There are many instances of this, of which, perhaps, the most celebrated is the collective resignation of 1746.[1] The geography of the royal palace seems to have favoured this habit: the ministers with access to the closet gathered by themselves in an ante-room, where they could prime each other before they went in, or report on the king's mood and expressions as they came out.[2] But language in the closet could also be concerted from the country houses of England.[3] It was a well recognized practice, and we should therefore remember that the Cabinet with its minutes was not the only institution, though it was the most effective one, where ministers exerted their collective influence and developed their solidarity.[4]

Much has been written about the origins of the Cabinet: historians have been at pains to trace, to date, and to explain the first development of the Cabinet out of the Privy Council and that of the inner, or 'efficient' Cabinet out of the larger, or

George III, i. 189). Grenville referred again to the king's desultory habits of conversation in 1789 (ibid. ii. 169–70).

[1] For the resignation of 1746 see Newcastle's letter to Chesterfield, 18 Feb. 1745/6 in *Private Correspondence of Chesterfield and Newcastle*, ed. Lodge, pp. 108, 111. Other instances of artificial unanimity in the closet are found during George Grenville's ministry, in *Grenville Papers*, iii. 146, 166; during the first Rockingham Ministry, in *The Duke of Newcastle's Narrative of Changes in the Ministry*, ed. Bateson, pp. 43–45, 72–73.

[2] According to the story reported by Henry Fox (*Life and Letters of Lady Sarah Lennox*, i. 13), Pitt insulted Bute before 'the whole Cabinet Council', waiting in 'the inward room at St. James's', and kept the king waiting for him. Further light is thrown on the geography of this or another 'inward room' by a reminiscence of the third Lord Holland: while he and Windham, who were the last to go into the closet, waited 'in the outer room which is between the Closet and the ante-room', Windham started an embarrassing conversation which Holland feared the Lords of the Bedchamber, who were at the door (presumably between the ante-room and the 'outer room'), would overhear (*Memoirs of the Whig Party*, ii. 204).

[3] Temple, at Stowe, promised Bedford, at Woburn, to give the same answers as Rockingham (then in London) if the king should send for them (*The Duke of Newcastle's Narrative of Changes in the Ministry*, p. 134).

[4] The closet probably lost much of its importance in the reign of George IV, who spent much of his time, even in the parliamentary session, at Windsor or even Brighton, and often dealt with his ministers through private secretaries: Wellington

formal Cabinet.[1] We may safely accept Mr. Sedgwick's conclusion that the inner Cabinet—the direct ancestor of the modern
Cabinet—was in existence at least as early as 1740 and probably
some years before that. We cannot so easily date the withering
of the larger, or formal Cabinet. It certainly existed in 1761;[2]
but it was soon afterwards reduced to certain specialized sur-
vivals, such as the 'Hanging Cabinets' for receiving the reports
of the Recorder of London and the 'Grand Cabinet' for considering the king's speech at the beginning of the parliamentary
session.[3] Since these processes were almost complete before
George III began to reign, it would be beside my point to discuss at length the reason why successive layers of formality were
thus peeled off in order to reach the kernel of intimacy and confidence. No doubt many causes coincided. The king or the Prime
Minister wished to separate those whose advice he wanted from
those others whose advice he had to pretend to want because of
their social eminence or political power. War, then as now, required institutions of special secrecy.[4] George I's and George II's

once complained that he had sometimes passed five months without seeing the
king (*Journal of Mrs. Arbuthnot*, ed. Bamford and the Duke of Wellington, i. 99).

[1] D. A. Winstanley, 'George III and his First Cabinet', *English Historical Review*,
xvii. 678–91; H. W. V. Temperley, 'Inner and Outer Cabinet and Privy Council',
ibid. xxvii. 682–99; Sir William Anson, 'The Cabinet in the Seventeenth and
Eighteenth Centuries', ibid. xxix. 56–78; H. W. V. Temperley, 'A Note on Inner
and Outer Cabinets', ibid. xxxi. 291–6; R. R. Sedgwick, 'The Inner Cabinet from
1739 to 1741', ibid. xxxiv. 290–302; and the vast mass of undigested fact in E. R.
Turner, *The Cabinet Council of England, 1622–1784* (Baltimore, 1930–2).

[2] George Grenville was admitted to the outer Cabinet, Feb. 1761 (*Grenville
Papers*, i. 359), but he would not have seen any papers if Jenkinson had not, at
Bute's command, sent him abstracts (ibid. 361). In Bentham's phrase, he was in
the Cabinet, but not 'with the Circulation'.

[3] Lord Colchester described George III as holding a 'Grand Cabinet' or
'Honorary Cabinet' to read the King's Speech in Jan. 1806 (*Diaries*, ii. 26), and
Mrs. Arbuthnot reported in Feb. 1829 that 'The Duke and all the Council' (by
which, I think, she meant the 'Grand Cabinet') are gone down to Windsor to
settle the speech with the King' (*Journals*, ii. 234).

[4] Even within the 'efficient Cabinet' a secret inner circle sometimes negotiated
peace or directed a campaign without the knowledge of their colleagues: thus there
were concentric circles of secrecy in 1762 (*Letters of George III to Lord Bute, 1756–1766*,
pp. 94, 119, 125). In 1782 the king, Shelburne, and Grantham kept the negotiation
in their own hands, to the great annoyance of Richmond (*Correspondence of George III*,
nos. 3918, 4055). During the conferences at Lille in 1797 the Cabinet minutes were
specially edited so that the outer circle might know little or nothing of Malmesbury's
secret discussions with Maret (*Hist. MSS. Comm., Dropmore MSS.* iii. 337, 342–3):
this must have been more effective than the device mentioned by Canning in
Diaries and Correspondence of Lord Malmesbury, iii. 416, note, which looks like a joke

absences from Hanover made it convenient to establish a standing committee to correspond with them about secret affairs. Perhaps, moreover, it is no accident that the definitive establishment of the 'efficient' Cabinet took place not long after the death of Queen Caroline, when George II no longer possessed the force to impose his decisions upon the politicians.

The king himself sat at the Hanging Cabinets and the Grand Cabinets for the speech, but only summoned the efficient Cabinet to his presence on specially important political emergencies. George did so on 21 June 1779, and declared, in a long speech, his intention to carry on the American war to the bitter end; his real purpose was to deter North's enemies from their eternal sniping at the Prime Minister.[1] He presided at another Cabinet in January 1781, to discuss the question of accepting mediation; some of the members showed that they were uncertain about the drill for a meeting in the sovereign's presence, which is not surprising if such a meeting was a rarity.[2] He was present again on 26 January 1784, at the height of the political crisis, and spoke with agitation of his determination to abdicate rather than 'be put bound hand and foot into the hands of Mr. Fox'. This time, again, he meant to stiffen his ministers' resolution rather than take their advice.[3]

The king had a right to the Cabinet's advice if he asked for it. He could command a Privy Councillor to attend Cabinet, even though that Privy Councillor did not regularly sit there by right of office.[4] Ministers in dudgeon often vapoured about refusing to go to Cabinets in future. This could be tolerated when they only meant to demonstrate their hostility to their colleagues; but the king might treat it as a breach of duty to himself. That is why George III expelled Devonshire from the Privy Council in 1761. Devonshire, out of mere faction, wished to escape the responsibility for the peace treaty, although he could have had no objection to the terms, by refusing to come to Council; George III rightly treated him as having broken his councillor's

---

of Canning's). In the same Ministry Grenville considered it a mistake to discuss military affairs in a big Cabinet, and many decisions were taken by smaller groups (*Hist. MSS. Comm., Dropmore MSS.* iv. 224, v. 217, 247, 270, 487).

[1] *Correspondence of George III*, nos. 2670, 2674; *Hist. MSS. Comm., Various Collections*, vi. 260, 267.   [2] Ibid., p. 272.

[3] *Political Memoranda of Francis, Fifth Duke of Leeds* (ed Browning), p. 96.

[4] *Bedford Correspondence*, iii. 41.

oath.[1] Yet there might be occasions when not only particular ministers, but the whole Cabinet would withhold its advice. Something of this sort happened in the obscure dispute over the Regency in 1765. George III wished to make his ministers responsible in parliament for the Regency Bill; they seem to have resolved to avoid this responsibility, either because they genuinely thought that a proposal which only concerned the royal family was no business of theirs[2] or because they feared that the king would want power to name his unpopular mother as Regent.[3] At first they held a Cabinet, at his command, and approved the proposal generally; but when they foresaw trouble in the House of Commons, they tried hard to escape from further responsibility. The king spoke of referring the matter to Council, and asked Grenville whether he thought the Council would give him their opinion; Grenville replied that those who knew of the proposal already (that is, the Cabinet) might do so, but the other members might demand time for consideration. A few days later, the Cabinet itself went on strike: the Lord Chancellor refused to attend another meeting on this question, saying he had given his opinion already; Mansfield thought the subject improper for a Cabinet but would not object to an informal meeting. Such a meeting was held, but the members would only deliver a verbal opinion through a Secretary of State, instead of the written minute for which the king clamoured. As a result

---

[1] *Letters from George III to Lord Bute, 1756–1766*, pp. 143–4; see also Bute's letter to Granby, Add. MSS. 36797, f. 20, and his letter to George Townshend, quoted by Namier, *England in the Age of the American Revolution*, p. 433. Devonshire was expelled from the Council after his dismissal from his post as Lord Chamberlain; but he had committed his offence before it, at a time when he was a member of the formal Cabinet though he had withdrawn from the efficient Cabinet. The king had also inquired in Sept. whether Mansfield, Lord Chief Justice, had been at the Cabinet— 'if he has not, it is the greatest mark of disrespect ever showed to my commands' (*Letters from George III to Lord Bute, 1756–1766*, p. 131).

[2] North did not take this line about the Royal Marriages Bill.

[3] I think this is the true explanation: it would account for their otherwise unintelligible references to Bute, whom most people associated in their minds with the Princess of Wales (*Grenville Papers*, iii. 162). George III accounted for Grenville's ill will by admitting that he had consulted Bedford and the Lord Chancellor first, and then made the matter worse by telling him that 'in ministerial affairs he might perhaps have a colour tho' no reason to complain if not the first consulted, yet in affairs of a family concern & wherein the good of the nation at large was concerned that was not so' (*Correspondence of George III*, no. 139). But this would not account for the obstructiveness of the Ministry as a whole; evidently they felt that, as Lord Granby expressed it, a 'snare' had been set for them, and congratulated themselves on getting out of it.

of all this informality and indecision the ministers contradicted each other in parliament, and everybody was made to look ridiculous. The whole episode was a cause, though not the proximate cause, of their dismissal in the summer of that year.[1]

The king, then (this exception notwithstanding) had a right to demand the Cabinet's advice. It was more doubtful whether he had a duty to do so. Shelburne once defined the proper procedure as follows: 'I conceive the natural course of business to be, first for the Department to submit any business to Your Majesty, and to be consider'd afterwards by the Cabinet under Your Majesty's reference.' George III replied, 'the Minister of the Department used always to ask the permission of the King to lay such a point before the Cabinet, as he cldnt chuse to venture to take the direction of the Crown upon without such sanction; then the advice came with propriety'.[2] If neither the king nor the departmental minister saw the necessity for such reference, none could be claimed; as Carteret once said, 'he knew very well that the King might take a foreign measure with his secretary of state only, but that if the King referred the matter to the council the opinion of the majority of the council was the measure'.[3] George III and his ministers continued to act upon this plan for many years. In 1775 Rochford referred to a departmental decision which the king had approved, and added that whether Suffolk agreed with it was 'now immaterial, as Cabinet need not be consulted upon it'.[4] In 1799 the king and Dundas agreed to ratify the Duke of York's capitulation with the French; Lord Grenville would have liked to complain, but recognized that they were within their rights in taking this decision without consulting the Cabinet, and that he had nothing to say to it.[5] Ministers might urge the king to refer matters to Cabinet; indeed, they often did so,[6] especially when they disagreed with his opinion. Jenkinson, at a time when North's Ministry was at sixes and sevens and half its members were

---

[1] *Correspondence of George III*, nos. 48, 52–54, 56–59, 139; *Grenville Papers*, iii. 25–37, 125–62.

[2] *Correspondence of George III*, nos. 3699, 3700.

[3] Quoted by D. A. Winstanley, *English Historical Review*, xvii. 691.

[4] *Correspondence of George III*, no. 1617.

[5] *Hist. MSS. Comm., Dropmore MSS.* v. 502–4.

[6] For example, Barrington appears to have done so in 1778 and Sandwich in 1781 (*Correspondence of George III*, nos. 2155, 3404).

trying to run away, entreated the king 'not to suffer any great question of policy to rest singly on discourses in your closet between Your Majesty and Lord North, or any one of your Ministers, but to refer the same to your council for their deliberation, with orders for them to report to your Majesty their opinion thereupon'.[1] But this was originally in the king's discretion, and his alone.

At some time, however, in George III's reign, the Cabinet must have established its right to consider matters or, at least, formed the habit of considering matters without any reference from the king. This change, perhaps the most important in the history of the institution, has never been dated exactly, so far as I know. Very likely the Cabinet may have taken liberties of this sort during the lax administration of Lord North, if not earlier.[2] But the right seems to have been claimed expressly for the first time in the second Rockingham Ministry. Shelburne's and George III's statements of the proper procedure, quoted above, were protests against what they considered as an innovation attempted by Rockingham or Charles Fox. 'Certainly', said the king, 'it is quite new for business to be laid before the Cabinet and consequently advice offered by the Ministers to the Crown unasked.' There are other indications, though slight ones, that Fox, at least, claimed for the Cabinet an initiative independent of the king's permission.[3] It would be consistent with his known principles to do so, and it would explain one of the mysteries of his career. No evidence has yet come to light,[4] to show why Fox was so much surprised when the king procured the defeat of his East India Bill in 1783. He privately accused George III of 'treachery', and one of his newspapers asserted that the king had expressed his concurrence with the bill 'a

[1] *Correspondence of George III*, no. 3504.

[2] Sandwich apologized in 1779 for sending off a Cabinet instruction to an admiral before the king could see it (ibid., no. 2741); but this is not quite the same thing as bringing a question before the Cabinet without the king's approval.

[3] Possibly I am reading too much into an exchange between the king and Fox in June 1782; but it looks as though George III instructed Fox to refer a matter to the Cabinet before offering any opinion on it, and Fox replied, with special intention, that he had always meant to do so (ibid., nos. 3803, 3809). George III himself encouraged these ministers' tendency to discuss matters first among themselves; for he disliked personal intercourse with them so much that he usually told them to send a Cabinet minute without attending him (ibid., nos. 3630, 4316).

[4] I wish to thank Professor Herbert Butterfield for helping me, though without result, to clear up this mystery by consulting the Windsor archives on my behalf.

thousand times in the closet'. Fox himself, however, never dared to claim this in public; perhaps this was because he knew that even if the Cabinet had formally had the king's permission to bring in a bill (which it must have had, or the subject could not have been mentioned in the King's Speech), it had done so without ever explaining the contents properly to him or getting from him his explicit consent.[1]

Pitt undoubtedly used the same liberty as Fox, though perhaps without making any formal claim to it. It is not easy to find traces of this, for informality of procedure almost amounted to disintegration in the later years of his long Ministry.[2] But the celebrated misunderstanding about Catholic Emancipation illustrates very well the length to which this licence had gone. Pitt had received every warning of George III's prejudices about this subject, and he knew what those warnings meant;[3] yet a body which Castlereagh (who could not have been mistaken) regarded as the Cabinet, took, in the autumn of 1799, a decision which authorized the Lord Lieutenant to give vague, but far from meaningless, assurances to the Irish Catholics. The same body held set debates upon this subject in September and December 1800. The king may have suspected that this was going on—though even that is not certain; but he never had any official knowledge of it and, indeed, the Cabinet, as such, never made any official communication to him about Catholic

---

[1] *Memorials and Correspondence of Charles James Fox*, ii. 221; *Parl. Hist.* xxiv. 153. Burke wrote, in the *Annual Register* for 1784–5, p. 69, that 'it seemed to the last degree improbable that they [the ministers] should have adopted a measure of such infinite importance, without knowing, or contrary to the inclinations of the king'. This passage (to which Miss L. S. Sutherland has kindly drawn my attention) is more likely to be a polite way of saying that the king was consulted than an attempt to conceal the fact that he was not. But since the king, at this time, tried to avoid all discussions with Fox, and Fox had no wish to encourage his interference, it is unlikely that the matter was fully explained between them.

[2] I shall touch upon this later, pp. 161–2.

[3] George III had pointedly warned him on this subject in 1795, adding that he did not believe a Cabinet of ministers could carry this point 'without previous concert with the leading men of every order in the state' (Stanhope, *Life of Pitt*, ii. Appendix, p. xxv). He did not, however, say on that occasion that he would never consent. In 1798 or 1799 the king suspected that Pitt was entering into some engagement, but did not know it, and had to ask Dundas, who replied, in effect, that the question was still open (R. Mackintosh, *Life of Sir James Mackintosh* (London, 1835), i. 170). Pitt told Grenville in Feb. 1799 that he would write to the king 'to remonstrate a little against the notions which he seems forming every day, more and more, of excluding the Catholics in case of an Union' (*Hist. MSS. Comm.*, *Dropmore MSS.* iv. 468).

Emancipation before he burst out and forbade it to do so.[1] With every allowance for the demands of the war and the nervous breakdown from which Pitt had long suffered, one cannot regard this as pure inadvertence or pure cowardice: the Cabinet must have been in the habit, at this time, of taking the old king's consent for granted, in great and small matters, and discussing whatever it thought proper without his previous permission.

George III was not ready to put up with the loss of his control over the Cabinet's deliberations: thereafter he began to ask ministers to bind themselves not to propose measures which he could not accept. He obtained such a promise, in effect, about Catholic Emancipation from Pitt in 1804; but he had to waive his request for a pledge against proposals for army reform in 1806, and when he asked for a similar one against Catholic Emancipation next year, he aroused a storm of outraged whig virtue. The Cabinet of All the Talents declared:

the absolute impossibility of their thus fettering the free exertion of their judgment. Those who are entrusted by your Majesty with the administration of your extensive empire, are bound by every obligation to submit to your Majesty without reserve the best advice which they can frame to meet the various exigences and dangers of the times.[2]

More significantly, the 'tory' Spencer Perceval prevailed with George III not to ask for a pledge in 1809, representing that the presence of some anti-Catholics in the Cabinet would be a suffi-

---

[1] *Memoirs and Correspondence of Viscount Castlereagh*, iii. 418, iv. 8–12, 20–21, 83. There was a controversy whether the question had ever been submitted to Cabinet and approved there by a majority. Lord Grenville asserted that it had (*Courts and Cabinets of George III*, iii. 129); and this is consistent with his repeated statement that only Cabinet ministers were obliged to resign when their advice was disregarded (*Hist. MSS. Comm., Dropmore MSS.* vi. 436). Loughborough, Portland, and Dundas, on the other hand, denied this (see George III's letter to Addington in Pellew, *Life of Sidmouth*, i. 305, and *Diaries and Correspondence of George Rose*, i. 302–3). This contradiction can best be explained by supposing that there was a meeting, whose formal status was never defined because it did not result in an immediate submission to the king. George III's surprise seems to have been genuine (see his letter to Addington (Pellew, *Life of Sidmouth*, i. 285), in which he seems not to know Pitt's opinion). He reproached Grenville for the omission to consult him beforehand (ibid. i. 298).

[2] This minute is printed by Lord Holland in his *Memoirs of the Whig Party*, ii. 319, and in *Hist. MSS. Comm., Dropmore MSS.* ix. 119. See also Brand's resolution to the same effect which the House of Commons rejected (*Parl. Debates*, ix. 284–348).

cient guarantee against any attempt to bring forward Catholic Emancipation as a Government measure.[1] Perhaps the most remarkable statement of the Cabinet's freedom to consider whatever it liked came from Lord Chancellor Eldon in 1812.

As to the Proposal that the Roman Catholic claims should be taken into consideration by Cabinet, I conceive it to be the duty of Government to consider in Cabinet the claims of any body of His Majesty's subjects, and to decide upon them bonâ fide whenever the attention of Government is called to that consideration by any member of Cabinet acting upon his sense of public duty.[2]

Not a word of the king's previous permission; yet Eldon, even more than Perceval, may be considered as a tory. The Cabinet was well on the way to the nineteenth-century procedure, by which any of its members could cause it to meet upon any subject within his department. Only on special occasions did prudence suggest the expediency of first obtaining the sovereign's permission before calling upon the Cabinet to entertain a proposal which he was known or suspected to dislike—as Wellington asked George IV to sanction a series of preliminary and confidential consultations before the question of Catholic Emancipation was even put to the Cabinet,[3] or Gladstone submitted the heads of the Irish Church Disestablishment Bill to Queen Victoria before he discussed it with the Cabinet.[4]

The opinions which the ministers put before the king were usually the collective sense of the Cabinet; but nobody denied his right to ask for separate opinions in writing. George III and his successor sometimes did so at Cabinet crises.[5] In 1825 George IV required separate answers in writing about the Cabinet's South American policy; he received a collective Cabinet minute, but

---

[1] Spencer Walpole, *Life of the Rt. Hon. Spencer Perceval*, ii. 23–6.

[2] *Correspondence of George IV*, ed. Aspinall, no. 90. Lord Holland's description of Cabinet practice (the best we have for this period) gives the same impression that the king's consent might be given but was not necessary: 'There are no precise laws or rules, nor even any well-established or understood usages which mark what measures in each department are or are not to be communicated to the Cabinet. ... There is nothing but private agreement or party feeling generally, or the directions of the King accidentally, which obliges even a Secretary for Foreign Affairs to consult his colleagues on any of the duties of his office, before he takes the King's pleasure upon them' (*Memoirs of the Whig Party*, ii. 85).

[3] *Wellington, Despatches (Continuation)*, iv. 564, 573, v. 253, 268.

[4] *The Queen and Mr. Gladstone*, ed. P. Guedalla (London, 1933), i. 151.

[5] George III did so in Jan. 1806 (C. D. Yonge, op. cit. i. 207), George IV in May 1812 (ibid. i. 393; *Correspondence of George IV*, ed. Aspinall, nos. 84, 86–93).

the Prime Minister did not pretend that the demand for separate opinions had been improper—he only argued that it was needless to comply with it because his colleagues were agreed, after a full discussion, upon the answer to be returned.[1] Nor was it usually thought improper for the king to ask his ministers to report the opinions expressed in a Cabinet discussion. North, for example, told him in December 1777 which ministers had voted for and against a certain decision.[2] According to Mrs. Arbuthnot (who had it from Wellington), George IV asked Liverpool, in December 1824, whether the Cabinet was unanimous in a recommendation it had lately sent him, and Liverpool 'fairly told him all the shades of difference'.[3] More objection might, perhaps, be taken to the practice of reporting incomplete discussions in the Cabinet, especially when this was done by ministers who possessed the king's special confidence but were not titular Prime Ministers. Northington and Egmont sometimes sent George III such reports in the first Rockingham Ministry and Shelburne in the second.[4] But there is only one suggestion, in George III's correspondence, that anybody would have considered this a violation of an obligation to secrecy. This was in a Ministry dominated by Charles Fox, whose opinion on the relations of the king and the Cabinet was abnormal at the time.[5]

Indeed, some of George III's ministers claimed the right to lay protests or dissenting minutes before the king. The elder Pitt tried to induce him to accept such a protest in October 1761,[6]

---

[1] *Journal of Mrs. Arbuthnot*, i. 373–4; *Wellington, Despatches (Continuation)*, ii. 403.

[2] *Correspondence of George III*, no. 2126. There was a curious incident a little later in the same year: the Cabinet directed Lord George Germain to report its advice orally to the king, and North sent a note (which seems to have been lost) which he hoped the king would read before Germain arrived (ibid. 2153, 2156).

[3] *Journal of Mrs. Arbuthnot*, i. 367.

[4] *Correspondence of George III*, nos. 102, 446 (misplaced in Fortescue's edn.), 303, 304, 307, 3676, 3693, 3785, 3824.   [5] Ibid., no. 3824.

[6] 'Mr. Pitt brought his paper, or rather protest, this day to the King, and offered it to his Majesty, who declined accepting it. My Lord Bute was present, and said "As you, Sir, have given your reasons, it is but reasonable that those who dissent from you should give theirs also." And I think it was agreed that Mr. Pitt's paper should be inserted in the minute with our dissent' (Newcastle to Hardwicke 21 Sept. 1761, printed by Albemarle in *Memoirs of the Marquess of Rockingham*, i. 371; the paper is printed by P. C. Yorke, op. cit., iii. 275). Newcastle thought this a very improper proceeding: Pitt would be wanting to publish the protest in the House of Commons (ibid., iii. 323). That was just what Pitt did want, according to Horace Walpole—indeed, he went further and suggested in parliament that it would be a

and Conway in 1766.[1] Lord Grenville told the king in 1795 that he did not agree with the Cabinet minute he was sending, and the king replied that he was sorry when his ministers disagreed but did not wish them to conceal it.[2] A little later, Pitt had to transmit a dissenting minute by Grenville;[3] Windham would have liked to dissent but did not know the procedure for doing so, and we hear of a dissenting minute from Lord Pelham in 1801 and a sort of *caveat* from Canning in 1821.[4] Perhaps the most mischievous minute of dissent was that of Wellesley in 1812, who contrived to show the Prince Regent that he would have liked to grant him a larger Civil List than his colleagues would allow.[5] On none of these occasions did the dissentient minister resign, nor—which is more important—did the king take advantage of the division of opinion to prefer the minority's view to that of the majority, or even to have the question reopened.

Separate opinions and dissenting minutes were exceptional; as a rule, the strength of the Cabinet lay in the fact that its advice was collective. We have not much evidence as to the procedure which brought forth these minutes; no doubt, one Cabinet differed from another then, as now. It seems to have been understood that the departmental minister, in charge of the business referred to the Cabinet, would open the discussion and give his colleagues a lead—at least, when Halifax failed in this duty, they complained of his 'deadness', though Sir James Harris reported that, at a Cabinet dinner which he attended by special invitation in 1787, the Foreign Secretary was almost the only person who said nothing upon a question of foreign policy.[6] The other ministers then gave their opinions 'seriatim', and the minister in charge drew up a minute which the other members

good thing if every Cabinet minister had to sign his opinion separately, as the repealed clauses of the Act of Settlement had enjoined (Horace Walpole, *Memoirs of the Reign of George III*, ed. Russell Barker, i. 74, 103; ii. 186). The elder Pitt's opinions of ministerial responsibility were heterodox, as I shall show later (*v. infra*, p. 166 note 1).

[1] *Correspondence of George III*, nos. 482, 483 (printed by Fortescue in inverted order). This was not so much a protest as an alternative scheme; George III disregarded it.

[2] *Hist. MSS. Comm., Dropmore MSS.* iii. 50.

[3] J. Holland Rose, *Pitt and Napoleon*, p. 242.

[4] *Hist. MSS. Comm., Dropmore MSS.* v. 306, viii. 486; *Diaries and Correspondence of Lord Malmesbury*, iv. 73; Yonge, op. cit. iii. 33.

[5] Spencer Walpole, op. cit. ii. 231.

[6] *Grenville Papers*, ii. 515; *Diaries and Correspondence of Lord Malmesbury*, ii. 303.

had some opportunity of amending.[1] An absent minister could have his name recorded in it if he agreed with the conclusions— for, after all, it was his share of the collective responsibility that counted rather than his presence at the meeting.[2] He might have his opinion delivered for him by another, or even give his proxy to another—though instances of this are rare.[3] The minute was then transmitted to the king by the departmental minister or the Prime Minister. George III kept these minutes and his ministers sometimes kept copies.[4] Very often—especially in later years—the meeting did not result in a minute, but in the approval of a dispatch to an ambassador, a colonial governor or a military commander. Such dispatches, if also approved by the king, were regarded as covered by the responsibility of the Cabinet, and Lord Auckland once suggested this explanation for the fact that a British Foreign Secretary did his business through his own agents abroad rather than foreign ministers at the Court of St. James: a dispatch engaged the collective responsibility of his colleagues before parliament more definitely than a conversation.[5]

[1] Grafton, *Autobiography*, p. 230. George III seems to have congratulated Hillsborough on his fairness and skill in doctoring a Cabinet minute (*Correspondence of George III*, no. 598).

This incident relates to the circular letter of 21 April 1768; that of which Grafton complains to the circular of 9 May 1769.

[2] Ibid., no. 3172.

[3] Ibid., nos. 652, 4421; *Hist. MSS. Comm., Dropmore MSS.* ii. 403.

[4] *Political Memoranda of Francis, Duke of Leeds*, ed. Browning, p. 173. In 1790 Thurlow wished the Cabinet minutes of 1783 could be recovered, as they would settle a disputed question; but he did not speak as if there were any means of doing this (*Hist. MSS. Comm., Dropmore MSS.* i. 576).

[5] *Bedford Correspondence*, iii. 137; *Journal and Correspondence of Lord Auckland*, ii. 394. On occasions, however, Secretaries of State did not consider themselves absolved from personal responsibility by this collective sanction. In 1761 the elder Pitt thought of making his fellow Secretary sign a dispatch which he disapproved, as an alternative to resigning (Add. MSS. 32028, f. 299); Leeds did this, and the younger Pitt suggested it as a compromise which might make it unnecessary for Lord Grenville to resign at once (*Political Memoranda of Francis, Duke of Leeds*, pp. 158, 166; *Hist. MSS. Comm., Dropmore MSS.* ii. 54, iii. 30). This was all wrong: when Egremont argued that '*his head* was concerned in writing a proper letter to Spain upon this occasion', Lord Royston remarked that 'every Minister at the Board was equally responsible to his country for the advice he gave, and for the manner in which that advice was carried into execution' (Albemarle, *Memoirs of the Marquess of Rockingham*, i. 58). Sometimes, on the other hand, the Secretary of State's colleagues suspected him of misrepresenting their sense in his dispatches, or altering them after the Cabinet had approved of them; their best protection was to insist on a formal Cabinet minute as a more unequivocal record of the decisions than any dispatch. The elder Pitt's colleagues threatened to do this in 1761 (Add. MSS. 32926, f. 187).

This procedure was followed more exactly in certain Cabinets than in others. It was much relaxed in the later years of North's Ministry and in that of the younger Pitt. North's memory and his will were breaking down, he could not make up his mind, and he was too much given to taking decisions in holes and corners with two or three colleagues—perhaps underlings—whom he found congenial. We hear of an important dispatch read out when some of the members were on their feet to go away, or had even gone. Hillsborough complained of Lord North's 'flimsy way of doing business' and Sandwich had to recommend to the king that 'the advice to be given to your Majesty from the meetings should (as was usual before) be reduced into writing, and when a question is agitated there it ought to be decided one way or the other, and not put off as now most frequently happens, without any determination'.[1]

Pitt was even more inclined to do business with special intimates. Leeds might complain of the 'marble' in his composition, and Thurlow or Richmond of the want of confidence and communication within the Cabinet;[2] these great colleagues were necessary to him, but he never cared for them. Even his cousin Grenville only wrote and received from him such letters as one man of marble might write to another who was engaged in the same cause. It was Pitt's men of business and, above all, his young men, who had his real confidence and saw his real face. He scarcely ever rode with Dundas without doing some business, and once shut himself up with him for ten days at Wimbledon in order to master the complexities of the Bengal revenue settlement; now he called in Auckland to help him with the finances, and now Addington; at another time he is described as transacting everything in 'a sure little junto', with 'Ryder and young Jenky'. These men were treated to the persiflage of his intimate letters, the bad jokes of which even Canning complained, the habit of 'quizzing things away' which so much shocked the solemn Windham; the dazzling personal charm which sprang forth, unprompted, in the libraries of country

---

[1] *Correspondence of George III*, no. 2775; *Hist. MSS. Comm., Bathurst MSS.*, p. 18. Many were the complaints, at this time, against 'Lord North's interior Cabinet' (*Hist. MSS. Comm., Stopford-Sackville MSS.* i. 266; *Lothian MSS.*, p. 343; *Abergavenny MSS.*, pp. 26, 28).

[2] *Political Memoranda of Francis, Duke of Leeds*, pp. 102, 148–9; *Diaries and Correspondence of Lord Malmesbury*, ii. 257.

houses or at other accidental times and places. It was this charm, and the semi-official confidences reposed almost casually now in one ally or henchman, now in another, which made them compete so fiercely—almost like rival sultanas—for his favour and, after his death, for his political heritage. But it was a bad way of doing business. Moreover the king was too old to pull the Ministry together as he had done in Lord North's time.

At no time, however, did the Cabinet cease to meet and to give its advice in the form of Cabinet minutes. It was an open question whether the king was constitutionally bound to take this advice. George III and some of his ministers spoke, from time to time, as if he might exercise a right to reject it;[1] but it is much harder to point to occasions when he actually did so, and most of these concern particular departments over which he was recognized as having special control. For instance, even Charles Fox hardly liked to join issue with the king for rejecting a Cabinet minute about his eldest son's allowance, and North's Ministry seem to have acquiesced in his rejection of their recommendation about sending a regiment to Jamaica.[2] Catholic Emancipation is not a perfect example of the exercise of this right; for no Cabinet minute was ever presented in 1801, and the Catholic Bill of 1807 was withdrawn because the king's consent had been obtained by a misunderstanding.[3] In the subsequent controversy about the pledge, the Cabinet did not claim more than the right to submit whatever they thought proper 'for your Majesty's decision'.[4] Nevertheless, it would probably be true to say that

[1] According to Gilbert Elliot, the king told Pitt in 1761 that even if the Cabinet had been unanimous in recommending war with Spain, he should have been very unwilling to agree to it (G. F. S. Elliot, *The Border Elliots*, p. 367), and in the next summer he said he did not see how he could take his ministers' advice when he was sure it was wrong (*Letters from George III to Lord Bute*, p. 127). A Cabinet at which only three ministers were present asked him to refer their recommendation to a fuller Cabinet rather than reject it (*Correspondence of George III*, no. 3410), and Lord Grenville wrote in 1796 as though it was not inconceivable that the king might refuse to comply with a Cabinet minute (*Hist. MSS. Comm., Dropmore MSS.* iii. 169).

[2] Fox excused himself for giving way in the dispute over the Prince's allowance, saying 'everybody will not see the distinction between this and political points so strongly as the Ministers have done' (*Memorials and Correspondence of Charles James Fox*, ii. 116; see also *Correspondence of George III*, nos. 4380, 4384–6, 4390, 4391, 4393). The king rejected the Cabinet's advice to send a regiment to Jamaica in Jan. 1779. Lord George Germain was annoyed but docs not seem to have been able to do anything (*Hist. MSS. Comm., Various Collections*, vi. 155).

[3] Perhaps, rather by sharp practice (M. Roberts in *English Historical Review*, l. 69.)

[4] The minute is in Lord Holland's *Memoirs of the Whig Party*, ii. 312–15. A similar

he was expected to accept the Cabinet's advice, and would find great difficulty in avoiding it. He was aware of this, and it was one of the reasons why he resented the behaviour of Lord Grenville, whom he suspected of presenting all business for the first time in the form of Cabinet minutes which had to be accepted.[1] When he wanted the Cabinet to take account of his opinion, he tried to express it early before his ministers had formed their own; and when they had done so, he acquiesced in it even when he thought it scarcely consistent with national or personal dignity.[2] He might demand a reconsideration or a personal explanation; but in the last resort he yielded.[3] Thus, before the end of his political life, his ministers—and not only his 'whig' ministers—were coming to believe that if they sincerely thought it necessary to insist upon their own opinion, the king must follow it. Canning expressed their doctrine in 1809, when he assumed that every member of the royal family was in the same position as the king, namely that the Cabinet was not responsible for him unless he took its advice *in toto*.[4]

This responsibility of the Cabinet for advice given to the king, and accepted by him, was its primary responsibility. It was concerned with the king's service. The general well-being of the country, the improvement of social conditions or political machinery, were not immediately related to that service unless they touched public finance or commercial treaties. A Cabinet minister was bound to propose, and even, perhaps, to insist upon, anything which was, in his opinion, necessary for the

controversy about the Cabinet's right to propose measures of army reform had come to a similar conclusion: Lord Grenville had been content with the liberty of proposing, and admitted that the king decided in the last resort (*Hist. MSS. Comm.*, *Dropmore MSS.* viii. 9).

[1] This is apparent in the king's complaint and Grenville's excuse about the dissolution of parliament, Oct. 1806 (ibid. viii. 382–4). There is (ibid., pp. 380–2) a very curious letter in which the Prince of Wales recommends Grenville to spring the decision upon the king at the last moment. Charles Fox must have thought of a Cabinet minute as a kind of sanction against the king, for he promised to let George III off one if he would accept his own (Fox's) letter as having the force of one (ibid. viii. 50).

[2] Ibid. iii. 170, 173–4, 256, 284, 327, 330. On some of these occasions the king was only giving his ministers rope, for he was sure the French would not agree to the terms proposed. Even so, his pride was mortified. He reserved his liberty of action as Elector of Hanover; for that his ministers were not responsible (ibid. iii. 134, 228, 311).

[3] Ibid. iii. 230; vi. 258, 277–9.

[4] Spencer Walpole, op. cit. i. 322.

king's service; he was not equally bound to insist upon anything which he thought right in itself. This distinction is clear, for example, from the younger Pitt's behaviour over Catholic Emancipation in 1801. He had to resign office when the king would not even let him propose a measure necessary for his service; but, even before he gave his celebrated pledge against raising the question again, he did not think of going down to the House of Commons and moving a resolution. Nowadays a politician would not lose twenty-four hours before doing so, if he thought the measure right; but Pitt had never considered the question in terms of right, only in terms of expediency for the king's service, a mattter on which he had changed his mind but now made it up, and could not have his advice rejected without resigning.[1] Grenville's attitude in 1807 was much the same; he had come to the conclusion that the war could not be won without recruiting more Catholic soldiers in Ireland for general service, and that this could not be done without altering the army laws; and it was because the king would not even listen to advice proposed for his own service that Grenville accused him, in effect, of violating the constitution.[2]

This is an important distinction, for it explains what we find hard to understand in the attitude of politicians to legislation. We are inclined to accuse Pitt of lukewarmness in the cause of humanity and reform, or to marvel at the curious arrangement by which Catholic Emancipation remained an open question for seventeen years within the Cabinet. But these were not generally considered as being matters of government, as government was then understood. The king's service very seldom required legislation—except, of course, financial legislation. When it did, the bill would be gone through in Cabinet, in order to make sure that the ministers should not contradict each other in Parliament.[3] But very few of the proposed laws which we consider, in

---

[1] Pellew, op. cit., i. 293; *Memoirs and Correspondence of Viscount Castlereagh*, iv. 39. When Grenville said (*Hist. MSS. Comm., Dropmore MSS.* vi. 436) that he hoped very few ministers not in the Cabinet would resign, he probably had the same thing in mind. The Cabinet ministers were responsible for advising the king what was necessary for his service, and could not remain if it was not taken. Castlereagh and Cornwallis were more definitely pledged to the Catholics than Pitt and Grenville, more convinced supporters of Catholic Emancipation; yet they were both back in office long before Pitt and Grenville—nor did many people think this odd, for they had not been Cabinet ministers.　　　　[2] *Parl. Debates*, ix. 243.

[3] George III recommended that the second Rockingham Cabinet should go

retrospect, to have been most important were Cabinet measures. Parliamentary reform was not, though Pitt and Richmond would have liked to make it so.[1] The abolition of the slave trade was not: though Pitt spoke of treating Dolben's bill and, later, another compromise bill as a Cabinet measure, it does not appear that he ever had to do so; and we only hear of a Cabinet on any part of this business, when the slave trade to the conquered colonies had to be considered—strictly an executive affair.[2] Even Fox and Grenville only did, in 1806, what Pitt is so much blamed for doing—they tried to get a measure agreed by the Cabinet for the abolition of the slave trade, but when they found they could not, they brought in a bill as individuals.[3] Wellington sat for many years in Cabinets which had agreed to consider Catholic Emancipation as an 'open question' because they did not consider it as a matter of government and there were so many other matters of government on which they did agree. Individual ministers spoke for Catholic Emancipation; other individual Ministers spoke against it. Only when it became

through Burke's Economical Reform Bill clause by clause, in order to prevent discrepancies (*Correspondence of George III*, no. 3648). No doubt his real object was to give Shelburne, Thurlow, and Ashburton an opportunity of moderating the bill and tying Rockingham's hands.

[1] *Political Memoranda of Francis, Duke of Leeds*, p. 99. Much has been written about Pitt's attitude to parliamentary reform in 1785 (e.g. by D. G. Barnes, *George III and William Pitt*, pp. 125–30). Considering that Pitt had promised to do everything in his power 'as a man and *as a minister*' for reform, it is certainly curious that he should have thought his honour satisfied by the king's promise not to influence anybody against it; and this may possibly be an example of his alternations of over-confidence and helplessness. But it is clear that he could not have made it a Cabinet question without changing his Cabinet; he may have inherited his father's views about the responsibility of ministers for parliamentary measures (*v. infra*, p. 166, note 1); and above all, his behaviour was, as I have tried to show, not at all unusual for the times. It is worthy of remark that he was satisfied not only with the king's neutrality but with that of his own Secretary of the Treasury (*Diaries and Correspondence of George Rose*, i. 35–37).

[2] Pitt was extremely nettled by Thurlow's opposition to Dolben's bill (*Journals and Correspondence of Lord Auckland*, ii. 221; *Hist. MSS. Comm., Dropmore MSS.* i. 342) and would have made it a Cabinet question if he had not got his way. He is said to have thought of making some compromise on this question a Cabinet measure in 1799 (Bagot, *Canning and his Friends*, i. 151). For Cabinets on the slave trade in the conquered colonies, see *Hist. MSS. Comm., Dropmore MSS.* v. 173, viii. 168.

[3] It appears from Grenville's letter to Sidmouth (ibid. viii. 168) that he would have liked to make it a government measure; but in the end this was not done (*Parl. Debates*, ix. 279). Fox had said that Pitt was a rogue to speak for the abolition of the trade but let Dundas speak on the other side (*Memorials and Correspondence of Charles James Fox*, iii. 131).

a matter of government—that is, of civil war and destruction of property—Wellington insisted on making it a Cabinet question. All this was quite well recognized.[1] Lord Barrington, in George III's early years, argued that 'this bill is brought before the House by an officer of the Crown, but not in consequence of a consultation of the ministers. There will, therefore, be no triumph over administration by getting rid of it.'[2]

[1] Sir H. Cavendish, *Debates*, ed. Wright, i. 25; *Parl. Debates*, ix. 268. I must confess that the distinction I have drawn does not account for all the examples of ministerial insubordination: for example, it does not explain George Grenville's attempt to oppose the Peace of Paris and retain his Secretaryship of State (see my book, *War and Trade in the West Indies*, p. 605), or the flagrant insubordination of Chatham's House of Commons ministers in 1767. Chatham's own opinions on ministerial solidarity seem to have been unusual, or at least archaic. Ministerial discipline in the House of Commons had been extremely slack in Henry Pelham's and Newcastle's time; but this does not excuse the elder Pitt for supporting the West India interest against Legge's sugar tax in 1759 (ibid., p. 511), or for his attempts to make Newcastle responsible for the cost of the war while he took the credit for the successes (*Chatham Correspondence*, i. 305; P. C. Yorke, op. cit. iii. 316; Add. MSS. 32918, f. 467; 32922, f. 21). He seems to have thought, in 1760, that there was some difference between the responsibility for proposing things in the Cabinet himself and for agreeing to the proposals of others (Add. MSS. 32904, f. 259; 32923, f. 65) and, in 1765, that if he were Secretary of State he would have to insist on his own foreign policy, but need not do so if he held any other Cabinet office (Albemarle, op. cit. i. 202). One might argue that worse things than this have happened in coalition Ministries; but that does not explain Chatham's behaviour in his own Ministry of 1766–7. He did not think it right to try to carry through an agreed policy of the Cabinet on the East India question or on American questions. According to Horace Walpole (who probably got his information correctly from Conway) Chatham refused, at an early stage, to hold a Cabinet for deciding upon a parliamentary campaign on the East India question (*Memoirs of the Reign of George III*, ed. Russell Barker, ii. 278). Finding, a little later, that he could not get agreement among his colleagues, he declared that ministers ought to leave this '*capital object of the publick*, upon which Lord Chatham will *stand* or *fall*' to the decision of parliament without giving any lead at all. 'Parliament is *the only place* where I will declare my final judgement upon the whole matter, if ever I have an opportunity to do it. As a servant of the Crown, I have no right or authority to do more than simply to advise that the *demands* and the *offers* of the Company should be laid before Parliament, referring the whole determination to the wisdom of that place' (Grafton, op. cit., pp. 116–17, 124). He even advised Shelburne to treat a somewhat less difficult American question in the same way: 'it ought, on no account, to rest on the advice of meetings of the cabinet, and the course of office: but . . . to be laid before parliament, in order that his Majesty may be founded in, and strengthened by, the sense of his grand council' (*Chatham Correspondence*, iii. 215). This abdication can only be explained in one of two ways: either he was already half mad, or he held opinions about the relations of the executive and the legislature which were less modern than those of any contemporary.

[2] Barrington's speech in Cavendish, *Debates*, ed. Wright, i. 25. Sometimes a Cabinet minute was drawn up for the express purpose of obtaining unanimity in parliament. George III himself demanded one for this purpose (*Correspondence of*

So far, I have discussed the Cabinet as though it were then, what it is now, a separate body standing over against the king. Some Cabinets, indeed, considered themselves in that light. Grenville, Halifax, and the Bedfords may have disliked and suspected each other, but they did their best to make a common front against the king, and to insist on their rights as a Ministry.[1] The Rockingham and Fox Cabinets represented a mutual admiration society of certain great families who thought of the king as an outsider and of themselves as his constitutional advisers rather than his servants. Later, the circle of Pitt's political heirs, fortified by long experience of business and of each other, felt a certain solidarity in their dealings with George IV, originally their political enemy, often absent at Brighton, and never a master whom they could love or respect very much. But there were other Cabinets whose relations with the king were more intimate; and it would be wrong to speak of these as normally conflicting with him or even altogether distinguishable from him. The likelihood of conflict or even of separation would depend, above all, on two things: the composition of the Ministry, that is, its relation to parliamentary parties, and its structure, that is, the relation of the chief minister to his colleagues.

Very few Ministries, as I have already remarked, were composed of the members of a single party. These Ministries, as the precursors of the modern Cabinet, have a certain constitutional significance: for the chiefs of the party met, sometimes as such,

George III, no. 2161). But it should be remembered that in its original form, collective responsibility was only for advice given to the king.

[1] When Bute had constructed the Ministry which was to succeed him, he adjured them to 'enter thoroughly into the necessity of a strict union, not only amongst yourselves, but with all the other parts of the defenders of Government, and this as the only means of supporting the King's independency' (*Grenville Papers*, ii. 40). It was very naïve of Bute to suppose that a strict alliance among the ministers would increase rather than diminish the king's freedom of action. This Ministry, which seems to have been the first to hold regular Cabinet dinners, though for the inner circle only (ibid. ii. 489), was conspicuous for its efforts to maintain its solidarity *vis-à-vis* the king. The members of the inner circle sometimes concerted their language in the closet beforehand (ibid. ii. 498, iii. 166), and Grenville made a point of forcing Weymouth down the king's throat just because he had promised to do so (*Correspondence of George III*, no. 139, p. 165). Yet they disliked each other: there are many proofs of their mutual jealousy in the *Grenville Papers*, and the king truly said that 'the Duke of Bedford and Mr. Grenville were inflexible, not loving each other, and only agreeing to give him the law' (ibid. iii. 193). After it was all over, Grenville reminded Halifax 'that union was their crime and not division' (ibid. iii. 222).

and sometimes as the king's confidential advisers. (Where the ministers were not all of a party, they would not meet in the former capacity at all.) Rockingham's first Ministry only decided to take office in a party sanhedrin;[1] his appetite for consultation and his inability to give a lead imparted to both his Cabinets the character of what the imperious Shelburne called 'a round-robin administration', and account, in all probability, for the inordinate time they consumed in quite minor details of patronage.[2] The party meeting, however, was never completely merged in the Cabinet, and this fact embarrassed Egmont and Northington, who belonged to the latter but not to the former. The Lord Chancellor had to inquire, more than once, what kind of meeting it was: if it was a Cabinet, he would feel himself bound to give his opinion on the advice to be offered to the king; if it was only a meeting of party chiefs, he declined to give any, and felt no scruple about reporting the proceedings to George III.[3] This distinction between a Cabinet council for the purpose of advising his Majesty, and a meeting of ministers for the purpose of talking things over with each other, seems to have persisted in the next Administration; for there was some dispute in the House of Commons whether the decision to recommend the expulsion of Wilkes had been taken at the one kind of meeting or at the other, and Conway said (as if the distinction was a perfectly familiar one), 'Whether the gentlemen alluded to met as counsellors, or as his Majesty's servants, it is so long ago, I cannot possibly charge my memory.'[4] Fox may have alluded to it in 1806 when he said that there were different kinds of Cabinet meetings—'For affording to the members an opportunity of consulting with each other and stating their ideas reciprocally on points connected with their several departments,

[1] Albemarle, op. cit. i. 218–20; *The Duke of Newcastle's Narrative of Changes in the Ministry*, ed. Bateson, p. 25.

[2] Shelburne could not bear the idea of 'a round-robin administration, where the whole Cabinet must be consulted for the disposal of the most trifling employments' (*Political Memoranda of Francis, Duke of Leeds*, p. 70). Fox's friend Hare admitted that 'the time of the Cabinet is as much taken up in settling the Vice-Treasuryship as the Kingdom of Ireland' (*Memorials and Correspondence of Charles James Fox*, i. 328).

[3] *Correspondence of George III*, nos. 446 (misplaced by Fortescue), 279, 303, 304; *The Duke of Newcastle's Narrative of Changes in the Ministry*, p. 60. (Even Newcastle ended by threatening to ask the king to allow him 'to withdraw from the private meetings of his ministers'.)

[4] Sir H. Cavendish, *Debates*, ed. Wright, i. 440.

but with no intention of communicating the result to his Majesty. . . . On other occasions the Cabinet Council meets to advise His Majesty in person.'[1] This distinction may be said to have opened the way for the development of the Cabinet's functions as a general organ of government without special regard to the king's wishes; and it is probably no accident that we hear most of it in the Cabinets which were most nearly party Cabinets.[2]

Cabinets of that sort were the exception, not the rule. In most Cabinets there were distinguishable parties or 'caves'. It would be a mistake to exaggerate the significance of inner circles of leading ministers, such as that of Hardwicke and the Pelhams, or the younger Pitt, Grenville, and Dundas, who met together to prepare the business of the full Cabinet meetings; such circles have often existed, and there is nothing extraordinary in them. The same thing may be said of the casual groupings of ministers on one side or another of an internal controversy within the Cabinet—such as the pacifist 'cave' who annoyed Bute by dining together in the summer of 1761, or the brothers-in-law Grenville and Egremont who made so much trouble for him the next year that one or other of them had to be removed from the Secretaryship of State. These 'caves', however, sometimes

[1] *Parl. Debates*, vi. 312. Temperley, who quoted this passage (*English Historical Review*, xxvii. 692, note), was entirely wrong in supposing that Fox was here distinguishing the 'conciliabulum' from the 'outer Cabinet'. But I confess that I am not sure whether Fox was alluding to extra-official meetings of the party leaders who happened to be the king's ministers, or to his favourite doctrine that the Cabinet had a right to take action independently of the king. His pointed allusions to Castlereagh suggest that he may have been thinking of the Cabinet's promises to the Catholics in 1800, to which I have referred above, p. 155.

[2] When Rockingham formed his second Administration, Burke wrote him a rather mysterious letter, in which he said, 'I never was more pleased with anything than with your resolution of forming a cabinet on a new system; I mean the cabinet you propose for your own particular advice and support. It will not only strengthen you in the resolutions which you may *take upon yourself* in another place; but it may, under the appearance of coercing you, carry you through things of a disagreeable nature . . . which you could not, with any hope of success, assume personally' (*Works* (1852 edn.), i. 489). It is hard to know just what to make of this. It may mean that Rockingham still hoped on 22 March to make a 'monolithic' Ministry which would always back him up against the king; if so, the closet is meant by 'another place'. This interpretation is possible, and the phrase 'but *one* ministry' later in the letter, seems to confirm it. But it may mean that Rockingham had already resigned himself (as he certainly had done two days later) to having Thurlow and Shelburne in the Cabinet; if so the Cabinet itself is 'another place', and Rockingham's 'cabinet on a new system' is a private junta of his own party leaders.

represented more permanent differences; for many of the Cabinets were in effect alliances rather than fusions of distinct parties. Thus there was a Bedford 'cave' in most of the Cabinets from August 1763 to 1788, a Shelburne 'cave' within the second Rockingham Ministry, an Addingtonian 'cave' for some months in 1805, three separate ones in the Ministry of All the Talents, and attempts at a Canning 'cave' from 1822 to 1828. This might be improper: Wellington, for example, denied

the expediency and desireableness of having two members of the same family or party in the Cabinet. Whether it is a fault or otherwise, I assure you that in the existing Cabinet such a confederacy does not exist, and if it did it would be useless. I have never known two members of the existing Cabinet go into the Council determined to be of the same opinion.[1]

This, however, was not only a very flattering picture of Liverpool's administration;[2] it was a doctrine which even the king denied,[3] and many party politicians had contravened in the past.[4]

Burke was not the only man to suggest that George III encouraged divisions of this sort—that he preferred 'weak, divided, and dependent administrations'. I think that in certain circum-

---

[1] *Wellington, Despatches (Continuation)*, ii. 132. Lord Liverpool too said in 1823 'I cannot bear the idea of the Cabinet being a collection of little *knots of parties*' (*Correspondence of Charles Arbuthnot*, ed. Aspinall, p. 45).

[2] According to Arbuthnot, Peel was already complaining, three weeks earlier, of Liverpool's 'subjection' to Canning (*Hist. MSS. Comm., Bathurst MSS.*, p. 543), and he continued to do so (*Journals of Mrs. Arbuthnot*, i. 285). When Wellington himself was Prime Minister, he particularly objected to the Canningite 'cave', and this was his real reason for accepting Huskisson's resignation so promptly: see his letters in *Despatches (Continuation)*, iv. 452, 454, and, especially, 470, where he says 'these transactions . . . have shewn that these gentlemen had never amalgamated with your Majesty's other servants, but had continued as a party in your Majesty's government'; also Huskisson's letter, iv. 199, and Bathurst's, iv. 298.

[3] *Journal of Mrs. Arbuthnot*, i. 254.

[4] For example, Gower, when he refused to enter Chatham's Ministry unaccompanied by any other member of the Bedford party (see his letter in Grafton's *Autobiography*, p. 100). It was, of course, unusual for one party in the Cabinet positively to obstruct the measures of another; but even this might happen on occasion: Carteret was strongly suspected of encouraging underhand the opposition to Pelham's sugar tax in 1743 (Pares, *War and Trade in the West Indies*, pp. 509–10) and Newcastle's House of Commons ministers opposed his measures from the Treasury Bench in 1754–5. In 1762 Charles Yorke advised Newcastle to oppose Bute from within the Ministry rather than resign, and somebody—said to be Burke—gave Charles Fox very similar advice in 1782 (*Memorials and Correspondence of Charles James Fox*, i. 455–8).

stances he did so. When he was dealing with people like Grenville, Rockingham, and Charles Fox, who thought of the Administration as their Administration, not his, he thought it right to keep the different elements apart. George Grenville had a suspicious mind; but he can hardly have been altogether mistaken when he thought the king was trying to play him off against the Bedfords.[1] In the first Rockingham Ministry there can be no doubt that Egmont and Northington constituted a 'cave' of George III's particular friends.[2] He cautioned Grafton against the Bedfords, though he later came to prefer them to him. In the second Rockingham Ministry he treated Shelburne as a joint Prime Minister, and their correspondence shows that neither of them considered himself to owe any loyalty to Rockingham, whose intelligence they despised.[3]

It is more questionable whether George III encouraged dissension in other Ministries which he regarded as more truly his own—in those of North and the younger Pitt. Hillsborough told Leeds in 1781 that 'when any faction appeared even among the ministers he (the king) instantly put an end to it, and that this was a system H.M. was determined to preserve'.[4]

Not everybody believed that George III's practice conformed to this system. Indeed, it was the later years of North's Ministry that re-established the legend of the 'secret Cabinet' and the 'secret adviser' Charles Jenkinson. The publication of a large part of George III's correspondence enables us to set this accusation in a truer light. The king, who talked incessantly and wrote much, undoubtedly uttered some 'asides', which might indicate to one of his advisers what he thought of another; they are not unduly numerous for a period of twenty years. From 1778 to 1782 there was something more: North suffered from a

---

[1] It was particularly easy to do this, for Grenville claimed to be Prime Minister and the others would have liked to dispute the claim, or at least its consequences in the field of patronage (*Grenville Papers*, ii. 207, 219, 222, 489, 494, 512, 513). Grenville ended by believing 'that the King had been taught that *division* was the art of Government' (Harris, *Life of Lord Chancellor Hardwicke*, iii. 454).

[2] *Correspondence of George III*, nos. 446 (misplaced by Fortescue), 279, 303–4, 307, 310, 318–20, 335.

[3] Ibid., nos. 3582, 3635, 3645, 3647, 3651, 3676, 3677, 3692, 3693, 3704, 3737–8, 3741–6.

[4] *Political Memoranda of Francis, Duke of Leeds*, p. 46. Hillsborough was, of all George III's ministers, the most convinced 'King's Friend'. I do not know what particular incidents he had in mind: perhaps the king's harangue to the Cabinet in June 1779, for the purpose of stopping the intrigues against North.

nervous breakdown, for he could not resign[1] and could not tell
the king that he disagreed with his policy,[2] so he became distracted, unapproachable, and unable to make up his mind. A
Prime Minister so situated would, in any case, have been surrounded by an atmosphere of whispering and backbiting—service ministers trying to cast the blame on each other, rats trying
to leave the ship or at least to throw the captain overboard.
George III authorized a secret correspondence between Charles
Jenkinson—not a Cabinet minister, but one in whom he had
special confidence—and John Robinson, North's *homme de con-
fiance*.[3] The object of this correspondence was, in part, to find
out what North himself really intended to do, and to give the
king an opportunity of giving him a shove at the right moment
so as to make him do something; in part, to get wind of the
manœuvres of North's enemies in the Cabinet. The correspondence was in no sense hostile to North, nor even a usurpation
of any right which he was capable of exercising. Indeed, it
seemed to be the only way of keeping the Ministry together and
getting anything done.[4] Nevertheless, the king was, perhaps, ill

[1] Probably this was because it would be ingratitude after George III had paid
his debts (as Professor H. Butterfield suggests in *George III, Lord North and the
People*, p. 18). I am convinced, however—and Professor Butterfield appears to
agree—that the king had no calculation of this sort in his mind when he paid them.
His letter to North upon this occasion (*Correspondence*, no. 2059) shows his character
at its most pleasing. It would not have been human nature, however, if he had
abstained from referring to North, at the time of the coalition, as 'that *grateful* man,
Lord North'.

[2] I do not agree with Lord John Russell (*Memorials and Correspondence of Charles
James Fox*, i. 212) in thinking that North referred to the American question, in
Sept. 1779, when he said that 'he holds in his heart, and has held for three years
past, the same opinion with Lord Gower'. It seems clear to me that he was talking
about a coalition of parties, and that George III never understood that North
wanted to give up the contest with America until December 1781 (*Correspondence of
George III*, no. 3475). No doubt he had a remarkable capacity for not taking a hint.
North's contemporaries knew quite well that he had continually sacrificed his convictions to those of the king; and this is what Pitt meant by implying that North
had had 'the meanness to act upon the advice of others', and 'the hypocrisy to
pretend, when the measures of an administration in which he had a share, were
deserving of censure, that they were measures not of his advising' (*Parl. Hist.* xxiv.
294). Charles Fox did not try to defend North against this charge (ibid., p. 367).

[3] The letter sanctioning this 'unreserved correspondence' between Robinson and
Jenkinson in Mar. 1779 is calendared in *Hist. MSS. Comm., Abergavenny MSS.*, p. 24.

[4] I cannot give all the references to the *Correspondence of George III* upon which I
found my opinion of the essential harmlessness of these transactions. The reader
must consult the correspondence itself, from early 1779 to the end of Mar. 1782,
and form his own conclusions.

advised to allow it, for it must have increased the unhappy North's obsession with the cobweb of intrigue that surrounded him, and possibly his resentment may have had some part in persuading him into the coalition with Charles Fox. It gave Fox an opportunity to thunder against the secret advisers of the Crown in the great debates of 1784—a libel on George III, who was remarkably capable of taking decisions and finding things out for himself.[1] Even Pitt may have suspected, at one time, that these secret advisers really existed: at any rate, he rather ostentatiously cold-shouldered Jenkinson, and did not readmit him to office for some time. There is no reason to think that George III later encouraged disunion in Pitt's Cabinet; on the contrary, he was at some pains to reconcile Pitt and Thurlow, by no means an easy thing to do. Sidmouth, no doubt, spoke quite truly in 1807, when he said that neither he nor Pitt had ever had any trouble from secret advisers.[2]

If the 'secret influence' was mostly mythical in George III's reign, the same thing cannot altogether be said of the king's own political ambitions. George III did not try to control the everyday operations of government in person from beginning to end of his reign. At first he aimed only at conferring this power upon the adored Lord Bute. But when he had to part with his 'dearest friend', there is something significant in his repeated declaration that he looked upon his subsequent ministers as 'tools'.[3] They were tools, however, that he knew not how to handle; and, unless the loss of part of his correspondence has created a misleading impression, he did not take a very active part in

[1] *Parl. Hist.* xxiii. 671, 703; xxiv. 695.

[2] *Parl. Debates*, ix. 400; see also Pitt's own remarks in 1784, *Parl. Hist.* xxiv. 294. Yet it is fairly clear from the correspondence quoted by Professor D. G. Barnes (op. cit., p. 124) that the king was in correspondence with Lord Sydney, a member of the Cabinet who disliked Pitt's proposals for the reform of parliament; and when George III assured Pitt that he had not influenced anybody against those proposals he must have forgotten that he had let Sydney know that he shared his dislike of them. Sidmouth himself, knowing that George III was likely to look more kindly upon him than upon his colleagues, preferred the post of Lord Privy Seal to that of Lord President in 1806, as the latter gave more frequent access to the king, and he did not want the other ministers to suspect him of colloguing with the king behind their backs (Pellew, op. cit. ii. 416). A few months later, however, he became Lord President, and seems to have alarmed the king about his colleagues' proposals in favour of the Catholics. It is probable, however, that he acted fairly, and even Lord Holland seems to have thought so (ibid. ii. 455–64; *Parl. Debates*, ix. 393–403; Holland, *Memoirs of the Whig Party*, ii. 210–12).

[3] *Letters from George III to Lord Bute, 1756–1766*, pp. 208, 220.

administration during the Ministry of Grenville, or even of the feeble Rockingham—still less during that of the superman Chatham, to whom, in all probability, he was prepared genuinely to look up.

From some time between 1767 and 1770, however, his printed correspondence becomes much fuller of administrative detail, and it is apparent that more and more is submitted to the king's decision. Probably he never claimed this, but it came about because Grafton was indolent and North unable to make up his mind. We find the king deciding what admiral shall command a squadron, and how many ships shall sail to the West Indies.[1] He also acts, one might say, as Secretary-at-War: having approved a secret expedition against Goree, he undertakes to provide the soldiers, saying: 'I trust with a little consideration I shall be able to chalk out means of effecting what I look on as so essential a service.'[2] He twice dismisses a Lord Chancellor when Grafton or North is unequal to the task.[3] He composes quarrels in the Cabinet, and once conducts a Cabinet reshuffle, with the air of a householder distributing domestic tasks among some rather difficult servants with a special eye to the comfort and prestige of the major-domo.[4] He gets North out of a difficulty about some law promotions and twice warns him not to promise offices without consulting him first.[5] Some of his ministers treat him as one might treat a Prime Minister who did not happen to be at the Cabinet: Rochford sends him confidential reports of Cabinet discussions and primes him for his conferences in the closet,[6] Lord George Germain (apparently) asks whether he has any particular commands as to the line he should take at a Cabinet meeting.[7]

Indeed, one might well ask, who was Prime Minister at this

---

[1] *Correspondence of George III*, nos. 2320, 2325, 2330.

[2] Ibid., no. 2430. As Lord George Germain pointed out (in 1777) to a discontented general, it was the king who decided upon operations; and, indeed, this was only too true, for Germain himself was extremely annoyed, a short time afterwards, when the king and Amherst overruled him in a military matter. 'If the King and Lord Amherst like this new arrangement', he said, 'it must be their measure, not mine'—language such as one would use about a Prime Minister rather than a king (*Hist. MSS. Comm., Various Collections*, vi. 132–3, 157).

[3] Grafton, op. cit., p. 245; *Correspondence of George III*, nos. 2262, 2307.

[4] Ibid., nos. 1740–56.

[5] Ibid., nos. 2299, 2369, 2407.

[6] Ibid., nos. 843–52 (the correspondence deals with the Falkland Islands crisis).

[7] Ibid., no. 1859.

time—George III or Lord North? Some interesting letters passed between them on the subject of the Prime Ministership. North urged 'That in critical times, it is necessary that there should be one directing Minister, who should plan the whole of the operations of government, and controul all the other departments of administration so far as to make them co-operate zealously & actively with his designs even tho' contrary to their own.'[1] North admitted that he did not possess these qualities,[2] and complained that he had no authority. George III must have suspected North of claiming constitutional rights (he once accused him of 'aping the Prime Minister')[3] and asked him what kind of authority he lacked. North dodged a controversy by saying that he had referred to moral authority and ascendency of character.[4] But George III himself did not hold that all his servants were equal: he too had a conception of the rights of a chief minister, though it was not the same conception as North's. He claimed that:

from the hour of Lord North's so handsomely devoting himself on the retreat of the D. of Grafton, I have never had a political thought which I have not communicated unto him, have accepted of persons highly disagreable unto me, because he thought they would be of advantage to his conducting public affairs, and have yielded to measures my own opinion did not quite approve.[5]

George III thus recognized that the Prime Minister was, by

[1] Ibid., no. 2446.
[2] On another occasion (ibid., no. 2845) he almost made a merit of it, and described his relations with his colleagues as follows: 'They have always known all that I knew, unless I was forbid to communicate anything to them which has been very seldom. I have never interfered in any of their departments. I have never clash'd with their views.' In short, he thought the only fair accusation they could make against him was 'That I am not equal in abilities to the station which I ought to hold, as the place next the director of publick affairs at this time.' In judging the sincerity of this last phrase, we should remember that North was writing to the king.
[3] H. Butterfield, op. cit., p. 68.
[4] Correspondence of George III, no. 2452.
[5] Ibid., no. 2451. George III claimed with some justice to have confided his political thoughts to North (this was before the days of the Robinson–Jenkinson correspondence). In Mar. 1778 he said, 'I shall write every thought as it occurs in this slight manner to Lord North' (ibid., no. 2243). He required similar confidence from North: 'where', he asked, 'can you repose your undigested thoughts more safely than in the breast of one who has ever treated you more as his friend than Minister?' (ibid., no. 2369). When North did confide a difficulty to him, he was delighted: 'it had the appearance of unbosoming to a friend' (ibid., no. 2615).

rights, the king's chief confidant, whose opinions and convenience, in a parliamentary monarchy, must be studied; but nothing more.

The Prime Minister's office was more distinctly recognized than it had been in the preceding generation, when the House of Commons barely acquitted Sir Robert Walpole of the charge of being a Prime Minister, a post unknown to the constitution, and he defended himself by inducing his colleagues to testify to the truth of his disclaimer.[1] But the development of this institution, as of all others which are affected by personal ascendencies or deficiencies in this quarter or in that, must not be thought of as continuous—as when we perceive, in the heart of a fog, a whitish blob which curdles into a tram and advances along the lines, growing larger and more distinct, until it stops obediently at our feet. The history of the Prime Minister before 1832—and perhaps after it—is more like that of the Cheshire Cat: sometimes there is almost a whole cat, sometimes no more than a grin, and it is not always the same end that appears first.

Sir Robert Walpole was in some ways more of a modern Prime Minister than Henry Pelham, in other ways less: more, because he kept better discipline in the House of Commons and endured rivals in the Cabinet less willingly;[2] less, because he was, as his son rightly observed, a court minister rather than a House of Commons minister—he acted upon the Commons in the interests of the court, whereas Henry Pelham acted rather upon the court in the interest of an aggregation of groups in the Commons.[3] But it was not altogether clear that Henry Pelham was above his elder brother the Duke of Newcastle: Newcastle disliked Pelham's constant use of 'the first person on all occasions', but Hardwicke (perhaps out of flattery) sometimes

[1] *Parl. Hist.* xi. 1182, 1232, 1296.

[2] His control over his colleagues in the Cabinet seems to have broken down from 1739, and he certainly was not master in his own house at the time of the Convention and the Spanish war. I attribute this partly to increasing age and nervous strain, but still more to the loss of his private line to the king *via* Hervey and the queen.

[3] Henry Pelham's brother the Duke of Newcastle was often considered as a court minister; but when he was piqued by his young friend Rockingham's inattention to him in 1765–6, he frequently criticized him for 'depending so much upon the stability of court favour' (*The Duke of Newcastle's Narrative of Changes in the Ministry*, pp. 38, 41–42). This may be mere inconsistency; but I think Newcastle had always imagined that he governed by 'weight, credit, and real reputation in the Kingdom'.

referred to Newcastle himself as having the chief power, even during his brother's lifetime;[1] and certainly Newcastle had some of the notes of a Prime Minister, such as the almost undisputed control of Church promotions. Yet there is one thing which seems to prove that Henry Pelham was a Prime Minister: at his death, everybody behaved as if an epoch was at an end and the Government had to be reconstructed.[2] Newcastle was not, in all senses, a Prime Minister even after 1754: the king once told him he was not, and he himself, in a panic fear of responsibility, once or twice disclaimed being more than a departmental chief.[3]

The elder Pitt's ideas on Prime Ministership, as on other subjects, are confused and hard to interpret. He seems to have been just as uncertain as the historians whether he was Prime Minister in the coalition of 1757—indeed, whether there was one at all. On the one hand he treated Newcastle, rightly I think, as having the chief interest in the closet; but he also said that he would not defer to the opinions of any colleague, but the sovereign must decide between them.[4] He went on to say, in the next breath, 'The rights of my office are not enough for me', and he declared in public, after it was all over, that he had resigned 'in order not to remain responsible for measures which I was not allowed to guide'. Though he tried later to explain this away by saying that he had only referred to the affairs of his own department, this excuse does not ring true, if one considers the almost megalomaniac contempt which he expressed for his late colleagues and the phrases about borrowing Newcastle's majority to carry on his policy, and so forth: he is said to have owned to Bute that 'he felt in his breast a superiority and a right to lead'.[5] In the Ministry of 1766, on the other hand, he clearly cast himself for the part of superman[6]—though a sick superman, who soon became unable to take decisions.

[1] Ilchester, *Henry Fox, First Lord Holland* (London, 1920), i. 100; P. C. Yorke, op. cit. ii. 22, 96. Henry Pelham himself once spoke of his brother as being 'at the head of business'.

[2] One might, perhaps, say that there was very nearly as great a change when Castlereagh died in 1822—and he was clearly not Prime Minister. Yet I think the comparison would be strained.

[3] Ibid. ii. 218, 223, 306.

[4] Ibid. iii. 315; Fox's memoir in *Life and Letters of Lady Sarah Lennox*, i. 9; G. F. S. Elliot, *The Border Elliots*, pp. 363–4.

[5] Ibid.; *Chatham Correspondence*, ii. 158.

[6] Charles Townshend, his Chancellor of the Exchequer, complained in Aug.

No Prime Minister ever made more fuss about his rights than
George Grenville; and, since he had no originality of mind, we
may suppose that the conception of those rights had already
begun to crystallize. He was interested, above all, in the control
of patronage—a matter which created much difficulty at that
time within the Cabinet: the line between the general patronage
of the Cabinet or of the Prime Minister and the particular
patronage of departmental chiefs was not an easy one to draw.[1]
Grenville had some success in persuading George III to back
him against his colleagues, but he seriously weakened his position by a quarrel with Bute's brother, for whom the king had
reserved the Scottish patronage, and this was probably one of
the things which impaired his relations with the king in 1765.[2]
He finally disgusted George III by declaring that he would

1766 that 'everything proceeds from Lord Chatham to the king, from thence, without any intermediate consultation, to the public, and I am confident that no other
man has the least previous knowledge or influence' (*Hist. MSS. Comm.*, *Stopford-
Sackville MSS.* i. 67).

[1] Some Secretaries of State claimed the right to appoint and remove diplomats
or colonial governors in their departments without reference to the Prime Minister.
Grenville objected to Halifax's attempt to remove Sir Joseph Yorke from his post
at The Hague; but I think this was because Yorke was a member of parliament,
so that Grenville ought to have been consulted as leader of the House (*Grenville
Papers*, ii. 219). Later, when Grenville was no longer Prime Minister, he declared
in the House of Commons that Secretaries of State had the right to appoint ambassadors, &c. (ibid. iv. 217). Chatham annoyed Conway by appointing an envoy
to Russia without telling him in 1766 (H. Walpole, *Memoirs of the Reign of George III*,
ed. Russell Barker, ii. 258). Shelburne resigned in 1768, primarily because the king
supported Grafton against him in a dispute over the appointment of a Minister at
Turin. (*Correspondence of George III*, nos. 658, 661). Much later, Liverpool told
Bathurst that the great embassies and colonial governorships were the Prime
Minister's patronage as much as the Secretary of State's (*Hist. MSS. Comm.*,
Bathurst MSS., pp. 605–6). A Secretary of State might offer to share his depart-
mental patronage with the Prime Minister, as Sydney offered to share his with Pitt
(Stanhope, *Life of Pitt*, i. 229), but another minister might try to encroach upon the
general patronage; Lord Grenville accused Dundas of having done this (*Hist. MSS.
Comm.*, *Dropmore MSS.* viii. 307). Grenville's own disputes and those of other
ministers with Windham over patronage are a very undignified example of inter-
departmental jealousy (ibid. viii. 18, 140, 183, 189). On the whole the Prime
Minister's patronage tended to increase at the expense of the departments. The
Chief Secretaryship of Ireland is a good example of this: originally the Chief
Secretary was the personal secretary to the Lord Lieutenant, chosen by him with
little or no reference to the wishes of any other minister. But in 1801 Addington
appointed Abbot Chief Secretary before it was certain that Hardwicke would
accept the Lord Lieutenancy (*Diaries and Correspondence of Lord Colchester*, i. 234–41)
and in 1812 Liverpool appointed Peel without asking the Duke of Richmond
beforehand (C. D. Yonge, *Life and Administration of Lord Liverpool*, i. 425).

[2] *Grenville Papers*, 207, 211–12, iii. 124; *Correspondence of George III*, no. 139.

not serve an hour if people presumed to talk business (by which I think he meant patronage) to the king without his leave.[1]

Rockingham presented George III with yet another aspect of the Prime Minister's claims in 1766: he demanded that the king should discipline the minor office-holders, the 'King's Friends', into voting conformably to his (Rockingham's) wishes in the House of Commons. I have dealt already with this controversy,[2] and I will only say that Rockingham probably credited the king with more power over these people than any one possessed. Any reader of Horace Walpole's or Cavendish's reports of parliamentary debates can see that the House of Commons, and even the Treasury Bench, was a bear garden: every man was his own expert on law and procedure, and pundits like Dyson or Welbore Ellis could spontaneously traverse the designs of their leaders out of pure, unprompted pedantry.

In the years between Chatham's failure and his son's rise, the Prime Ministership seems to have developed little, if at all. North probably had not the courage of his convictions, Rockingham's was a round-robin administration with two almost co-ordinate Prime Ministers, and even Shelburne, though imperious and dictatorial, had so little control over his own Cabinet that he hardly dared assemble it for fear it should disagree. Portland, as a catspaw for Charles Fox, presented the greatest claims yet made on paper; for there can be little doubt that his demand for the king's 'confidence' meant not only a free hand in the composition of the Ministry but the principle that the king must accept the Cabinet's advice so long as he retained it in office.[3] But this was just the reason why George III determined to get

---

[1] Ibid.; Jenkinson also mentions this as one of the things that most annoyed the king, in his memorandum on Grenville and Bute (*Jenkinson Papers*, p. 399).

[2] *V. supra*, p. 108.

[3] This, at least, I take to be the meaning of such remarks as: 'If it is his Majesty's pleasure to place me at the head of the Treasury, it is impossible to suppose that He means to withhold from me any part of his confidence' (*Correspondence of George III*, no. 4206), and 'many difficulties occur to the submitting a Plan for His Majesty's inspection until they can flatter themselves that His Majesty is graciously disposed to listen to the recommendations which it may be their duty to offer him' (ibid., no. 4236). George III seems to have understood Portland's demands in the same sense: 'he [Portland] expected that on his coming to the head of the Treasury, I should rely on his making no propositions but such as he thought necessary for my affairs and consequently that I should acquiesce in them' (ibid., no. 4268, p. 325).

rid of Portland, and it remained for the younger Pitt to continue the development of the Prime Ministership.

Everybody knows Pitt's celebrated definition of it: he spoke of

the absolute necessity there is, in the conduct of the affairs of this country, that there should be an avowed and real minister possessing the chief weight in council and the principal place in the confidence of the King. In that respect there can be no rivality or division of power. That power must rest with the person generally called the First Minister; and that minister ought, he thinks, to be the person at the head of the finances. He knows to his own comfortable experience, that notwithstanding the abstract truth of that general proposition, it is no ways incompatible with the most cordial concert and mutual exchange of advice and intercourse amongst the different branches of executive departments; but still, if it should come unfortunately to such a radical difference of opinion that no spirit of conciliation or concession can reconcile, the sentiments of the Minister must be allowed and understood to prevail, leaving the other members of administration to act as they may conceive themselves conscientiously called upon to act under such circumstances.[1]

The remarkable thing about this definition is that it claims no rights against the king. An American scholar wrote a book, not long ago, to show that Pitt's relations with George III were not what most historians had supposed: that the king was by no means 'in shackles' to Pitt, and that Pitt did not even try to obtain the king's active support for all his policies.[2] Professor Barnes's conclusions are sound, but they need not surprise anybody who attends to what Pitt said. Pitt, like his father, came into office as the champion of the king's right to choose his minister: how, then, could he claim the right to impose his will upon his master? When he was quite convinced that the king was not merely neutral but hostile to the measures proposed as necessary for his service, Pitt's position became untenable and he had no choice but to resign, as his father had done.

Pitt's claim to power, like his father's, was one which it is hard to fit into the constitutional scheme of the eighteenth century: it is the claim of ability[3]—the claim of the man who can govern

[1] Pellew, op. cit. ii. 116. The words are Melville's, not Pitt's; but they purport to be, and probably are, an accurate report of Pitt's conversation.

[2] Donald G. Barnes, *George III and William Pitt*.

[3] This was recognized at the time: in 1792, when the Duke of Leeds was trying to negotiate a coalition, Lord Chesterfield, who favoured the proposal, said 'we

to be allowed to do so. It involves subordination of colleagues—and I do not think anybody denies that Pitt insisted upon this—but it does not necessarily involve encroachment on the king's rights—at least, Lord Chatham and his son did not think so. Yet, in practice, a king and a Prime Minister who both feel themselves able to govern and responsible for governing are not likely to work together very long. Chatham's co-operation with George III only lasted eight months, and was only possible because the king was still diffident and looked up to the man who could make even Charles Townshend feel himself an 'inferior animal'. Chatham's son started with the advantage of agreeing with the king on those things which they both regarded as matters of government—peace, retrenchment, restoring discipline and keeping out Charles Fox. But this harmony might not have lasted so long if George III's strength had not been declining, especially after 1788, and if Charles Fox had not seemed to be the only alternative. As I have already argued, the incident of 1801 shows how far Pitt's Cabinet had come to reckon without the king and to rely on his assent to anything which was presented to him cut and dried as a Cabinet minute; and the successors of Pitt, as much as the successors of Fox, habitually acted on the principle that the king must do what his ministers wanted. 'I am no Whig', Lord Liverpool is reported to have said, 'and tho' I have proved that on a point where I feel that I am right, I can press and insist, I will not urge a measure on my sovereign when my own conscience tells me I am wrong.'[1] A trifling concession to the monarchy indeed.

cannot go on well unless we have some acres added to our abilities' (*Political Memoranda of Francis, Duke of Leeds*, p. 199).

[1] This is quoted from a letter of Liverpool to Canning 1826, which Mrs. Arbuthnot purports to have seen (*Journal of Mrs. Arbuthnot*, ii. 39).

VI

THE DECLINE OF PERSONAL MONARCHY

IN these lectures I have been trying to describe the ruling interests and motives of British politics in George III's reign; to explore the king's uncertain and undefined relations with the House of Commons; and to illustrate the conflicts which this uncertainty and want of definition produced from time to time. The historians of the last century treated those conflicts in a crudely dramatic style. Those of this generation, justly revolted by that style, have either argued that the rights and wrongs of the conflicts were not what their forefathers believed, or have denied that there were any conflicts at all. The first of these two theses seems to me more acceptable than the second. True, the conflicts only once rose to a crisis, in the years 1782 to 1784, and that only by grace of a unique national disaster. True, also, that even in those years two-thirds, at most, of the House of Commons was engaged in the conflict at all;[1] that the average member of the House was not then a party man, even in the sense in which he was a party man in 1832; that the collisions between king and politicians, which had some constitutional significance, often arose out of the collisions of one group of politicians with another, which had none.[2] Yet it seems to me that, when George III disputed in the closet with George Grenville (or with his son) about the ministers' right to deprive him of his freedom of choice, or when he defended against Charles Fox his right to choose his ministers at all, there was a conflict between a more and a less personal conception of constitutional monarchy.

[1] The divisions of Jan. to Mar. 1784 were big, but not exceptionally big; those of Dec. 1783 (before the country gentlemen had come to town) were decidedly small, considering the gravity of the issues.

[2] This is true of the collision with the Rockinghams in the second half of 1766 which induced Burke to formulate that party's theory in the *Thoughts on the Cause of the Present Discontents*. Rockingham had not much to complain of in his direct relations with the king during his first Ministry (so, at least, George III believed him to have admitted, *Correspondence of George III*, no. 342). But when George III gave his enthusiastic support to Chatham's attempt to pulverize parties, which culminated in the Edgcumbe affair, then he got more than his fair share of the party's venom, and Burke began to complain of 'administrations constructed upon the idea of systematic discord'.

It is more profitable to argue that the constitutional doctrines of Fox and Burke were newer, and less well founded in history, than those of George III. Yet even here, one can see how the king came to be considered as the innovator. He may have claimed no right that his grandfather had not claimed, but he exercised, in his prime, rights which his grandfather had not exercised in his old age. I do not see how anybody can believe that George III's relations with North were the same as George II's relations with the Pelhams. Newcastle was always afraid that George II would snap at him; and some of George II's prepossessions, especially his Hanover interests, greatly influenced British policy. But in the last resort, I think, Newcastle governed George II and George III governed North. The differences were personal, but the constitutional history of this country, above all in this department, is made up of personal differences.

The historian of a conflict can hardly feel quite satisfied unless he can answer the question 'How did it end?' and even, perhaps, the question 'Who was right?' These are two questions, not one: to say that the winner (if we can spot him) is always right is, indeed, a definition of right, but not the only one in which historians can interest themselves. Moreover, we must explain what we mean when we talk of a 'winner' at all. George III undoubtedly beat Charles Fox in 1784, and trampled on his ghost in 1807; but our politicians act, today, on Charles Fox's constitutional principles, and Lord Liverpool was already beginning to act on them in 1815, although he was an adversary of Charles Fox. Who, then, was the winner—George III or Charles Fox?

The decline of personal monarchy was, in part, a personal decline. George III himself was decaying after his attack of madness in 1788. We need not take very seriously the celebrated letter in which he told Pitt that he should thereafter keep only a 'superintending eye' over the administration;[1] for the first thing he did, when he had recovered his faculties, was to renew the quarrel with Lord Buckingham over the Irish military promotions, almost where he had left it off. Indeed, his continued interference with military organization—much less so with strategy—showed that he had by no means lost

[1] *Diaries and Correspondence of George Rose*, i. 97.

his command of detail; and the crises of 1801 and 1807 proved that he could still have the last word on a question of high policy. Yet, in spite of violent eruptions of letter-writing from time to time,[1] an old, blind man, distracted by quarrels in his family and afraid of losing his wits for good and all, could not hope to keep control of the machine as he had done in his prime.

Still less was George IV, with his tears and his tantrums, and his long, opalescent lies, man enough to maintain a consistent control over a set of ministers who felt little personal affection for him and had proved, by the experience of a successful war, that they were well able to govern the country without his help. As Wellington remarked, 'he liked to talk grandly to make people imagine that his Prime Minister was a sort of maitre d'hotel which he might dismiss any moment that it happened to suit him'.[2] He might threaten to take 'such measures as the Government will be the least prepared to expect', or ask 'can the present Government suppose that the King will permit any individuals to force upon him at this time a line of policy of which he so entirely disapproves'?; but it all ended in smoke, and he accepted even from a Cabinet which he knew to be divided the assurance that an overruling sense of duty induced them to press their advice on him against his known opinion.[3] The collapse of his resistance to Catholic Emancipation made his impotence still more evident. He had made his opposition to the measure far more public than his father had ever done, yet he yielded, after a monologue of an hour and a half about the story of his life and a good cry.[4]

It is not enough, however, to ascribe the rapid decline in the influence of the monarchy to the old age of one king or the unmanliness of another. The conditions of political life were changing, and the power of the Crown was not what it had been.

[1] e.g. at the beginning of Addington's Ministry.

[2] *Journal of Mrs. Arbuthnot*, i. 79. She gives an instance of this (ibid. i. 278), and there are others in *Correspondence of George IV*, ed. Aspinall, nos. 867, 878–80, 1189. On the other hand, Wellington was equally sceptical about Liverpool's periodical threats of resignation.

[3] *Wellington, Despatches (Continuation)*, ii. 401, 403.

[4] *Journal of Mrs. Arbuthnot*, ii. 245–6, 262. Perhaps the comparison between George IV and his father is a little unfair at this point: it is not easy to see what resources George III could have exerted in 1829 without starting another civil war in his empire.

Not everybody saw this. In the controversies over the reconstruction of the Ministry in 1812, people might blame or praise the Prince Regent for refusing to exchange Perceval and Liverpool for Grey and Grenville, but nearly everybody assumed that he could have done it if he had chosen. Soon afterwards, however, the consolidation of the country's patriotic and Conservative forces in the revived tory party created a bloc so powerful, and (in spite of the friction over Catholic Emancipation and Canning's personal ambition) so well united that the king's power to divide or desert it began to be questioned: Mrs. Arbuthnot, for example (perhaps too strong a partisan to be a good judge) remarked in October 1820, 'I am quite sure we may be thankful to our own power as a party & not to the King's good will for our places'.[1] This was put to the test in 1827, when George IV flouted the party's wishes by choosing Canning for his minister.[2] He made good his choice, but the Cabinets of Canning and Goderich were two of the weakest of the nineteenth century. This weakness was advantageous, in some ways, to the king; for the Ministry's life depended on the continued

[1] Ibid. i. 42. Liverpool cannot have agreed with her: a few months after the fright over George IV's plan for dismissing the Ministry, he started the negotiation for bringing in the Grenville party, of which the purpose is revealed in Castlereagh's phrase, 'In this way you will be sure of taking this connection out of that central position in the House of Commons which invites intrigue, and might facilitate an intermediate arrangement' (Yonge, op. cit., iii. 163). No doubt Castlereagh had in mind the danger of an 'intermediate arrangement' made by the king. See also Charles Arbuthnot's remarks, in his *Correspondence*, ed. Aspinall, p. 24. For a further discussion of this important move, v. infra, p. 191.

[2] George IV was not anxious to meet this challenge; indeed, he tried to avoid it by getting the Cabinet itself to name a successor to Liverpool, until Peel persuaded him that this would be throwing the apple of discord at it (*Formation of Canning's Ministry*, ed. Aspinall, p. 49; *Journal of Mrs. Arbuthnot*, ii. 98). But he was nettled by the injudicious conduct of the Dukes of Rutland, Newcastle, Buckingham, and (one must add) Wellington, for he was persuaded that the tory bloc was trying to intimidate him by a campaign of collective resignations (ibid.; *Wellington, Despatches (Continuation)*, iii. 611, 634, iv. 123; *Formation of Canning's Ministry*, ed. Aspinall, pp. 67, 75, 90). It is clear that Rutland and Londonderry were only 'King's Friends' so long as the king did what they considered the right thing, and that even Wellington held that his duty to the king was cancelled by the treason which he unjustly suspected Canning of committing against the party (ibid., p. xxix; *Journal of Mrs. Arbuthnot*, ii. 98, 102). But they used, in public, an argument of more loyal appearance: they proclaimed that the Prime Minister's views on the chief question of the day ought to be identical with those of the sovereign, which Canning's notoriously were not (*Formation of Canning's Ministry*, ed. Aspinall, p. 76; *Wellington, Despatches (Continuation)*, iv. 5–6, 23).

manifestation of his favour,[1] and he was able to insist on those little personal concessions which Liverpool had so rigidly resisted. Goderich, indeed, might be described as George IV's Grafton and Herries as his Jenkinson; and if the king had been a young man of good repute and constitution, instead of an old, broken *roué* soaked in laudanum, there is no telling what might have happened.[2] Yet the whole experiment failed: the co-operation between the middle wings of the two parties was always on the point of breaking down, and after nine months of 'intermediate arrangements' depending on his own favour, George IV was only too glad to have recourse once more to Wellington and the main body of the tory party.[3]

This was by no means an unqualified defeat for the king, since Wellington was, in principle, a 'King's Friend'—indeed, his maxim that the king's or queen's government must, above all, be carried on, was the fundamental principle of the 'King's Friends'.[4] Moreover, so far as Wellington was a politician at all, his tory convictions should have given the king as much hold over him as he had over the king: obsessed with the fear of revolution, he believed that the Cabinet and even the aristocracy ought to bear all from the king rather than give up the

---

[1] So much did Canning depend on exhibiting his master's implicit confidence, by the usual method of disciplining office-holders and candidates for office who voted the wrong way, that he withdrew from his friend Bagot the offer of the Governor-Generalship of India, because Bagot's brother had given his proxy against the Corn Bill in the Lords (Bagot, *Canning and his Friends*, ii. 405, 412) and catechized Dean Percy (whose relations had voted against the bill or at least not voted for it) as to his political intentions before he would recommend him for a bishopric (*Correspondence of George IV*, ed. Aspinall, no. 1359).

[2] Perhaps one should not believe all Mrs. Arbuthnot's stories about George IV making bishops and governor-generals without the ministers' knowledge and consent (*Journals*, ii. 151), but he certainly wrote to Goderich *en maître* about bishoprics and the composition of the Cabinet (*Correspondence of George IV*, ed. Aspinall, nos. 1400, 1404, 1420). I doubt if Liverpool or Wellington would have allowed C. R. Sumner to be translated to the see of Winchester so soon after he had got Llandaff.

[3] Wellington's Cabinet was, like every other since 1807, neutral or divided on the Catholic question; but it contained no whigs at first.

[4] When Liverpool invited him to join the Cabinet in 1818, Wellington only accepted on the condition that he should not be expected to follow his colleagues into opposition if any circumstance should occur to remove them from power. Liverpool, though more of a party man, agreed with him in principle (Yonge, op. cit. ii. 378–9). No doubt, as Wellington pointed out, his feeling was coloured by his military experience: it would have been difficult for anybody to rise to the head of an organized profession, above all the military profession, without coming to think something of the sort.

government to whigs and Radicals.[1] Nor did he underrate the influence of the Crown. Mrs. Arbuthnot never saw him so angry as when he heard of the interview in which George IV had told Eldon that he would have resisted Catholic Emancipation if he could.

He said that such conduct on the part of the King wd totally destroy the Govt & that he was certain it could not last after this Bill was over; that the King had now told seven or eight very influential Tory peers that this measure had been forced upon him & shewn clearly that he hated his Ministers. The consequence, the Duke said, wd be that the Tory Party wd abandon him, & as he was determined he wd give up the Govt rather than stay to be supported by the Whigs, he wd go to the King & tell him he had broke down his Govt by his conduct & language & might make another as he cd.[2]

Wellington knew quite well that his best hope of circumventing the king's escape was a coalition with some of the whigs: indeed, the king saw it too, and showed marked jealousy of the negotiations which brought Rosslyn and Scarlett into the Ministry, thinking it the kind of encircling movement which had so often threatened his father's liberty of action.[3] But Wellington never seriously intended anything of that kind: his experiences with the Canningites in the previous year had sickened him of coalition Cabinets.[4] Thus, if George IV had known how to use his advantage as king of the tories, he could have retained at least as much control over policy as his father had exercised in the time of the younger Pitt.[5]

---

[1] See his letter to Liverpool, 26 Oct. 1821, in his *Despatches (Continuation)*, i. 195; and his rebuke to Londonderry in 1827, ibid. iii. 655. (On this last occasion, Wellington had just set a bad example by resigning the command of the army; but, however much he might defend this action afterwards, it was clearly an aberration caused, above all, by his uncontrollable dislike of Canning).

[2] *Journal of Mrs. Arbuthnot*, ii. 261. It is pretty clear from this report, and from Eldon's account of the interview (Twiss, *Life of Eldon*, iii. 83) that nobody was thinking of any possible accident to the bill still in the House of Lords—it was too late for that. According to Eldon, George IV neither enjoined nor forbade him to try to provide an alternative Government; but it is certain that Eldon could not have done it, for the reason which had made a purely 'Protestant' Ministry impossible since 1812: there might be enough votes on the 'Protestant' side, but there was not enough parliamentary talent.

[3] *Journal of Mrs. Arbuthnot*, ii. 273.

[4] Ibid. ii. 275, 293 (Wellington was referring here to a coalition with the 'Ultras' as a separate party; but the principle was the same).

[5] Wellington claimed (ibid. ii. 245–6) that he had offered at the beginning of the

The episode seems to show how little the politicians had changed the terms in which they thought of political power: Wellington's outburst against George IV's damaging indiscretion reminds me of the complaint which Bedford made in 1765 against the improper distribution of George III's 'smiles and frowns'.[1] Yet ideas of this sort were beginning to be out of date, even before the Reform Act. Wellington himself was the first Prime Minister since Addington—perhaps one should even say, since Shelburne—to part unwillingly from his sovereign at the behest of parliament; William IV's attempt to change his Ministry in 1834 met with no permanent success; and when Peel refused to take office in 1839 he probably attached more importance than he ought to the marks of royal 'confidence' which Queen Victoria refused him.

There were several reasons why, in spite of appearances, the influence of the Crown had declined. One of these was George IV's own conduct. Not only had he forfeited the personal popularity which his father's private virtues had always gained for him outside London; but he had destroyed his own party. The most significant thing about his 'great betrayal' of 1812 was not his failure to come to terms with Grenville and Grey, which he probably never meant to do, but the abandonment of any attempt to make Moira his Lord Bute, and the consequent annihilation of the separate Carlton House party.[2] Most of the promises he had made to his personal followers were cancelled by the rigid constitutional propriety of Lord Liverpool; and, though he might like to single out one minister or another by an injudicious particularity of friendship, the 'King's Friends', as a party, almost ceased to exist.[3] The only estimate, however rough,

session, to fight Catholic Emancipation if the king wanted. There is no trace of this in their printed correspondence, but it is quite consistent with the duke's conception of the way business should be conducted. He could not have guaranteed success. Nor would his resignation have freed the king's hands as that of Pitt freed the hands of George III in 1801 (*Correspondence of George IV*, no. 1557). There were too many differences between 1801 and 1829: the House of Commons was against yielding in 1801, for yielding in 1829, and the wishes of the Irish could not have been ignored in 1829 as George III rightly supposed they could in 1801.

[1] See my article in *Trans. Royal Hist. Soc.*, 5th series, i. 148.

[2] Soon afterwards, the relegation of Moira to the lucrative exile of Calcutta put it out of the Prince Regent's power to turn to him in an emergency as his father had turned, once or twice, to Bute.

[3] According to Mrs. Arbuthnot, Wellington found George IV's ostentatious partiality a nuisance (*Journal*, i. 300). Egmont or Northington would not have

of their number which I can find during his reign is thirty-seven.[1] This is very much smaller than Charles Fox's 180 'Supporters of the Chancellor of the Exchequer for the time being' in 1805, and shows no trace of the loyalty, or the facility, which gave George III's new ministers, in March 1807, a majority of thirty-two against the 'Talents' in a House of Commons which the 'Talents' themselves had just chosen.

The reasons for this decline were more than personal. Ever since the first Economical Reform Act of 1782, one Minister after another had been chipping away at the excrescences of Government patronage, and the House of Commons had become almost obsessed by the desire for retrenchment whenever war expenditure had called for heavy taxation.[2] It is unwise to pay very much attention to a particular minister's complaints of this state of affairs, for Lord North used to say, just like the Duke of Wellington fifty years later, that he never had an opportunity of conferring a place on a friend of his own. But there can be no mistake about the number of boards and offices reduced, even if other boards or offices had to be created, upon occasion, for the performance of new services.

Moreover, promotion in the public services was becoming more strictly professional, so that it could no longer be given away as a political reward—at least, not by the Prime Minister.[3] Church preferment, too, was ceasing to be a means of paying off the political services of lay politicians. George III, indeed, had

thought it so. In this respect, the tory politician certainly outweighed the 'King's Friend' in Wellington's composition.

[1] Sir Robert Wilson said in 1827 that a favourable Crown would carry Catholic Emancipation by seventy votes in the House of Commons (*Formation of Canning's Ministry*, ed. Aspinall, p. 37). Since it had just been defeated by four votes, this must mean that thirty-seven M.P.'s would change sides at the word of command from the king—if it means anything at all.

[2] The best treatment of this subject is that of Archibald S. Foord, 'The Waning of the Influence of the Crown', *English Historical Review*, lxii. 484–507. But the improvements were only partial and perhaps accidental (see A. Hope-Jones, *Income Tax in the Napoleonic Wars* (Cambridge, 1939), pp. 58–64).

[3] Wellington complained, in 1829, of a Treasury regulation which reserved promotion to the Collectorships of the Customs for men who had served in the inferior offices of the Customs. This automatically transferred the patronage from the First Lord of the Treasury, who had appointed the Collectors, to the Commissioners of the Customs, who filled the inferior offices (*Despatches (Continuation)*, v. 407). The operation of the same causes is illustrated by a letter of that inveterate patronage-monger Windham: he wished to have an additional under-secretaryship in his office, instead of a clerkship, whose present incumbent he could not remove (*Hist.*

never liked considering it as such; and even George IV, in spite of such incidents as the Sumner affair, was known to declaim that 'great learning, orthodox principles, and general good conduct' were a more satisfactory reason for making a man a bishop than 'political motives, or his having been tutor to a Duke'.[1] The Prime Ministers themselves were beginning to take the same view. Liverpool claimed that he had never had any connexion with the bishops he had made, and had not even known some of them, and Wellington spoke of himself as 'necessarily obliged to select those who have distinguished themselves by their professional merits'.[2] These withdrawals from the field of political patronage must have diminished the number of 'supporters of the Chancellor of the Exchequer for the time being', and, to that extent, limited the king's freedom of choice.[3]

That choice was also limited in another way. At certain times in George III's reign—notably from 1763 to 1770 and from 1801 to 1812—there had been as many as four or five independent political groups, each ready to offer, by itself or in conjunction with others, the prestige of its noblemen and the parliamentary talent of its commoners as a shield to the humbler corps of administrators who did most of the business under the king. On some occasions—for example, 1763 and 1767—the variety of the possible combinations was almost embarrassingly rich; and the sovereign might profit by the freedom of choice which this

MSS. Comm., Dropmore MSS. viii. 33). See also Peel's remarks in 1841: he had nothing to dispose of, but Household offices, parliamentary offices, and chance seats falling vacant at a Board of Revenue—every other appointment required previous service in a subordinate situation or professional qualifications (Correspondence of Charles Arbuthnot, ed. Aspinall, p. 234).

[1] Correspondence of George IV, ed. Aspinall, no. 1139. The king, who had never forgotten Liverpool's inconvenient scruples about Sumner, took this opportunity of rebuking him for some incautious expressions in a letter of recommendation; but I do not think that Liverpool's general practice deserved the rebuke.

[2] Yonge, op. cit. iii. 10; Wellington, Despatches (Continuation), iv. 300. Wellington did not, however, exclude the possibility that the Lord Chancellor might have something to bestow upon a nobleman's son; and even where bishoprics are concerned, he does not come well out of the controversy with Liverpool about his brother Gerald. Liverpool insisted that a clergyman who was separated from his wife without taking any steps to divorce her could not be promoted to a bishopric without scandal, no matter how powerful his relatives; but his virtue was not austere, for he bestowed upon Gerald Wellesley one of the richest Crown livings.

[3] When Gladstone was considering the further reform of the Civil Service on professional lines in 1853, a former chief whip pointed out that he could not be expected to like it (Edward Hughes, 'Sir Charles Trevelyan and Civil Service Reform, 1853–5', English Historical Review, lxiv. 67).

variety allowed. But now the proprietary political groups were melting away into the two great parties. Nuances of Grey and Lansdowne could still be distinguished on the whig side, or of Canningite and anti-Canningite on the tory side; but the fact remains that the last independent group—the Grenvilles—had attached themselves to the tories in 1821 and that the tory Prime Minister had negotiated this accession for the express purpose of reducing the king's liberty of choice.[1]

One cannot, at this period of history (or, perhaps, at any other) speak of more than a *tendency* to a two-party system: that tendency, which had set in after 1792, had been interrupted from 1801 to 1812, and even now, after the process of consolidation had been renewed, its permanence was not beyond question. The Huskissonians from 1828 to 1830, the 'Derby Dilly' for a few months in 1834–5, and the Peelites from 1846 to 1859 all threatened the revival of a middle group in parliament, though a very different kind of group from the Bedford or Rockingham whigs, or even the Sidmouth tories. (From 1828 to 1830 the situation was particularly confused, for there were moments when the whigs and the tories who had not consented to serve under Canning might have joined together against the whigs and the tories who had done so.)[2] Every such recrudescence might enlarge the sovereign's right, or duty, of choice: the leaders of the 'Derby Dilly' had it in mind to make themselves available to a call from William IV, and Queen Victoria never took a more active part in choosing a Prime Minister than when she laid her commands upon the Peelite Lord Aberdeen. These instances make it easy to see what was lost to the influence of the Crown when the two-party system consolidated itself.

Not only was the number of political groups being reduced once more to two, but these two groups contained, between

[1] *V. supra*, p. 185, note 1.

[2] See, especially, Londonderry's letter of 12 Aug. 1827 to Wellington, in the latter's *Despatches* (*Continuation*), iv. 84, and the various references in Mrs. Arbuthnot's *Journal*, ii. 178, 267, 273, 286, 290. Wellington, however, explained to her (ibid. 293) that this could never be: he would not take in any of the whig leaders and, unless he did so, he would 'never have more than those he paid', and so 'he must rest the strength of his Govt upon his measures & upon the honest & upright management of all the departments; that they were all filled by men with quite sufficient talent to do the business, & whenever vacancies arose, he wd fill them with those he thought most capable without at all excluding whigs'. (This is pure George III.)

them, an ever higher proportion of the House of Commons. Between 1807 and 1841, the man without a party label almost disappeared from the House of Commons as he is now disappearing from our elected municipalities. The process was gradual: as late as 1830, nobody knew who had won the general election even after it was fought, and it was not until 1868 that Disraeli confirmed, by a new constitutional convention, the assumption that everybody knew which party had won. There were other uncertainties. In the parliaments of the 1830's estimates of the strength of radicalism within the whig party varied widely, nor was it universally known in 1847 whether a particular Conservative M.P. was a Peelite or a Protectionist. Parliamentary discipline, moreover, was extremely loose, even among the acknowledged members of a party: Lord Liverpool was plagued with outbreak after outbreak of insubordination among the country gentlemen,[1] and it was not for nothing that the generation between the first and second Reform Acts was known as the golden age of the private M.P. Yet, though the parties of Grey's and Peel's time were loose and weak compared with those of Gladstone and Disraeli, they were, at least, pretty nearly inclusive; and this fact, too, was beginning to reduce the sovereign to registering the results of general elections.

This consolidation of the two-party system is not very easy to trace or to explain. It is sometimes ascribed to mechanical causes, such as the necessity of organizing the larger and better distributed electorate after 1832. No doubt that has something to do with it; but it does not explain why the separate proprietary groups within the parties had, to all intents and purposes, disappeared before 1830. Attempts have also been made to relate the political parties to the class structure, and to account for their increasing solidity by the formula of increasing tension between classes. This explanation has more to be said for it, but must be used with very great caution. The tories cannot simply be treated as the landowners' party nor the whigs as the industrial or trading party, even after the Corn Law of 1815 had introduced (perhaps for the first time) a conscious opposition between the agricultural and business interests. To treat the

---

[1] See Liverpool's complaints in *Correspondence of George IV*, ed. Aspinall, nos. 650, 772, and Wellington's in his *Despatches* (*Continuation*), i. 219, echoed of course, by Mrs. Arbuthnot in her *Journal*, i. 162–3.

tories as defending the classes which happened to be entrenched in political power and the whigs as championing other classes which tried to force their way in, is not much better. The whigs' Reform Act of 1832 may have strengthened the middle-class elements in the electorate, yet it did not increase—perhaps, indeed, it even diminished for a time—the number of middle-class men in the House of Commons, by abolishing the most venal and the most farcical constituencies, many of which were just those where moneyed men had found it easiest to buy seats against the wishes of the aristocracy. This can hardly have been unintentional, for Grey and his very aristocratic Cabinet were the political heirs of Lord Rockingham, who had complained of the intrusions of money into the preserves of 'legitimate influence'.

In any case, it is not very clear which classes were in power and which were out. The distribution of political power was fortuitous, and the opportunities for buying it, cash down, were many: while nearly all the land-holders in Scotland were disfranchised, London merchants bought seats in virtually agricultural constituencies in the south of England.[1] If hardly any manufacturers followed the example of the first Sir Robert Peel and bought their way into parliament, it can only have been because their time and their money were tied up in their factories, perhaps hundreds of miles from London, and because they stood to gain far less than the average financier, merchant, or ship-owner by contact with the ruling circles. Those middle-class men, who enjoyed such contact, had at least as much political power as was good for them. The agricultural interest may have been disproportionately represented in parliament, but it filled the air with unavailing complaints against the 'Squires of "Change Alley"' who hovered round the younger Pitt. Indeed, no British politician, not even Mr. Neville Chamberlain, believed more wholeheartedly than the men of Pitt's circle in

---

[1] The distribution of economic opportunity was scarcely less fortuitous, especially where it was regulated by law. This fact is exhibited by struggles between London and the outports, between the advocates of a regulated and a chartered African company, and, above all, between the East India Company and the private traders or even between the various 'interests' of the Company itself. An examination of the petitions in the *Commons Journals* for 1813 will show how many little trades and interests catered for, were protected by, and depended upon the Company's monopoly and how many others lived in hope of breaking it down (see also C. H. Philips, *The East India Company, 1784–1834* (Manchester, 1940), pp. 181–190).

1790 that the reputation and even, perhaps, the existence of their Government depended upon the continued prosperity of capitalist enterprise, and therefore upon peace.[1]

Yet the relation of parties to classes and ideas was, to some degree, sorted out between 1792 and 1794. For ten years before that time, it had been peculiarly confused. In the struggles of 1782–4 the parliamentary reformers had begun by supporting the adversaries of George III, as the only means of stopping the American War, but within two years most of them, like Wyvill, had decided that they disliked aristocracy even more than monarchy—and with very good reason, for, though the king's use of the political machine might be open to criticism, the machine itself was rather aristocratic. Each front bench in the House of Commons had exhibited a very 'advanced' leader with a number of reactionary henchmen and followers. The younger Pitt was George III's Prime Minister: but his political theory was at least as progressive as Fox's and his political economy much more so. Both of them began by thinking Burke's crusade for the old order a piece of romantic nonsense. But the panic of the 1790's brought about a different alignment. Portland, Loughborough, and Malmesbury did not join a reactionary Government; they rather made it reactionary by joining it. About parliamentary reform, the abolition of the slave trade, and the repeal of the Test Act they had differed not only from Pitt but still more from Fox, and they tried to turn the negotiations for a coalition between the two into an opportunity for exacting guarantees against reforms from both of them.[2] The Portland whigs, rather than Pitt's circle of professional administrators, were the real nucleus of the tory party. At the same time the great mass of the landholders and the middle class ranged itself behind the king and Pitt. The king, at least, deserved this. He had already been concerned for the maintenance of social discipline—of 'subordination'—when very few other politicians had been thinking in such terms; he had been an isolationist since 1783, but, once the great war against France had started, the unthinking tenacity which had destroyed his reputation in

---

[1] This comes out clearly in the correspondence of Auckland and Grenville (*Hist. MSS. Comm., Dropmore MSS.* ii. 93, 106, 113, 171–2, and *Journal and Correspondence of Lord Auckland,* i. 402–3).

[2] *Diaries and Correspondence of Lord Malmesbury,* ii. 460–1.

the American struggle was now to make him the most popular man in the kingdom (London, perhaps, excepted). Monarchy became the symbol for the self-preservation of a nation, and especially of a class.

In spite of the renewed confusion of the parties between 1801 and 1812, to which I have already referred, the effects of this new alignment were never wholly lost. At least the Conservative party of today can trace its ancestry back to it, and it must have been the social and national and class solidarity so created, which carried the once discredited remnant of the Pittites through their disagreements over Catholic Emancipation and the gratuitous troubles caused by Canning's personal ambition, to the triumphs of 1814 and the long, unquestioned ascendancy of Lord Liverpool. Yet this accounts much less satisfactorily for the survival of the whig party in spite of equally serious internal differences. The emergence of a two-party system may be, in part, due to some other circumstance of political life. Such a circumstance, perhaps, was the increased importance of legislation in politics.

I have tried to show that in the eighteenth century Cabinets existed to govern rather than to legislate, and parties to sustain government rather than legislation; that when a minister legislated, even on important matters, he often did so as an individual, not only technically but politically.[1] It did not often happen that a party's programme consisted of legislation,[2] or that the merits of a legislative proposal were, in any sense, put before the electorate.[3] Defeats on legislative proposals—even finance bills, did not usually involve the fall of the Government.[4] For half a generation between 1812 and 1828 the most celebrated political issue of the day, which necessarily involved legislation, was an open question within the Cabinet. This state of affairs, however, was changing. Other legislative measures, such as the

---

[1] *V. supra*, pp. 163–5.

[2] In Mar. 1782, however, three of Lord Rockingham's four points required legislation.

[3] Those of Fox's East India Bill were, however, discussed in the general election of 1784.

[4] Henry Pelham was defeated on the sugar tax in 1743, Charles Townshend made to reduce the land tax in 1767, and—most celebrated of all—Lord Liverpool's government defeated on the income tax in 1815, without resigning. But in 1819 Lord Liverpool made a point of the malt tax (*Correspondence of George IV*, ed. Aspinall, nos. 772–5).

Corn Bills, were introduced on the responsibility of the Cabinet as such; and the great spate of legislation which began in 1831 was, ever more and more, initiated and directed by the Government. This change was not complete before the age of Gladstone and Disraeli, when it was demonstrably connected with the completion of the party organizations in parliament and the country; but it was beginning before 1830, and it may have strengthened, even then, the tendency to a two-party system: for it is not possible to carry a series of bills, however rudimentary, through all their stages in parliament, without a more continuous discipline than is required for passing judgment, from time to time, on isolated acts of executive government.

A House of Commons which was coming, for whatever reason, under the control of two organized parties, did not offer the same scope for the free exercise of the royal choice as one where groups abounded and nearly half the members were without distinct party labels. Moreover the king was beginning to lose such control as he had exercised over the composition of the House itself.

I have already tried to explain that the Crown had very little direct control over the constituencies: that there were, at most, two or three dozen seats where any department of Government acted as the borough patron. These few seats were used, not so much for packing the House with votes favourable to ministers as for making sure that the necessary 'men of business' were elected.[1] Yet the Government always won general elections between 1742 and 1830. It did so, not by appealing to 'public opinion' but by making arrangements for using the electoral patronage of private persons. This was true, even when 'public opinion' was strongly on the Government's side. Although Mrs. George has shown, in a celebrated article,[2] that in 1784 Robinson's candidates did not win all the seats that he expected in the close constituencies and had more success than he expected in the open ones, yet it is clear that nobody could have won an election in the open constituencies alone, because there were

[1] Even they seem to have been expected to contribute part of the expense. From a letter of North to Robinson (*Parliamentary Papers of John Robinson*, ed. Laprade, p. 24) the normal contribution in 1774 seems to have been £1,000.
[2] *Transactions of the Royal Historical Society*, 4th series, xxi. 133–68.

not nearly enough of them; and, in fact, we can see Robinson at work, in his *Parliamentary Papers*, winning that election before it was even fought, persuading not only borough patrons to substitute new members for old but existing members already in parliament to retain their seats and vote differently in future.[1]

Secretaries of the Treasury were able to make such bargains, not because they had large sums of money at their disposal—for, as Sir Lewis Namier has pointed out, they had very little[2]—but because they could offer advantages of another kind. To the patron (or, if the candidate dealt directly with the electors, then to the candidate) they could offer the means of retaining his hold over the constituency by making him the sole channel through which its applications for small favours would be received. They could likewise induce him to risk his own money and efforts in the cause, by promising whatever he most wanted —perhaps a peerage or a sinecure for himself, or a Crown living for his brother, or a commission for his nephew. All they asked in return was that the member chosen should be, not necessarily a man designated by themselves, but a reliable friend to the Government. The Treasury stood as the intermediary between candidates of the right opinions who wanted seats and patrons of the right opinions who wanted candidates, and it had where-withal to induce the right opinions in both patrons and candidates: this was why a Secretary of the Treasury who knew his

---

[1] W. T. Laprade, 'The Parliamentary Election of 1784', *English Historical Review*, xxxi. 224–37. Professor Laprade is probably right in accounting for the reduction of Fox's majority, before Mar. 1784, by conversions of this sort. Robinson's papers, however, need some interpretation. The calculation printed on pp. 66–105 of *Parliamentary Papers of John Robinson* obviously was made before Pitt came to office, in the expectation of an immediate general election. Robinson predicted that many of the sitting members would be re-elected but would support Pitt instead of Fox in the next parliament, either because they were placemen or habitual supporters of the Ministry (for example, the members for Hythe, p. 81, for Anstruther Burghs and Culross Burghs, p. 99) or because their patrons could be induced to see that they changed sides (for example, the members for Dumfriesshire and Dumfries Burghs, p. 100). Many of these men probably changed their politics in Dec. 1783, when Pitt succeeded Fox; this (with the advent of the country gentlemen after Christmas) would explain why Fox's majorities were very much smaller in Jan. than in Dec. There were other constituencies where the patron promised not to change the attitude of the existing members, but to substitute others (for example, Liskeard, pp. 82–83, and Grampound, p. 83). These last were the reasons why there had to be a general election at all, and why Pitt won it so handsomely.

[2] *Structure of Politics*, i. 213–90.

business—no light matter[1]—could hardly fail to win a general election.

Three things were needed for this purpose: first, the electoral patronage must remain in the hands of the aristocracy, who must have no sufficient motive for withholding the use of it from the Crown; second, the sale of seats must be lawful, for not every patron could afford to bestow gratis upon the Government or its friends the use of electoral influence which cost him so much to maintain; and third, the Government must have enough patronage to procure the friendship of patrons and of candidates. All these conditions were necessary, and perhaps the third was the most necessary of all; for the borough patron was not an indispensable link in the chain and the Government could, in the last resort, still control the electorate by applying its patronage directly to the constituents, or enabling the candidates to do so, provided it still had something to offer both to candidates and to constituents.[2] The first of these three conditions existed, generally, until 1832; the second was abolished, at any rate in theory, in 1809; the third was diminishing all the time from 1782.

The gradual dwindling of these means of influence goes some way to explain how a Government could lose a general election, in peace-time, two years before the Reform Act. But perhaps there was a deeper reason still. Something else was taking the place which the Crown was losing, as the directing force in British politics. The British public was coming into its own.

This development was a slow one, and made up of a number of things. When George III came to the throne the phrase 'public opinion' meant so little as to be hardly worth using at all, except at those crises in war-time when explosions of almost universal anger could have made themselves felt even in an absolute monarchy. It then took a municipal form because there was no other form it could take: the municipal corporations might be controlled by some very queer people, but at least

---

[1] I have already adverted to the fact that even Robinson and Newcastle were only able to 'place', at any moment, about two-thirds of the House of Commons; if they did not know the business, who could?

[2] This, presumably, is what Lord Liverpool meant when he said (after Curwen's Act) 'Our friends, therefore, who look for the assistance of Government must be ready to start for open boroughs, where the general influence of Government, combined with a reasonable expense on their own part, may afford them a fair chance of success' (Yonge, op. cit. i. 444).

they had a certain status for expressing feelings which everybody held, and that is why it 'rained gold boxes'—freedoms of
corporations—upon Pitt and Legge in 1755-6. Above all, the
city of London had a public opinion of its own. It was the strong-
hold of Pitt and, later, of Wilkes. The enemies of those demagogues were probably mistaken in thinking that they had no
other support;[1] but they certainly had none which could be so
easily identified and organized. Twenty years later, the politically active 'British public' was already spreading to the pro-
vinces; the parliamentary reform movement and the revulsion
against Charles Fox were both nation-wide. There were several
reasons for this extension: above all, the discovery of new political machinery for expressing and mobilizing the opinions of
private people. I do not share Professor Butterfield's belief that
the growth of parliamentary reform associations in 1780 constituted a dangerous crisis or a revolution *manquée*; at least, there
is hardly any evidence that it worried the king or Lord North.[2]
But it is almost impossible to exaggerate the potential importance of this sort of agencies; and the even better organized
campaign of the humanitarians against the slave trade showed,
within a few years, that a public opinion thus mobilized could
procure Acts of Parliament. A little later again the newspapers
began to play a part in expressing this opinion. The mechanical
improvements, which enabled *The Times* to sustain a large circulation and to escape from dependence on the Treasury and
the theatre managers to the more impersonal patronage of the
advertisers, began the emancipation of the press from the position of a 'tied house'; and the growth of provincial reporting
(not really easy before the railways were built) meant that the
opinion which the London newspapers brought to bear on the
politicians was ceasing to be merely London opinion.[3]

To this opinion the politicians were becoming more amen-
able. For one thing, the public could see what the politicians
were doing. The absurdities of the Brass Crosby case in 1770

[1] Henry Fox always spoke as if this were true of Pitt (e.g. in *Life and Letters of
Lady Sarah Lennox*, i. 76–77). The Duke of Bedford, however, was roughly handled
by mobs of Wilkes's supporters at Exeter and Honiton in 1769 (see his journal
printed in Sir H. Cavendish, *Debates*, ed. Wright, i. 620–1).

[2] See my review of *George III, Lord North and the People*, in the *English Historical
Review*, lxv. 526–9.

[3] *The History of* The Times, i. (London, 1935), pp. 20, 115–17, 247, 413–14, 429–34.

did not directly establish the right of parliamentary reporting, for the galleries were still quite often cleared of strangers; but the outcry over the prosecutions of Gale Jones and Burdett made it almost impossible for the Houses to insist on doing so. Even the king, who was not supposed to hear what the members of parliament had said for fear of a breach of privilege, could now read it in the newspapers.[1] By 1826 there can have been very few people who remembered, like the Duke of Wellington, that the proceedings of the two Houses were technically private, or believed that 'Discussions, with open doors, and the publication of the discussions of a Legislative Assembly, however desirable, are not absolutely necessary for the existence of freedom or good government in any country'.[2] This publicity had its effect on the relations of ministers to parliament. Canning seems to have been the first British politician to use the House of Commons as a sounding-board for a wider public, just as he and Huskisson were the first to go speechifying up and down the country, to the great indignation of George IV who anticipated by more than half a century Queen Victoria's protests against the similar practices of Gladstone.[3] These speeches sometimes resulted in pledges, individual or collective, which might prove inconvenient and were, in any case, contrary to the older principle that a minister went into Cabinet with no obligation but to do the best he could for his country.[4] Canning and Huskisson foreshadow the middle-class prima donna in politics, with his

[1] George III referred for the first time to a newspaper report of a politician's speech in Nov. 1776 (*Correspondence of George III*, no. 1924). The fiction that it was a breach of privilege for a member of parliament to inform the king about debates was belied by the practice: it was the duty of the leader of each House to send him a daily report of the proceedings. George III referred to this as an established convention in 1767 (ibid., no. 414) and his printed *Correspondence* abounds in such reports, most of them very jejune.

[2] *Wellington, Despatches (Continuation)*, iii. 376.

[3] He asked Lord Liverpool in 1823 to suppress 'the passion which seems to exist for speech making out of time and out of proper place. What would Mr. Pitt have said if, in his days, sub-Ministers and others belonging to the Government had indulged in such inconvenient practices?' (*Correspondence of George IV*, ed. Aspinall, no. 1110).

[4] See Wellington's complaint against Huskisson's pledges (*Despatches (Continuation)*, iii. 343). See also Mrs. Arbuthnot's report (*Journal*, i. 400) of a Cabinet at which Canning declared beforehand that he would not agree to further coercion of the Catholics. 'The Duke of Wellington said he could not hear of such a pledge; that, if the circumstances arose, he was sure every member of the Cabinet wd do what was best at the time & no such engagement could be considered binding.'

thin skin and his obligations to 'his' public, so unlike Wellington and Peel who believed that a Government's duty was to govern in the light of the circumstances of the time, and that its followers' duty was to support it in so doing, regardless of past pledges. When the personal pledges were turned into party pledges—a thing which began to happen very soon after the Reform Act— the conflict between these two conceptions of government might even produce a catastrophe like that of 1846.[1]

The greater publicity of parliamentary proceedings, and the pledges which the leaders were beginning to give to the public, were not the only things which altered the conditions of parliamentary life. Members of parliament demanded, or received without demanding, more and more information about the proceedings of the Government and the state of the country; and that information was not merely laid, as before, on the table of the Houses but printed and published, so that the whole world could, if it chose, know what the member of parliament knew. Sometimes ministers themselves offered this information of their own accord: this was one of Canning's innovations. He made the laying of papers before parliament an instrument of foreign policy, to the alarm of Wellington, who argued in 1824 that: 'The moment the government lay papers before Parliament on any political question, the decision is no longer practically in their hands. Whatever may be the consequence in point of form, the decision of the government in point of fact cannot be independent'.[2] But even when the Government did not take the initiative, any back-bencher could demand the production of papers upon any subject; and, though the Ministry could refuse, it put itself in an awkward position unless it could claim that the papers related to an unfinished negotiation.[3] This reservation

---

[1] See N. Gash, in *Trans. Royal Hist. Soc.*, 5th series, i. 47–69.

[2] *Wellington, Despatches (Continuation)*, ii. 229. Wellington went on to argue, 'Foreigners who have witnessed and are aware of the caution and reserve with which we are in the habit of communicating papers of this description to Parliament, will see in this a desire to throw it out of our own hands', which was, no doubt, exactly what Canning intended.

[3] This was the doctrine of George Grenville and other supporters of the motion for the correspondence with France about the cession of Corsica (Sir H. Cavendish, *Debates*, ed. Wright, i. 58). There was a dispute between Spencer Perceval and Howick, in 1807, over the question whether it was parliamentary conduct to demand sight of papers without giving a reason (Spencer Walpole, *Life of Spencer Perceval*, i. 219).

was not nearly wide enough to satisfy the diplomats: as Hans Stanley (who had been on a foreign mission) pointed out, 'Ministers cannot speak out to ambassadors, if papers of this kind may be called for by parliament.' Yet even diplomatic documents continued to be called for and produced, though perhaps more sparingly than trade and financial returns, East India correspondence or dispatches about the condition of slaves in the colonies. Ministers and their agents were driven to rely more and more on private letters which, originally designed to withhold information from the king or from Cabinet colleagues, finally became most useful as a means of conveying information in a document of which parliament could have no official cognizance.[1]

---

[1] Ministers often entertained a private correspondence with agents of other departments, as Newcastle, when First Lord of the Treasury, exchanged letters constantly with Joseph Yorke, Minister at The Hague. Pitt, Secretary of State, obviously disliked this interference, just as he disliked Newcastle's talking diplomatic business with the French envoy in 1761; he therefore kicked up a fuss about Yorke's letters in 1759 (see Basil Williams, *William Pitt, Earl of Chatham*, ii. 75–76). Newcastle had shown some of Yorke's letters to George II, though the original purpose of this kind of correspondence was to convey information which need not be shown to the king; for, whereas a Secretary of State could not deny that he had received a dispatch, nobody could force him to produce a private letter, which nobody could convict him of having received. To show the king, or a colleague, one private letter, therefore, is not to admit the existence of private letters on other occasions. This is why the official correspondence of Secretaries of State is so often supplemented by unofficial correspondence with the same persons. When Lord Grenville became Foreign Secretary in 1791 he promised that he would not show the private letters of Ministers abroad to anybody except, occasionally, Pitt. (*Hist. MSS. Comm., Dropmore MSS.* ii. 101, 142.) Another sphere in which private letters were much used is the government of Ireland. Communication was so easy, so many British politicians had Irish property or relations, or were connected politically with Irish officeholders (as Portland was connected with the Ponsonbys) that almost everybody seems to have written to everybody, and there was great confusion. Thus we find Lord Buckinghamshire, the Lord Lieutenant, trying in 1779 to establish a private correspondence with the Secretary of State (apparently in order to say something which had better not be submitted to parliament); actually corresponding with Lord North; and complaining bitterly of the letters passing between the subordinate officeholders in Ireland and members of 'Lord North's interior Cabinet' (*Hist. MSS. Comm., Stopford-Sackville MSS.* i. 255, 266; *Lothian MSS.*, pp. 343, 359, 391). In 1782 Charles Fox, though very angry with Shelburne for interfering in his department, corresponded freely with Fitzpatrick and Portland about Irish questions, which were in Shelburne's province (*Memorials and Correspondence of Charles James Fox*, i. 388–418, *passim*); and next year, although he purported to be on much better terms with North than with Shelburne, he did the same thing again, and even told the Lord Lieutenant 'I wish, therefore, for the future, when you write for instructions on material points, that you or Pelham would write a private letter to the Duke of Portland or to me, letting us know how

This practice was allied to a new procedure of inquiry—the select committee of the House or, more rarely, of the Privy Council.[1] Back-benchers could use this instrument more purposefully than the mere right to fish in ministerial correspondence for what they might find. Everybody knows the celebrated story how Francis Place obtained, through such a back-bencher, a select committee on the Combination Laws, rigged all the evidence, and induced parliament to pass an Act of which neither it nor (as it turned out) Place himself understood the consequences.[2] This was an exceptional and not a very edifying incident. But the conduct of such select committees, and the consideration of their reports, must have brought members of parliament face to face with the interests and the facts, as the study of petitions and an occasional examination of witnesses at the bar of the House could not.[3] These members, pursuing their own inquiries, relying on evidence given in their own presence, and bringing in their own bills, often acted without much regard to the wishes of the Ministry; this is one reason why so much of the legislation, especially in questions of social welfare, continued to be the work of private members down to the middle of the century, or even later. But this work brought them into contact

---

far you consider each point as important to your plans or arrangements' (ibid. ii. 167). The correspondence of the Irish and British underlings, to which Fox had so much objected, continued for many years. Beresford's private letters to Auckland were particularly objected to, and probably accounted for Fitzwilliam's precipitation in dismissing him in 1795.

[1] Strictly this was not a new procedure, for there had been occasional committees earlier in the century; but it obtained a new political prominence in the 1770's, when a series of committees into East India affairs seem to have set the fashion. The celebrated inquiry of 1788 into the slave trade was conducted by a Privy Council committee: this had certain disadvantages, for witnesses could not be compelled to give evidence, and the Houses of Parliament might (out of *amour propre* or obstructiveness) insist on hearing the evidence all over again for themselves before they would take action (T. Clarkson, *History of the Abolition of the Slave Trade* (1808), i. 476, 508). One of the earliest occasions when a colleague tried to persuade the Prime Minister to establish a parliamentary committee in order to prepare the ground for legislation must have been 1782, when Richmond tried to make a bargain with Rockingham for a committee on parliamentary reform (Albemarle, *Memoirs of the Marquess of Rockingham*, ii. 481).

[2] Graham Wallas, *Life of Francis Place*, chapter viii.

[3] Something of the sort had existed earlier, for the House of Commons had often conferred upon committees the right to send for papers and examine witnesses, and they sometimes had their reports printed in its Journal or elsewhere for the benefit of members of parliament and the world at large; but this procedure was used far more widely after 1800 than before.

and even sympathy with the wishes and interests of the public, which was now able to watch and criticize them. Some of them were responsive to those wishes, long before they were responsible to any proper constituency; and this awareness of the public, together with the harder work, longer sessions, better-attended divisions, made the career of a British politician on the eve of 1830 very unlike what it had been in 1760. He was a public man, in a very different sense. Responsive to the wishes of the public, he need not, he could not heed the wishes of the Crown, or look to it for leadership as his predecessors had done.

I have tried to answer the first of the two questions—'Who won?' Neither the monarchy nor its adversaries won; both slowly lost ground to another force, which had supported the aristocrats against the king in 1780, the king against the aristocrats in 1784 and 1807, but was now becoming strong enough to claim power for itself. It would be misleading to call this force 'the middle class', but it might fairly be called 'the public'. Since this is so, perhaps it would be waste of time to discuss the other question, whether George III or Rockingham and Charles Fox were 'right'. Yet the constitution had a logic of its own: there was a sense in which George III was 'right' and another in which Charles Fox, with all his faults, was still more 'right'. It is too simple to say that George III was right with reference to the past and Fox right with reference to the future. But there was a deduction which could be drawn from the principles of the constitution which they both accepted. Charles Fox was right in thinking that this deduction must ultimately be drawn; George III was right in thinking that there was nothing, in the circumstances of his own time, which obliged him to draw it.

The House of Commons admittedly had the right to condemn the king's ministers. Charles Fox was not the inventor of the maxim that 'the king can do no wrong', and the habit of making the ministers generally responsible for the king's actions was well established before he was born. It does not matter that many of the most successful impeachments were of ministers whom the king had already more than half deserted, or that the issue was confused, even in these, by attempts to prove something that looked like an offence against the law instead of admitting that impeachment was the penalty for mere failure or unpopularity. When political sanctions finally took the place of penal sanctions in the middle of the eighteenth century, the doctrine of ministerial responsibility had reached something like its modern form. Perhaps, as Pitt argued in 1784, the House ought not to condemn ministers without assigning particular reasons and allowing them a fair period of office to prove their merits; but in the last resort it could condemn them, and it alone could judge the sufficiency of its reasons—as North told the king, the opinions of the House, 'whether just or erroneous, must prevail'. It possessed, in reserve, too many weapons to be resisted.

From the right of condemning ministers the right of designating them must, in the end, be deduced. Henry Fox might reject the deduction as improper or disloyal; but his son saw more clearly that those who possess the one right must necessarily possess the other—provided they were so constituted as to be able to exercise it. There was the rub. Any House of Commons could turn a minister out by a spontaneous revulsion, as North was turned out in 1782. Not every House of Commons could sustain, by a permanent and disciplined majority, a minister of its own choice. When a third of its members did not belong to any party at all, and could not even be relied upon to be present; when the remaining two-thirds were divided among three or more parties—even though the largest single group was that of those who would support almost any Ministry—the House of Commons had not usually the means of designating ministers for itself, though it might have the means of supporting a Ministry once designated. The only time, in George III's reign, that the House succeeded in performing this function of designating ministers, it was condemned by almost all decent people for perpetrating an 'infamous coalition'. Little wonder, then, that the choice of minister was habitually left to the king, and that the House of Commons confined itself to the negative role.

It could not take the positive role before the two-party system became its principle of organization; and, though there were earlier approximations to the two-party system, it was not well established before 1821 at the earliest. Fox and Burke talked about party, and the Macaulay dynasty afterwards praised them for their devotion to it; but the whig party of Burke and Fox only resembled very remotely the Liberal party of Macaulay. It did not even provide the talent necessary for governing—for, when Cumberland introduced Rockingham into the closet as the King's first minister, he seems to have recognized that he was only providing the great names while the king provided the administrative capacity from the ranks of his so-called 'friends'.[1] It did not provide the numbers in the House of Commons—the Rockingham party in 1765 cannot possibly have exceeded a hundred. It did not provide the organization in the country— the Rockinghams had no definable relation to public opinion except that of sitting with folded hands and waiting for it to fill their sails.[2] For a party so constituted to claim the right to hold the king to ransom was laughable, except at the rare crisis when the public demanded, at any price, some means of stopping the king's fatal American war. Even then, a coalition of parties was needed for maintaining the advantage gained over the king. George II had submitted to such a coalition; George III found that he need not do so.

For, in the last resort, even if parties had the means of holding the House of Commons steady, that would not have defended them against the king unless they could hold the electorate steady too. Neither the general election of 1784 nor that of 1807 was strictly necessary, for George III had already wiped out his enemies' parliamentary majority in 1784, and they never had one in 1807. But the turnover of seats was significant on each occasion, even though it was not accompanied by an exceptional number of contests.[3] Not until the election of 1835 or, at the

[1] *Jenkinson Papers, 1760–1766*, ed. N. Jucker, p. 370.

[2] Richmond once wrote to Burke 'The only way to cure this stupefaction is to lie by, and let people fight their own battles a little. I would look on quietly, and let the ministers alone; they will then do some crying injustice, and when they begin to feel, they will cry out, and come to us to implore our assistance' (Burke's *Works* (1852 edn.), i. 198). Burke and Fox, to do them justice, deplored this 'heresy of depending upon contingencies', though Burke recognized that it was just what might be expected of men of 'honest and disinterested intentions, plentiful fortunes, assured rank, and quiet homes'. He thought that Rockingham and his friends, 'though not thought so much devoted to popularity as others, do very much look to the people, and more than I think is wise in them, who do so little to guide and direct the public opinion' (ibid. v. 513). But although he was always preaching the necessity of organizing opposition out of doors, he had no practicable way of doing it, and when the parliamentary reformers invented one, they took very good care to prevent him from using it for his own purposes.

[3] Professor W. T. Laprade stated (*English Historical Review*, xxxi. 227) that the

earliest, 1830 was the king proved to have lost this resource—not only because he no longer possessed wherewithal to persuade candidates and voters, but because something else had come in to take his place.

Thus it was the modern party system, above all, which destroyed the more personal conception of constitutional monarchy and reduced it (though not so quickly as Bagehot supposed) to the role of 'encouraging, advising, and warning'. Party was the power which maintained in motion the irresistible weapons which the House of Commons possessed against the king. Without this motive power, any attempt to use those weapons consistently was an anachronism. In default of it, the moving spirit in politics and government could only be the will of the king himself. When his will was weak, politics almost disintegrated, as they did between 1748 and 1756, or again between 1827 and 1830. When it was firm and confident, as in the 1770's, it controlled the machine so effectively that the united will of almost the whole country could only succeed, after a convulsion of several years, in correcting a great mistake. Historians may be right in blaming George III's mistakes, but they are wrong in considering his career a failure; for he continued, nearly until the end of his political life, to do for his country what it had not yet the means of doing so well for itself.

number of contests in 1784 was not exceptional. Mrs. George has suggested (*Trans. Royal Hist. Soc.* 4th series, xxi. 135–8) that there were more contests than Professor Laprade was aware of; but this might have been equally true of the other general elections with which he compared that of 1784.

INDEX

Abbot, Charles, 27, 29, 36, 70, 141, 150 n., 178 n.

Aberdeen, Earl of, 191.

Addington, Henry, *see* Sidmouth, Viscount.

Adjournment of House of Commons, 96 n.

American question, 50, 68, 85, 90–91, 119–20, 172 n.

Anson, Lord, 20 n.

Arbuthnot, Charles, 83 n.

Arbuthnot, Mrs. Harriet, 12 n., 150 n., 185, 186 n., 187.

Army, the, 17–19, 144.

Ashburton, Lord, 88 n., 165 n.

Atkinson, Richard, 131 n.

Auckland, William Eden, Lord, 9, 12, 28 n., 29–30, 41, 81 n., 160–1, 194 n., 203 n.

Bagot, Sir Charles, 186 n.

Barham, Lord, 20 n.

Barnes, Professor D. G., 98 n., 180.

Barré, Isaac, 6, 128.

Barrington, Admiral, 21 n.

Barrington, Bishop, 25 n.

Barrington, Lord, 58 n., 144, 153 n., 166.

Bathurst, Earl, 13.

Beckford, William, 47.

Bedchamber, Lords of the, 41, 63, 146, 149 n.

Bedford, 4th Duke of, 56, 76, 81, 89–91, 101 n., 105 n., 106 n., 107 n., 108 n., 111 n., 116, 147 n., 152 n., 167 n., 188, 199 n.

Bedford, 5th Duke of, 59 n., 60 n.

Bedford Whigs, 72, 75–76, 81, 86 n., 87 n, 167, 170–1, 191.

Beresford, John, 203 n.

Berkeley of Stratton, Lord, 29.

Bishops, 23–25, 40–42, 144, 189.

Blackstone, Mr. Justice, 32.

Board of Trade, President of, 148.

Brand's Resolution (1807), 156 n.

Bristol, constituency, 3, 10, 50.

Bristol, Earl of, 77.

Brougham, Henry, 83.

Brown, Rev. John, 7, 71 n.

Buckingham, 1st Marquess of, 9, 18 n., 27, 38 n., 39, 110, 123, 144–5, 183.

Buckingham, 2nd Marquess and 1st Duke of, 36, 39, 185 n.

Buckingham Palace, 58 n.

Buckinghamshire, Earl of, 202 n.

Bulkeley, Lord, 41, 78 n.

Burgoyne, General, 22.

Burke, Edmund, 3, 6, 10 n., 11, 13–14, 15 n., 31–32, 43, 48–50, 51 n., 55, 57–60, 64 n., 75, 80, 84–85, 88 n., 96 n., 116–17, 124 n., 127 n., 129–30, 134, 155 n., 169 n., 170, 182 n., 194, 205, 206 n.

Burney, Fanny, 58 n., 65 n., 66.

Business men in politics, 15–16, 193–4.

Bute, Earl of, 5, 46–47, 56 n., 59 n., 66–67, 84 n., 86, 99–109, 113–15, 148 n., 150 n., 152 n., 158 n., 167 n., 169, 173.

Butterfield, Professor H., 172 n., 199.

Byng, Admiral, 21.

Cabinet, the, 20, 83, 121, 143–4, 149–70, 178, 185 n., 195.

Camden, Lord, 22 n., 50 n., 54–55, 56 n., 77, 96 n.

Canning, George, 10 n., 12, 27 n., 41 n., 42 n., 77, 81 n., 82 n., 86 n., 110, 140–1, 150 n., 159, 161, 163, 170, 185–6, 191, 195, 200–1.

Carmarthen, Marquess of, *see* Leeds, Duke of.

Caroline, Queen (wife of George II), 63, 151, 176 n.

Carteret, Lord, 44, 89 n., 94 n., 95 n., 97, 104, 148 n., 153, 170 n.

Carysfort, Lord, 138 n.

Castlereagh, Viscount, 81 n., 141, 147, 155, 164 n., 169 n., 177 n., 185 n.

Catholic Association, 53 n.

Catholic emancipation, 53 n., 60 n., 69, 91–92, 136 n., 137–9, 141–2, 155–7, 162, 164–6, 184–5, 187, 195.

Cavendish family, 58–59, 74, 99–100.

Cavendish, Sir H., 179.

Cavendish, Lord John, 58 n., 74.

Chamberlain, Neville, 94 n.

Charlotte, Princess, 136 n.

Charlotte, Queen, 65–66.
Chatham, Earl of, *see* Pitt, William, the elder.
Chesterfield, 4th Earl of, 62 n., 71 n., 88, 94 n., 95–96, 111.
Chesterfield, 5th Earl of, 180 n.
Church, the, 17, 23–25, 189–90.
Cinque Ports, 76 n.; Lord Warden of, 12 n., 80 n.
Closet, the, 148–9.
Committees, Parliamentary, 203.
Commons, House of, 3, 4, 17, 34–36, 40, 43–54, 62, 67, 72–74, 78 n., 93–94, 98, 122–7, 133–4, 148, 192–4, 205–6.
Conway, H. S., 6, 18, 47 n., 49, 70, 74, 85 n., 88 n., 90, 159, 166 n., 168, 178 n.
Cook, Captain, 20, 66.
Corn Law of 1815, 192, 196.
Cornwallis, Marquess, 145, 164 n.
Coronation oath, 140 n.
County constituencies, 8–9.
County meetings, 51–52.
Courtenay, John, 130 n.
Creevey, Thomas, 13.
Crosby, Brass, Case of, 199.
Cumberland, Duke of, 18, 63, 66–67, 109, 115, 117 n., 206.
Curwen's Act, 198.

Dartmouth, Earl of, 64.
Declaratory Act, 91.
'Derby Dilly', 191.
Devonshire, Duke of, 57, 59, 74 n., 96 n., 97, 99, 101 n., 151–2.
Disraeli, Benjamin, 192, 196.
Dissolution, right of, 134, 140.
Dodington, George Bubb, 101 n.
Dowdeswell, William, 14, 59, 97 n.
Dundas, Henry, Lord Melville, 6, 12 n., 122 n., 131 n., 140 n., 141, 153, 155 n., 161, 165 n., 169, 178 n.
Dunning's Resolution, 31 n., 119–20.
Dyson, Jeremiah, 12, 179.

East India Company, 26, 193 n.
Economical Reform, 120, 121 n., 127 n., 129–30, 165 n., 189.
Eden, William, *see* Auckland, Lord.
Edgcumbe affair, 84 n., 96 n., 116 n., 182 n.
Egmont, Earl of, 5 n., 84 n., 88 n., 107 n., 158, 168, 171.

Egremont, Earl of, 106 n., 160 n., 169.
Eldon, Lord, 11, 23, 132 n., 140 n., 147 n., 157, 187.
Elections, 8–9; General, 2 n., 134–5, 195–8, 206–7.
Eliot, Edward, 36.
Ellenborough, Lord, 138.
Elliot, Gilbert, 12, 14, 107, 108 n., 162 n.
Ellis, Welbore, 10 n., 179.
Erskine, Lord, 23 n., 140 n.
Exchequer, Chancellor of, 148.

Falmouth, Viscount, 29.
Fauconberg, Lord, 52 n.
Fitzpatrick, Richard, 122.
Fitzwilliam, Earl, 12, 59 n., 75, 82 n., 87 n., 132 n., 135 n.
Flood, Henry, 43 n., 53 n.
Fortescue, Sir John, 1 n.
Fox, Charles James, 10 n., 24, 29, 35 n., 38 n., 65, 72–5, 80 n., 81–82, 86, 88 n., 89 n., 91, 97, 98, 110, 120–30, 132–6, 137 n., 138–41, 143, 146, 150 n., 154–5, 158, 162, 163 n, 165, 167–9, 171, 173, 179, 181–3, 194, 197 n., 202 n., 204–5, 207.
Fox, Henry, 4, 9 n., 18, 21 n., 45–46, 55 n., 61, 63, 79 n., 89 n., 99, 100 n., 102–3, 148 n., 205.
France, wars with, 68–70, 135 n., 194–5.
Fremantle, W. H., 36, 39 n.

General Warrants, 91.
George I, 94 n., 150–1.
George II, 17, 44, 55 n., 61–64, 94–97, 99 n., 111 n., 121, 148 n., 150–1, 183, 206.
George III, 5, 7 n., 10 n., 11, 15 n., 17, 18 n., 19, 21 n., 22 n., 23 n., 28 n., 31, 34–35, 40, 45 n., 50, 57–58, 61–62, 64–72, 78, 79 n., 85–86, 90 n., 92, 95–175, 178–83, 184 n., 188 n., 194, 200 n., 204–7.
George IV, 41 n., 42 n., 87 n., 101 n., 110 n., 111 n., 121 n., 136 n., 142, 146–7, 149 n., 157–9, 162, 163 n., 167, 184–8, 200 n.
George, Mrs. M. D., 196, 207 n.
Germain, Lord George, *see* Sackville, Lord George.
Gladstone, W. E., 157, 190 n., 196, 200.
Goderich, Viscount, 185–6.

Gower, Earl, 10 n., 11, 76, 110, 116 n.,
122 n., 170 n.

Grafton, 2nd Duke of, 97.

Grafton, 3rd Duke of, 25 n., 40, 60, 65,
72, 86, 88 n., 89 n., 90, 110 n., 111 n.,
117–18, 160 n., 171, 174.

Granby, Marquess of, 96 n., 152 n.

Grantham, Lord, 150 n.

Grenville, family, 1, 37–39, 77, 82, 129,
145 n.; see also Temple, Earl;
Buckingham, Marquess and Duke
of.

Grenville, George, 5, 9 n., 13, 14 n.,
18–19, 21 n., 28, 38 n., 39, 45–46,
56 n., 68, 77, 79, 81, 82 n., 85 n., 90–
91, 98–99, 101 n., 105 n., 106, 107 n.,
108, 109 n., 113, 114 n., 116, 143,
145, 147 n., 148 n., 150 n., 152,
166 n., 167, 169, 171, 178–9, 201 n.

Grenville, James, 38 n.

Grenville, Thomas, 38 n., 39, 128.

Grenville, William Wyndham, Lord, 6,
9, 12 n., 20 n., 38 n., 39, 42 n., 69,
75 n., 81 n., 87 n., 88 n., 91, 98, 101 n.,
110, 111 n., 134 n., 137 n., 138–9, 141,
144–6, 148 n., 150 n., 153, 156 n.,
159, 160 n., 161–5, 169, 178 n., 185,
188, 202 n.

Grey, Charles (afterwards Viscount
Howick and 2nd Earl Grey), 12–13,
42 n., 75, 87 n., 101 n., 111 n., 141,
146, 185, 188, 193, 201 n.

Grosvenor, Thomas, 73.

Halifax, Earl of, 106, 159, 167, 178 n.

Hamilton, W. G., 90.

Hanover, 4–5, 151, 163 n., 183.

Hardwicke, 1st Earl of, 23, 37, 55 n.,
74, 95 n., 99 n., 101 n., 121, 169 n.,
176.

Hardwicke, 2nd Earl of, 37, 160 n.

Hardwicke, 3rd Earl of, 37, 178 n.

Harrington, Earl of, 95.

Harris, Sir James, see Malmesbury,
Lord.

Hawke, Sir Edward, 20.

Hawkesbury, Lord, see Liverpool, 2nd
Earl of.

Heir apparent, the, 101.

Herries, J. C., 186.

Herring, Archbishop, 23.

Herschel, Sir William, 66.

Hertford, Earl of, 18 n., 49 n., 66 n.

Hillsborough, Earl of, 58, 97 n., 117 n.,
160 n., 161, 171.

Hinchcliffe, Bishop, 25 n.

Holland, 3rd Lord, 141, 149 n., 157 n.,
173 n.

Hollis, Thomas, 54.

Household, Royal, 145; see also Bedchamber, Lords of the.

Howe, Lord, 20.

Howe, Sir William, 22.

Howick, Viscount, see Grey, Charles.

Huskisson, William, 12, 128, 170 n.,
191, 200.

Impeachments, 93.

Indian affairs, 16, 26, 47, 126–7, 131,
166 n.

Ireland, 3 n., 41 n., 53 n., 202 n.; Lord
Lieutenant of, 27, 64 n., 144, 178 n.;
Union with, 73 n., 145.

Irish M.P.s, 73.

Irish Volunteers, 53 n.

Jacobites, 71 n., 72.

Jamaica, 51.

Jenkinson, Charles, 1st Earl of Liverpool, 12, 73 n., 107, 150 n., 153,
171–3, 179 n.

Johnson, Dr., 19, 67 n.

Jones, Gale, 200.

Junius, 64–65, 117 n.

Kentish Petition, 51.

Kenyon, Lord, 140 n.

Keppel, Admiral Viscount, 21.

'King's Friends', 107–8, 117 n., 185 n.,
186, 188–9, 206.

Landowners, 192–3.

Laprade, Professor W. T., 197 n.,
206 n.

Leeds, Duke of, 25, 36, 98 n., 120 n.,
134 n., 159, 160 n., 161, 180 n.

Legal profession, 17, 22–23.

Legge, H. B., 46, 116 n., 199.

Legislation, 164–6, 195–6.

Leicester House, 101 n.

Lestock, Admiral, 21.

Liverpool, 1st Earl of, see Jenkinson,
Charles.

Liverpool, 2nd Earl of, 12 n., 39 n.,
139 n., 141, 146–7, 161, 170, 178 n.,
181, 183–6, 190, 192, 195, 198 n.

Locke, 33, 54 n.
London, City of, 54 n., 55 n., 199.
Londonderry, 3rd Marquess of, 185 n.
Lord Chancellor, 109–10.
Lords, House of, 35–36, 39–44, 60, 131.
Loughborough, Lord, 22 n., 41 n., 81 n., 126 n., 194.
Lowther, Sir James, 11, 36.

Macaulay, T. B., 205–6.
McIlwain, C. H., 32 n.
Mackintosh, Sir James, 141 n.
Malmesbury, Lord, 69 n., 81 n., 129 n., 134, 138 n., 139 n., 150 n., 159, 194.
Mansfield, Lord, 44 n., 55 n., 90 n., 152.
Markham, Archbishop, 24.
Matthews, Admiral, 20.
Meredith, Sir William, 11 n.
Middlesex Election, 49–50, 58 n., 70.
Moira, Earl of, 110 n., 146, 188.
Montesquieu, 31.
Murray, William, see Mansfield, Lord.
Mutiny Acts, 33 n., 134 n.

Namier, Sir Lewis, 1–2, 45 n., 58, 197.
Navy, the, 17, 19–22.
Newcastle, Duke of, 4 n., 24, 42, 44 n., 45–47, 55 n., 56–57, 62, 71–72, 76, 79, 81, 83, 85 n., 86, 89, 94 n., 95–97, 99, 101 n., 102, 104, 106, 108–9, 113, 114 n., 115, 148 n., 158 n., 166 n., 168 n., 170 n., 176–7, 183, 202 n.
North, Lord, 10 n., 13, 21, 27, 28 n., 34–35, 40, 47–48, 52, 67, 73, 77, 79, 81, 86, 88 n., 94 n., 104, 110 n., 112 n., 120, 122, 144, 146 n., 151, 152 n., 153–4, 158, 161–2, 171–5, 179, 183, 199, 202 n., 205.
North Briton, 19.
Northington, Earl of, 22 n., 23, 84 n., 88 n., 152, 158, 168, 171.
Northumberland, Earl of, 108 n.

Oczakoff Crisis, 23 n., 87.
Onslow, George, 50.
Oswald, James, 89 n., 103, 107.
Oxford, University of, 72 n.
Oxfordshire, Election of 1754, 8.

Paget, Berkeley, 147.
Palliser, Admiral Sir Hugh, 21, 67 n.
Palmerston, Viscount, 36, 80 n.

Parliamentary Reform, 43, 165, 192–4.
Parties, 71–92, 116–17, 190–5, 205–6.
Patriot King, 71.
Patronage, 6–7, 10–11, 16–30, 79–80, 178 n., 189–90, 198.
Patten's Motion, 137 n.
Peel, Sir Robert, 1st Bart., 193.
Peel, Sir Robert, 2nd Bart., 12, 83 n., 113, 121 n., 170 n., 178 n., 185 n., 188, 201.
Peelites, 191–2.
Peerages, 35–36, 57, 145.
Pelham, Henry, 4, 21 n., 44, 86, 89 n., 95 n., 121, 166 n., 170 n., 176–7, 195 n.
Pelham, Lord, 159.
Perceval, Spencer, 28 n., 81 n., 110 n., 139, 141, 147, 156–7, 201 n.
Percy, Dean, 42, 186 n.
Pigot, Admiral, 21.
Pitt, Thomas, 44 n., 48.
Pitt, William, the elder (later Earl of Chatham), 5, 9 n., 22 n., 23 n., 36, 38 n., 45–47, 54–57, 63, 66–67, 70, 72, 77–78, 81, 82 n., 84, 85 n., 89, 91, 96, 97 n., 99, 101 n., 102–3, 106–8, 110–17, 129, 148 n., 149 n., 158 n., 160 n., 166 n., 174, 177, 178 n., 181, 182 n., 199, 202 n.
Pitt, William, the younger, 9, 10 n., 11, 20 n., 27, 28 n., 36–37, 38 n., 42, 43 n., 48, 59 n., 69, 77–78, 81–82, 86, 89 n., 91, 97–98, 109 n., 110–11, 122 n., 125 n., 127–38, 141, 143–4, 155–6, 159, 160 n., 161–2, 164–5, 169, 171, 172 n., 173, 179–81, 193–4, 197 n. 205.
Place, Francis, 203.
Portland, Duke of, 59–60, 82, 84 n., 88 n., 110, 111 n., 121–3, 131, 133, 139 n., 146, 179–80, 194, 202 n.
Pratt, Sir Charles, see Camden, Lord.
Price, Rev. Richard, 54.
Prime Minister, 121, 123, 148, 171, 174–81, 185 n.
Prince Regent, see George IV.
Professions and professional men, 16–17.
Protestant Association, 52.
Prussia, 112.
Public opinion, 198–204.

Race-meetings, political importance of, 51 n.

Regency Bill (1765), 152–3.

Regency Question (1788–1812), 98, 134 n., 136, 137 n.

Reporting, Parliamentary, 199–200.

Responsibility of ministers, 93–94, 131–3, 139–40, 143.

'Revolution Families', 58, 100.

'Revolution Settlement', 33, 48–49.

Richmond, 3rd Duke of, 13, 15 n., 60, 78 n., 90, 110, 119 n., 120 n., 123 n., 132 n., 150 n., 161, 203, 206.

Richmond, 4th Duke of, 27 n., 178 n.

Rigby, Richard, 118.

Roberts, Professor M., 139 n., 146 n.

Robinson, John, 12, 35–36, 72, 87 n., 98 n., 131 n., 133, 172, 196–7.

Rochford, Earl of, 153, 174.

Rockingham, Marquess of, 6, 10 n., 15 n., 21, 25 n., 29, 37, 57–60, 72, 76, 80, 82–86, 90–91, 96, 97 n., 99, 101 n., 102 n., 106–10, 111 n., 113–21, 143, 154, 167–8, 169 n., 171, 176 n., 179, 182 n., 193, 195, 204, 206.

Rockingham Whigs, 44 n., 47, 55 n., 59 n., 68, 75–77, 85, 88–91, 96, 106, 108 n., 116–17, 129, 191, 206.

Rodney, Admiral Lord, 21.

Rose, George, 12, 73 n., 81 n., 82 n., 109 n., 165 n.

Rosslyn, Earl of, 187.

Royal Marriages Bill, 152 n.

Royston, Lord, see Hardwicke, 2nd Earl of.

Russell, Lord John, 111 n., 128 n., 172 n.

Rutland, 5th Duke of, 185 n.

Sackville, Lord George (later known as Lord George Germain and 1st Viscount Sackville), 13, 158 n., 162 n., 174.

St. Vincent, Admiral Lord, 22.

Salisbury, Marquess of, 25.

Sandwich, Earl of, 21, 64, 76, 114 n., 153 n., 154 n., 161.

Savile, Sir George, 14, 59.

Sawbridge, Alderman, 51.

Scarlett, Sir James, 187.

Schuyler, R. L., 32 n.

Scots, 41, 73.

Secretary-at-War, 20 n., 148.

Secretary of State, 148, 160, 166 n., 178 n., 202 n.

Secret Service Money, 45.

Sedgwick, Romney, 65, 71, 105, 150.

Selwyn, George, 99 n., 120 n.

Sheffield, Lord, 145 n.

Shelburne, Earl of, 6, 24 n., 30 n., 38 n., 62 n., 77, 78–79, 81, 85 n., 88 n., 91, 97, 99 n., 110, 120 n., 121–2, 123 n., 128, 130, 145 n., 148 n., 150 n., 153–4, 158, 165 n., 168, 169 n., 170–1, 178 n., 179, 202 n.

Sheridan, R. B., 101 n.

Sidmouth, Viscount, 24, 28, 79–80, 86 n., 87 n., 91, 109 n., 110, 128, 129 n., 136–8, 141, 161, 170, 173, 178 n.

Slave trade, measures against, 42, 165, 194.

Smelt, Leonard, 6 n.

Stafford, Marquess of, see Gower, Earl.

Stamp Act, 68, 91, 107 n., 108, 114.

Stamp Act Congress, 53.

Stanley, Hans, 14, 77 n., 202 n.

Stock-jobbing, 15.

Stormont, Lord, 41, 88 n.

Stuart Mackenzie, James, 105, 107 n., 178.

Sugar-planters, 16.

Sumner, Rev. C. R., 147, 186 n., 190 n.

Sunderland, Earl of, 102.

Sydney, Lord, 173 n., 178 n.

Sykes, Professor N., 42.

Temperley, H. W. V., 169 n.

Temple, 1st Earl, 38, 51 n., 101 n., 131 n., 145 n., 149 n.

Temple, 2nd Earl, 27, 38, 131–2; see also Buckingham, 1st Marquess of.

Thurlow, Lord, 22 n., 23, 25 n., 88 n., 110 n., 119 n., 122 n., 126 n., 130, 135 n., 160 n., 161, 165 n., 169 n., 173.

Times, The, 199.

Tone, Wolfe, 78 n.

Tories, 55–6, 71–72, 185–7, 191–3, 195.

Townshend, Charles, 37, 68, 177 n, 181, 195 n.

Townshend, Marquess, 37.

Townshend, Viscount, 94 n.

Treasury, Secretary of the, 76 n., 197–8.

'Treasury Boroughs', 75.

Triple Alliance, 112–14.

Verney, Lord, 76 n.

Veto, right of, 132–3.

Victoria, Queen, 146, 157, 188, 191, 200.

Wager, Sir Charles, 20 n.

Walcott, R., 2, 71.

Waldegrave, Earl, 18 n.

Wales, Frederick, Prince of, 64.

Wales, Princess of (mother of George III), 63, 68 n., 152.

Walpole, Horace, the elder, 4.

Walpole, Horace, the younger, 14, 18–19, 47 n., 72, 74, 90 n., 96 n., 99 n., 100 n., 117 n., 118, 158 n., 179.

Walpole, Sir Robert, 18, 28, 39, 87, 94 n., 103–4, 176.

Ward, J. W., 141 n.

Wedderburn, *see* Loughborough, Lord.

Wellesley, Hon. and Rev. Gerald, 190 n.

Wellesley, Marquess, 110, 159.

Wellington, Duke of, 12 n., 110, 128, 149 n., 157, 165–6, 170, 184–90, 191 n., 200–1.

Westmorland, Earl of, 110 n.

Weymouth, Viscount, 64, 76, 147 n., 167 n.

Whigs, 48–50, 55–60, 71–72, 192–3.

Whitbread, Samuel, 140.

Wilkes, John, 49–50, 55 n., 56, 67–68, 92, 168, 199.

William III, 33–34, 52, 126 n.

William IV, 53 n., 136 n., 146, 188, 191.

Wilson, Sir Robert, 189 n.

Windham, William, 20, 159, 161, 178 n., 189.

Wynn, Charles W. W., 39 n.

Wyvill, Rev. C., 43, 53, 194.

Yarmouth, Lord, 16 n.

Yorke, Charles, 22 n., 37, 50, 55 n., 56 n., 105 n., 147 n., 170 n.

Yorke, Charles Philip, 37 n.

Yorke, Sir Joseph, 178 n., 202 n.

Yorke, Philip, 9 n.; *see also* Hardwicke, 2nd Earl of.

Yorkshire Association, 24 n., 52–54.

Young, Sir William, 66 n.